THE TIMES

BRIEF LETTERS

to the Editor

Introduced by
Robert Thomson

TIMES BOOKS

HarperCollins*Publishers*
77–85 Fulham Palace Road
Hammersmith
London W6 9JB

The HarperCollins website address is
www.**fire**and**water**.com

First published 2002

Reprint 10 9 8 7 6 5 4 3 2 1 0

ISBN 0 00 712194 6

The Times is a registered trademark of Times Newspapers Ltd

British Library Cataloguing in Publication Data
A catalogue record for this book is available from the British Library

Text compilation and design by Clare Crawford

Printed and bound in Great Britain by Clays Ltd, St Ives plc

Introduction

A newspaper is only as good as its readers, and *The Times* is fortunate to have an intelligent audience whose tastes, as the letters in this volume testify, range from philosophy to nomenclature and cookery. Witty writing takes time and imagination, and it is clear that correspondents to our newspaper have thought long and hard about their subjects and their sentence structures. It is always intimidating for a newspaper editor to receive a missive from a reader whose knowledge of a subject dwarfs that of the paper's own specialist reporters. And it is always a pleasure to have a written conversation with a clever and amusing correspondent. We owe our readers a great debt.

Robert Thomson,
Editor, *The Times*,
London, 2002

Brief Letters
1997

JUST CLAWS

From Mrs C. Ennis

Sir, The idea of pets replacing husbands is not new ("Cats to replace husbands", January 30). When asked why she never married, the novelist Marie Corelli was said to have replied that she had three pets who took the place of a man – a dog that growled all morning, a parrot that swore all evening and a cat that stayed out all night.

Yours faithfully,
CELIA ENNIS,
Harrogate, West Yorkshire. February 5

BACK TO THE FUTURE?

From Mr Robert Vincent

Sir, In this remote corner of the Hampshire/Wiltshire border small commercial enterprises abound, having taken over and modified redundant ale houses, blacksmith shops, farmhouses, chapels and the like.

As it is in the nature of things for many businesses to cease trading after a number of years, one wonders if villages of the future will abound with dwellings such as The Old Aerobic Studio, The Old Desktop Publishing House, Old Computer Software Cottages, The Old Fitted Kitchen Shop and The Old Stripped Pine Furniture Forge?

Yours faithfully,
ROBERT VINCENT,
Andover, Hampshire
February 8

From Mrs S. Griffith

Sir, On the old route of the A5 near Oswestry, now bypassed, there is a single-storey house with a particularly large sitting-room. It is "The Old Little Chef".

Yours faithfully,
SUE GRIFFITH,
Denbigh, Clwyd. February 8

STOPS AND STARTS

From Mr Tom Courtenay

When trains near their destination nowadays, a strangled voice often announces: "We are now approaching so and so, where this train will terminate." No it won't. Surely in the majority of cases it will go on to have many more happy journeys.

Yours faithfully,
TOM COURTENAY,
c/o Wyndham's Theatre, London WC2.
February 22

From Prebendary Dr Chad Varah

Sir, Mr Tom Courtenay confuses two different uses of the word "train". In itself, it is a locomotive with a number of carriages or wagons in "train". Operationally it means, eg, the 14:48 from Paddington to Oxford.

On arrival, this particular use of the train terminates. It soon becomes a different train, or the collection of coaches or wagons may be shuffled.

The train in its existential sense will terminate only when the locomotive and all its "train" have gone severally to the scrapyard: in about 100 years, on past form.

Yours faithfully,
CHAD VARAH,
(Rector), St Stephen Walbrook,
London EC4. February 25

From Mr Graham Ramsay

Sir, I can understand Tom Courtenay's alarm on being told that his train would terminate at its destination. I am sure that he will sympathise with mine on being informed, a year or two back, that "the station now rapidly approaching is Swindon".

Yours faithfully,
GRAHAM RAMSAY,
Edinburgh. March 10

From Mr Tony Garland

Sir, Mr Graham Ramsay need have no concern about Swindon rapidly approaching his train. It all depends on your frame of reference, as Einstein might have said, possibly after inquiring of a porter at Euston: "Excuse me, does Crewe go past this train?" *Yours faithfully,*
TONY GARLAND,
North Shields, Tyne and Wear. March 13

From Mr Raymond Davern

Sir, Despite the fact that Einstein's lasting contribution to human knowledge pertained to what Aristotle called speculative rather than practical reasoning, I should have thought it likely that even he was concerned to discover not so much whether Crewe went past the train leaving Euston as whether, if it did so, it did so slowly enough for him to alight thereat.

Yours faithfully,
RAYMOND DAVERN,
King's College London, School of Law,
London WC2. March 18

TWO OF A KIND

From Mr John Kay

Sir, An Edinburgh genetics laboratory has apparently created, for the first time ever, a cloned sheep.

Having just returned from a visit to North Wales, I have to say I find it very difficult to believe their work is unique.

Yours sincerely,
JOHN KAY,
West Kirby, Wirral, Merseyside. February 28

From Mr K. L. Rawling

Sir, Perhaps we should bear in mind the words attributed to Ralph Waldo Emerson: "Never try to make anyone like yourself – you know, and God knows, that one of you is sufficient." *Yours etc,*
K. L. RAWLING,
Otley, West Yorkshire. February 28

From Miss Barbara Wanford

Sir, If human babies were produced by cloning from their mothers we could dispense with the whole of the male population. Most of the world's dictators, criminals, scientists and armies would disappear.

There would be no more wars.

However, before rushing headlong into this course of action, a word or two of caution should be noted. Who, for instance, would programme the video? *Yours faithfully,*
BARBARA WANFORD,
Bristol. March 15

From Mr Frank Rich

Sir, The task of programming the video would, of course, be performed entirely by grandchildren. Within a fortnight, however,

the world would be ruled by spiders living in bathrooms.   *Yours faithfully,*
FRANK RICH,
Hampton, Middlesex. March 19

From Mrs Caroline Zoob

Sir, Women trapped in the kitchen should investigate the possibility of cloning my husband.

We both work full-time yet he is an avid collector of supermarket reward points, an expert sorter of the laundry, utterly possessive of the ironing and his couscous and apricot stuffing is beyond Delia's wildest dreams. He not only uses the dishwasher, he cleans it. Even the cat is groomed daily. The house is filled with his wonderful piano playing and this morning freshly picked flowers (grown by him) appeared on my study desk.   *Yours sincerely,*
CAROLINE ZOOB,
London SE23. March 11

From Mrs Krzysia Gossage

Sir, I don't have the time to investigate the possibility of cloning Mrs Caroline Zoob's paragon of a husband. Could I just have him, please?   *Yours faithfully,*
KRZYSIA GOSSAGE,
Chinnor, Oxfordshire. March 12

From Mr David Elston

Sir, Along, I suspect, with most other husbands in the land, I am fervently praying that the Zoob family, particularly the apparently unbearable Mr Zoob, does not move in next door.   *Yours sincerely,*
DAVID ELSTON,
Edinburgh. March 12

From Miss Wendy Mullins

Sir, What a little gem Mr Zoob sounds. One is left to speculate whether this relaxed and biddable paragon shares his idyll with junior Zoobs. Or would he be driven to groom the couscous, eat the cat, stuff the dishwasher, clean the flowers and place a tasteful laundry arrangement on the freshly ironed desk?   *Yours sincerely,*

WENDY MULLINS,
Cambridge. March 13

From Mr Chris Hardy

Sir, Speaking as a long-time friend of Mr Zoob, could his exemplary behaviour be prompted by the imminent arrival of the cricket season?   *Yours sincerely,*
C. M. HARDY,
London SE23. March 13

SHORT FOR PROTESTER?

From Mr R. E. Nicklas

Sir, I am aware of the meanings of Yuppy and Nimby, but what is a Swampy (reports, April 1 and 2)?

Is it a Sincere Well-meaning Amiable Motorway Protester or one who Shirks Work and Argues Make-believe Politics?
Yours faithfully,
R. E. NICKLAS,
Cottingham, East Yorkshire. April 2

LONDON AQUARIUM

From Mr Michael Brown

Sir, Over 20 years of my working life were spent in London's County Hall (shortly to be turned into an aquarium). It is therefore gratifying to read your report that its present owners have reinstated its former use, as home to one of the biggest collections of sharks in the Western world.
Yours faithfully,
MICHAEL BROWN,
Highbridge, Somerset. April 4

SMALL IS BEAUTIFUL

From Mr Alan Millard

Sir, Thank you for featuring Rutland (report and photographs, March 31) with its delightful motto *Multum in parvo* – a lot in a little. As I am only five feet four inches tall, with a tendency towards rotundity, I have decided to adopt the motto for myself.
Yours sincerely,
ALAN MILLARD,
Lee-on-the-Solent, Hampshire. April 5

WITHOUT WORDS

From Mrs Judy Astley

Sir, Babyhood is not the only time that humans resort to communicating in sign language (article, April 15). Scientists would do well to come to my house and study "The teenager: non-verbal language skills".

The more common "signs" include the slouch n' scowl, which inevitably means denial, as in "No, of course I don't have any homework".

Eyes to ceiling/despairing shake of head means "Parents are a sad waste of space".

Then there is the smile and hover technique, by which hanging around the kitchen, generously rinsing one plate and grinning in a sickly way can only be interpreted as "I require money". *Yours faithfully,*
JUDY ASTLEY,
Helston, Cornwall. April 19

SPELLING IT OUT

From Mr George Harris

Sir, There may be other admirers of Patrick O'Brian of about my age who are hoping they can hang on until after the year 2000 so that they can emulate his hero Jack Aubrey and refer to "the year two".

I would think this distinctive style could operate only in single figures, or is it permissable to use, for example, "the year 34"?

I would think not. *Yours faithfully,*
E. G. B. HARRIS,
Plymouth, Devon. April 21

BLUEBELLS STRIKE BACK

From Mr Paul Roberts

Sir, You report that bluebells are easily damaged by the tread of feet (Mind and matter, April 28). But what about the tread of feet being easily damaged by the bluebells? My glissade on a patch of the little blighters has left me with a broken leg for the last six weeks. *Yours sincerely,*
PAUL ROBERTS,
Colchester, Essex. May 1

NORTHCOTE RECALLED

From the Earl of Iddesleigh

Sir, You underestimate my great-grandfather, Sir Stafford Northcote, when you refer to him as "prolific" (Diary, May 6). He had fathered ten, not eight, children when as Chancellor of the Exchequer he lived in No. 10 Downing Street, having exchanged houses with his Prime Minister, Benjamin Disraeli, in 1874.

His association with No. 10 does not end there. One of his granddaughters (not daughter), Dame Flora Macleod, was actually born in the house on February 3, 1878, and he himself died there on January 6, 1887, while waiting to see the Prime Minister, Lord Salisbury of the day. A unique treble, I think? *Yours faithfully*
THE EARL OF IDDESLEIGH,
Upton-Pyne-Hill, nr Exeter, Devon
May 14

REMINISCENCE OF LAURIE LEE

From Mr Christopher J. McManus

Sir, Your obituary of Laurie Lee told the bitter-sweet tale of Laurie going unrecognised in his own village of Slad – "Excuse us, could you tell us where Laurie Lee is buried?"

There was however one occasion on which he was recognised.

As Laurie told us himself at the Chelsea Arts Club one evening: "As I was walking down to the village pub I was approached by a little girl of about 9 or 10 who asked me if I were Laurie Lee. I said that I was, whereupon she said:'Were it you what wrote that poem teacher made us learn by 'eart?' I said with modest pride: 'Yes, I expect so.' The girl, taking careful and deliberate aim, then kicked me ferociously on both shins before running off as fast as her little legs could carry her." *Yours sincerely,*
CHRISTOPHER J. McMANUS,
Chelsea Arts Club, London SW3. May 22

"CROSS OF ST PATRICK"

From Major John FitzGerald

Sir, I have to declare a partial proprietary interest in the fate of the Union Flag.

That part of the flag, so sadly misnamed St Patrick's cross – the old boy was so busy chasing snakes that he clean forgot to get himself martyred and thus earn himself a cross – is the Geraldine saltire which was borne on Kildare and Desmond shields from the late 1300s until those families stopped rebelling against the English kings and quarrelling.

A Duke of Leinster in the 18th century allowed The St Patrick's Society to use the saltire in its badge, which is probably why the English, looking for something suitable to complete the Union Flag in 1801, nicked our saltire and mislabelled it.

If the Union Jack is to be re-cast, then can we please have our cross back, Mister?

Yours etc,
JOHN FitzGERALD,
York. May 27

STEERING COMMITTEE

From Mr T. P. Blenkin

Sir, You report that a prototype supermarket trolley with a self-centring steering system may eliminate "erratic trolley control".

Perhaps it will also dispel my long-held belief that the difference between a supermarket trolley and a non-executive director is that, while both hold a vast quantity of food and drink, only the trolley has a mind of its own.   *Yours faithfully,*
T. P. BLENKIN,
Blenkin & Co (chartered surveyors),
York. May 29

POLE POSITIONS

From Mr A. J. Saunders

Sir, My congratulations to the all-woman Polar expedition on their success. I have just one question: who did the map-reading?
Yours faithfully,

A. J. SAUNDERS,
Swindon, Wiltshire. May 29

From Mrs Anne-Marie Obolensky

Sir, Mr A. J. Saunders should understand that map-reading would have presented no problem to the all-woman Polar expedition, since they were travelling north. However, such an expedition to the South Pole, where the map would have to be held upside down, could be more of a challenge.
Yours faithfully,
ANNE-MARIE OBOLENSKY,
Pusey Faringdon, Oxfordshire. May 31

CLERGYMAN'S CRIB

From Mr Peter Hollindale

Sir, Speculation that the BBC might discontinue the Radio 4 *Sunday* programme (report, June 13) must dismay clergy in the Church of England, whose workload would be markedly increased by its loss.

I have listened to this programme on many occasions, only to find large portions of it retransmitted from the pulpit two hours later.   *Yours faithfully,*
PETER HOLLINDALE,
York. June 19

MIGHTY AS A MODEM

From Mr Charles P. F. Baillie

Sir, Within a week of your announcement of the acceptability of e-mail, you published a letter from me, written with a fountain pen that I received for success in your Saturday crossword some years ago. It is gratifying to know that we computer-illiterate reactionaries, for whom the shoehorn represents the apotheosis of technology, are not therefore denied the hospitality of your columns.   *Yours faithfully,*
C. P. F. BAILLIE,
Weston-super-Mare, Somerset. June 28

SIGN-OFF OF THE TIMES?

From Mr Adrian Dodd-Noble

Sir, For more than 60 years I have considered myself as your obedient servant and shall, I hope, continue to remain *Yours faithfully*.

Now there is e-mail I shall be on the lookout for "bye-bye for now" or similar valedictory tags.   *Believe me, Sir*,
ADRIAN DODD-NOBLE,
Hexham, Northumberland. July 3

From Mr Babar Mumtaz

I hope Mr Adrian Dodd-Noble does not spend too much time looking out for strange valedictory tags for e-mail letters: netiquette requires neither opening nor closing salutations.

BABAR MUMTAZ,
London NW3. July 8

From Mr David Staples

Sir, Mr Adrian Dodd-Noble suggests the "your obedient servant" is perhaps an unsatisfactory closing for an e-mail.

Could I be the first to conclude an e-pistle to the editor with a "smiley".   *Yours* :)
DAVID T. STAPLES,
London N8. July 9

From Mr Henry Robinson

Sir, The march of technology must not be allowed to erode courtesy and civilisation. In a civilised society, any written communication should be signed off with a suitably courteous salutation, whatever "netiquette" – or perhaps nerdiquette – may or may not require.

I remain, Sir, Yours truly and electronically,
HENRY ROBINSON,
Waterlooville, Hampshire. July 9

URBAN DERELICTION

From Mr Paul J. Hickey

Sir, Suburbs have nothing to do with geography but are states of mind.

For example, Golders Green is a suburb while Hampstead and Highgate are not. Indeed, if you told any of the illuminati who run the Heath and Old Hampstead Society that they lived in a suburb, they would prob-

ably come round and pebble-dash your house . . .   *Yours faithfully*,
PAUL J. HICKEY,
London NW2. July 4

FURTHER TO YOUR LETTERS . . .

From Mr Nicholas D. W. Thomas

Sir, When you published a letter from me in 1987 on the subject of aunts I, unlike Mr Adrian Taylor, received no written responses. However, a then casual acquaintance read the letter in Kathmandu a day or so later and, as a result, subsequently became my wife.   *Yours faithfully*,
NICHOLAS D. W. THOMAS,
Bebington, Wirral. July 5

From the Honourable Julian Guest

Sir, Your correspondents today are lucky; the only response I ever got to a letter published in *The Times* was a telephone call from my Mother informing me that I had entirely spoilt her breakfast.

Yours faithfully,
JULIAN GUEST,
Norham, Berwick-upon-Tweed. July 5

From Mrs Jacqueline Worthington

Sir, After you published a missive of mine in August 1994, which described how a ladybird had eaten a crumb of gingerbread and drunk a drop of tea off my plate, I was inundated with letters from all over the world, including one from a Belgian gentleman with a poem he had written to celebrate the ladybird's teatime visit.

Incidentally, I have since discovered that ladybirds are very fond of shortcake and chocolate biscuits as well as gingerbread.

Yours faithfully,
JACQUELINE WORTHINGTON,
Stansted, Essex. July 5

From Professor Irving Benjamin

Sir, Last year I wrote a letter about church music. My cousin in Israel, with whom I had not been in touch for 41 years, read *The Times* that day because she could not get her usual daily paper, recognised my name and wrote to me. We then kept in contact by e-mail, and I have since been reunited, not only with her, but with two cousins in Australia and one in London.

Yours sincerely,
IRVING BENJAMIN,
London W13. July 5

From Mr V. E. Scottpadgett Truss

Sir, My own experience is that every letter that I have written to *The Times* has prompted a response. Unfortunately in my case it has always been in the form of a small note of rejection.   *Yours faithfully,*
VICTOR SCOTTPADGETT TRUSS,
Braintree, Essex. July 5

From Mrs Eileen Hocking

Sir, You published a letter of mine in the summer of 1986 about a Volcano kettle in which, lacking dry twigs, we had boiled water for tea with one copy of *The Times*. I received over 50 letters, most asking where such a kettle could be found, but some interesting ones which told me of people's experience with this useful article. I replied to all, typing brief information as to where they would find it, and long replies to those who had taken the trouble to write such interesting letters. It was a very happy time.

Yours etc,
EILEEN HOCKING,
Falmouth, Cornwall. July 10

From Mr Richard Need

Sir, My first letter in *The Times*, a one-liner printed in 1971 on Labour disunity over Europe, brought me, by airmail from Bermuda, a fan letter from Sir Terence Rattigan.

Judging by some of the responses I have had to later efforts, I wonder whether I should have quit at my peak.

Yours faithfully,
RICHARD NEED,
Cheam, Surrey. July 10

From Mr Alan Liddicoat

Sir, A letter of mine you published in Janu-

ary 1986 brought me hundreds of letters. For a few days the postman delivered in sacks.

I had joined in a light-hearted banter you ran about junk mail. I supported the stuff because it brought the postman to me each day as one who was "old, isolated, and alone".

At the time I was old, a lone widower, in the remote Devon countryside. The combination of those three words had a dramatic effect. Kind letters came from all sorts of people from all over the world, although chiefly from southeast England. A high proportion were written by doctors, teachers and children (at the behest no doubt of adults).

Every child in one class of 12-year-olds in the Midlands, encouraged obviously by an imaginative teacher, wrote individually the most charming letters. Many hard-pressed GPs scribbled a few kind words on prescription forms. One lady in Scotland said she made it a rule to write to someone every day before she had breakfast. A child said my letter reminded her that she did not write to her grandparents enough. There were tips from businessmen on useful lucrative occupations. Large numbers of elderly people suggested pen-pal relationships.

To my intense embarrassment someone writing anonymously from France arranged with Fortnum & Mason to send me a parcel of brandy and cigars. The firm refused to disclose the name of my benefactor.

I received no proposals of marriage nor, interestingly, any letters from the clergy. One lady of slight acquaintance wrote to express disappointment that I had not let her know I was lonely. Letters came, mostly anonymously, in decreasing numbers for a couple of years.

Now I am very old, married again, and live in a town. The junk mail comes in greater volumes but I do not have time to look at it.   *Yours faithfully,*
ALAN LIDDICOAT,
Holt, Norfolk. July 15

From Mr Roger Cookson

Sir, Please publish this letter. I am old, sad and unbearably lonely, and would derive maximum benefit (on all fronts) from an anonymous Fortnum & Mason hamper.

Yours, in anticipation of imminent relief,
ROGER COOKSON,
London NW11. July 16

AS OLD AS YOU FEEL

From Mr J. W. Scott

Sir, By describing Camilla Parker Bowles, aged 49, as being "in late middle-age", Jane Shilling (article, July 8) may be betraying the number of her own years, since middle-age is, throughout life, always about ten years older than you are yourself. I am slightly older than Mrs Parker Bowles and, from my own viewpoint, she has yet to reach even early middle-age.

However, if middle-age is also defined as the time when you have either achieved your every ambition or come to terms with the fact that you will not do so, then I think that Jane Shilling herself, judging by the tone of her article, would agree that the phrase was inappropriate.   *Yours faithfully*,
JONATHAN SCOTT,
Bournemouth, Dorset. July 12

From Mrs Peter Halliwell

Sir, I understood that middle-age was that period of life when parents and children caused equal amounts of worry.

Yours faithfully
ROMY HALLIWELL,
Winchester, Hampshire. July 18

From Mr Harry Whitham

Sir, As a middle-aged 65-year-old, I believe the definition of middle-aged given in Chambers dictionary – "between youth and old age, variously reckoned to suit the reckoner" – to be the most accurate.

Yours faithfully,
HARRY WHITHAM,
Wakefield, West Yorkshire. July 18

From Sir Bryan Thwaites

Sir, The onset of middle-age can, in my experience, be quite precisely dated. It is when you are incapable of understanding how to send a letter to *The Times* by e-mail even though you have such an address. (Please do not send me your usual charming letter of acknowledgement by e-mail – I won't know how to retrieve it.)

Yours faithfully,
B. THWAITES,
Winchester, Hampshire. July 21

From Mrs Pam Robinson

Sir, There is an expression used by the medical profession that confirms our entry into middle age.

Last week I was admitted to hospital for a minor operation. The nurse who took my blood pressure announced that it was "excellent . . . for your age". I am 51.

Yours sincerely,
P. ROBINSON,
Sandbach, Cheshire. July 21

From Mr D. C. Burrows

Sir, Another sign of middle-age: questions begin with the words "Are you still . . .?"

Yours faithfully,
D. C. BURROWS,
Burton Overy, Leicestershire. July 26

From Dr Grace Marshall

Sir, The middle-aged are easy to identify. They are the ones who look at the rain teeming down and say: "That'll be good for the garden."   *Yours faithfully*,
GRACE MARSHALL,
Southampton, Hampshire. July 28

From Dr Anthony Field

Sir, Middle-age is surely that one year in your life after your doctors keep telling you that "you'll grow out of it" and before they tell you to "learn to live with it".

Yours truly,
ANTHONY FIELD,
Pulborough, Sussex. July 28

VOLUNTARY EUTHANASIA

From Dr Richard Gordon

Sir, How much easier was life, and death, before people started striking attitudes and forming associations about ethical problems.

Some 50 years ago, as a newly qualified houseman with a tortured conscience, I ventured to kill off my first patient. I instantly and solemnly told the ward sister: "I've just turned off the drip on No 16." "Oh, yes, doctor", she said, "that patient's already been dead for half an hour."   *I am, etc,*

RICHARD GORDON,
Garrick Club, London WC2. July 25

SIGN OF THE TIMES

From Mr Christopher Holborow

Sir, I have heard the return of Hong Kong to China spoken of as the end of the Empire.

It is clear to me, however, that the Empire actually ended a couple of years ago when the tourist attraction sign at Junction 3 on the M3, which used to say "Windsor Castle. Royalty and Empire", was changed to read "Windsor Castle. Legoland".

Yours faithfully,
CHRISTOPHER HOLBOROW,
Witham Friary, nr Frome, Somerset.
July 30

HERE IS THY STING

From Mr Jeremy Billingham

Sir, In the light of recent coverage on the subject of euthanasia, readers of pensionable age living on the Kent/Sussex border should know of a service currently advertised in our local newspaper, *The Courier:*

Wasps nests destroyed   £20
O.A.P.s   £15

Yours faithfully,
JEREMY BILLINGHAM,
Wadhurst, East Sussex. August 2

STRANGE BEINGS

From Mr Peter Hungerford-Welch

Sir, A notice in a local DIY store, inform-ing customers that the store would no longer stock a particular model of lawn-mower, made for alarming reading. Apparently, the mower was "de-ranged".

Yours faithfully,
PETER HUNGERFORD-WELCH,
Tonbridge, Kent. August 12

From Professor Gerald Goodhardt

Sir, Notices around the Elephant and Castle warn that the parking meters are "alarmed". Maybe they have heard about the "de-ranged" lawnmowers of Tonbridge.

Yours faithfully
G. J. GOODHARDT,
London NW8. August 13

From Colonel J. I. G. Capadose (retd)

Sir, Mr Peter Hungerford-Welch is alarmed by reading of "de-ranged" lawn-mowers in Tonbridge.

Let him not come up the road to Sevenoaks, where "mad tiger prawns" are sold over a supermarket fish counter. This exotic, if disconcerting, title appears on the little label spewed out by the weighing and pricing device, which cannot manage "Madagascar".

Perhaps his fears of Kentish vendors would be allayed, on the other hand, by buying a portion of the more prosaic and comforting "trad undyed hadd".   *Yours faithfully,*
JAMES CAPADOSE,
Westerham, Kent. August 14

From Miss Sarah Mulholland

Sir, Still pondering over the intriguing images of de-ranged lawnmowers, alarmed meters and mad prawns, I am now wondering whether to take up the offer of a local hairdresser to cut my hair "while-u-wait". Given the hectic pace of life, however, perhaps I should after all simply leave it in to be cut while I pursue other tasks.

Yours faithfully,
SARAH MULHOLLAND
Sherwood, Nottingham. August 18

From Dr G. L. Bolt

Sir, The "de-ranged" lawnmowers, alarmed parking meters and mad prawns are surely outnumbered by the floods of disabled toilets.   *Yours faithfully,*
G. L. BOLT,
King's Lynn, Norfolk. August 19

From Mrs Shirley M. Large

Sir, Perhaps the alarmed parking meters and de-ranged lawn mowers are concerned at the threat of the "large plant crossing" roadways under construction.

Yours faithfully,
SHIRLEY M. LARGE,
Little Wolford, Warwickshire. August 19

A NEW AGE?

From Mr Nigel Sarjudeen

Sir, Surely an encouraging sign for all those clamouring for the modernisation of the Establishment is the fact that the prime minister who read the lesson at Diana's funeral is younger than the pop star who sang.

Yours faithfully,
NIGEL SARJUDEEN,
Hove, East Sussex. September 10

A LOVESOME THING

From Mr Robert Hargreaves

Sir, Readers who advocate wilder gardens should remember the country vicar who greeted one of his toiling parishioners with the remark: "It's a wonderful thing that God can do with a garden."

"Maybe so, Vicar," replied the gardener. "But you should have seen it when He had it to Himself".   *Yours sincerely,*

ROBERT HARGREAVES,
Winchelsea, East Sussex. September 12

NO 10 AND BISHOPS

From the Reverend Peter Haughton

Sir, The Prime Minister has every right to appoint and disappoint bishops.

Yours faithfully,

PETER HAUGHTON,
London SW15. September 18

THE BOOKER BOOKED

From Mr John O'Byrne

Sir, Now that the season of "Booker" is upon us how about some enterprising first-time novelist attempting a grand theme on the prize itself?

The ingredients could include obsession, thwarted ambition, rejection, loss, disillusionment, and some damn close-run things. But what should be the title?

Yours literarily,
JOHN O'BYRNE,
Harold's Cross, Dublin. September 19

From Mr Ian Brammer

Sir, The title of a Booker prize novel will depend more on timing than on plot.

Before the competition *Great Expectations* or *Vanity Fair* would be appropriate. After the judging the unsuccessful authors could choose between *The Grapes of Wrath, Hard Times, Decline and Fall* and *The Long Goodbye*. The winner would select *Victory* or *Brave New World*.   *Yours faithfully,*
IAN BRAMMER,
Macclesfield, Cheshire. September 24

From Mr Tim Nagley

Sir, In his search for a title, Mr O'Byrne should perhaps avoid *The Booker Book*, which was used by Simon Brett in 1989 as the title for his most entertaining novel about an enterprising first-time novelist attempting to win the prize.

Yours faithfully,
TIM NAGLEY,
London NW6. September 24

WORLD-WIDE WEB?

From Mr Hamish Carmichael

Sir, Every morning the paths in our garden are newly blocked by orb-spun cobwebs of unprecedented magnificence, each with a large resident spider. I cannot remember another autumn like it. Friends have made similar comments. What does it mean?

Yours faithfully,
J. W. S. CARMICHAEL,
Surbiton, Surrey. October 7

From Dr Stanley Solomons

Sir, Mr Hamish Carmichael draws attention to the unusual number of exceptionally large spiders' webs this autumn and asks what it could mean.

Hopefully, it means very bad news for the flies.   *Yours sincerely,*
S. SOLOMONS,
London NW3. October 9

From Mr Christopher Ellis

Sir, Mr Carmichael's spiders are simply following the example of the Government - spinning like crazy.   *Yours faithfully,*
CHRISTOPHER ELLIS,
Farnham, Surrey. October 9

HORSES FOR COURSES

From Mr Christopher Nutt

Sir, Today your Sport section has articles on rugby by Hands, on horses by Barnes and, best of all, "Groins add to the strain" by Truss.

Is this some employment policy? If so, I am glad not to be assignable by you, as I remain   *Your obedient servant,*
C.Y. NUTT,
London SW6. October 15

EXCUSES, EXCUSES

From Mrs Ian Campbell

Sir, Many years ago my son, a young subaltern in the army, was told that the best way to avoid wrath on losing expensive equipment was to send a message "Regret the loss of six water-bottles down a ravine".

After several weeks had elapsed a further message should be sent saying "Referring to my earlier message, for water-bottles read tanks".   *Yours faithfully,*
PATRICIA J. CAMPBELL,
Yelverton, Devon. October 16

From Sir Laurence Martin

Sir, Mrs Patricia Campbell's advice on how to explain away lost military equipment brought back happy memories of being a National Service officer in the RAF. In those days remarkable things could be done by tidying your inventory with something called a conversion voucher.

By sequentially exploiting overlaps and inconsistencies in categories of equipment you could go a long way. The record was reputedly held by a squadron leader said to have changed a "hangar, aircraft", supposedly in his care, to a "hanger, coat".

Yours faithfully,
LAURENCE MARTIN,
Newcastle upon Tyne. October 18

HEARD ON THE HIGH

From the Reverend David Copley

Sir, My brother-in-law once told me of a snippet of conversation he heard when he was passing two men talking to each other in Oxford. "But of course the later history of Sparta ..." were the magic words.

With that in mind I thought I would pick up a wise word or two when one day in Oxford in the late 1940s I saw A. L. Rowse (obituary, October 6) deep in conversation with a companion coming towards me. As they passed I heard Rowse say: "Yes, my braces are always getting in a twist too."

Yours faithfully,
DAVID COPLEY,
Halesowen, West Midlands. October 17

From Mr Jonathan Lamb

Sir, The Reverend David Copley's letter on learned conversations overheard in Oxford streets brings to mind the contributor to a radio programme some years ago who said he had seen two gowned figures approaching him on the High, deep in conversation.

As they passed him he heard only two words: "And ninthly ..."

Your obedient servant,
J. C. LAMB,

The United Oxford and Cambridge University Club, London SW1. October 20

From Mr Huon Mallalieu

Sir, May I offer another Oxford tale to accompany those of the Reverend David Copley and Mr J. C. Lamb.

In the mid-1960s my tutor, the late historian John Cooper, was observed walking in the Broad with his two-year-old son Oliver dependant from one hand. The latter, named for Cromwell, was bawling inconsolably. In the true spirit of Oxford his father was heard to plead: "Oh, Oliver, DO be reasonable."

Yours faithfully,
HUON MALLALIEU,
London N1. October 28

From Mr John B. Harris

Sir, Not far away on the banks of the Isis: "Eight men with but a single thought!"...
"If that." *Yours faithfully,*
JOHN B. HARRIS,
London W11. October 28

LOST IN TRANSLATION

From Señor Ernesto Aguirre

Sir, Reading today your report about tonight's match between Aston Villa and Athletic de Bilbao, I see with surprise that you call Bilbao airport Llegadas, when that is the Spanish word for Arrivals. The real name of the airport is Sondica.

Yours sincerely,
ERNESTO AGUIRRE,
Madrid. October 23

FELLOW FEELING?

From Mr Bryan Gabriel

Sir, Interesting to read your report today about the lawyer who escaped being savaged by a shark in Australia.

Professional courtesy, perhaps?

Yours faithfully,
BRYAN GABRIEL,
Dorking, Surrey. October 30

AGAINST A FEARFUL PARRIS

From Dr Edward Young

Sir, Matthew Parris uses a lengthy article to explain that though he is a firm non-believer, fear still makes him superstitious.

The 18th-century poet Dr Edward Young (no relation) was more succinct: "By night an atheist half believes a God" (*Night Thoughts*, 1742-45). *Yours faithfully,*
EDWARD YOUNG,
Reading, Berkshire. November 6

SCIENTIFIC SPIN

From Mr Patrick Green

Sir, You report (November 7) that spinning black holes (or other matter) can distort time and space.

Is this a coincidence of scientific and political discovery? *I remain, Sir, yours,*
PATRICK GREEN,
London EC4. November 12

AN EVERYDAY TALE

From Mr Jon Massey

Sir, Is the plan to sacrifice children's Radio 4 in favour of an extra episode of *The Archers* the first example of the dum-di-dum-di-dum-di-dumbing-down of the BBC?

Yours etc,
JON MASSEY,
Plymouth, Devon. November 20

PEDAL POWER

From Mr Philip Tooke

Sir, You report today that Queen Beatrix of The Netherlands "never wears a crown and rides a bicycle". May I applaud this cautious approach to travel. *Yours faithfully,*
PHILIP TOOKE,
Leeds, West Yorkshire. November 21

IN A FLAT SPIN

From Dr David B. Cook

Sir, Along with a number of other gifted and hard-working people, my wife has a PhD, which involved the study of the magnetism due to the spin of electrons and nuclei.

Both of us find the current campaign of vilification aimed at spin-doctors thoroughly offensive.   *Yours sincerely,*
D. B. COOK,
University of Sheffield, Sheffield.
November 22

BACK OF THE STALLS

From Dr John H. Greensmith

Sir, I read recently that a cinema in Bolton is to open 24 hours a day (News in brief, November 8). When, I wonder, are they going to Hoover the carpet?

I can see it now:"Excuse me, love, can you just lift your feet up while I get under that seat...Tut, you ought to be out in the fresh air on a nice day like this . . ."

I don't believe they've thought it through.
Yours faithfully,
JOHN GREENSMITH,
Downend, Bristol. November 27

WARM FRONT?

From Mrs Eileen M. Clarke

Sir, November 28 and my husband is still not wearing his vest.

Is this clear evidence of global warming?
Yours faithfully,
EILEEN M. CLARKE,
Stonesfield, Oxfordshire. November 29

SENSE OF DIRECTION

From Mrs Janet Whitby

Sir, Your Science Briefing (December 8) concludes that "men learn to pay attention to direction more than women but women are just as good at it, given the motivation."

After many years in the passenger seat being told to "stop reading that map, women have no sense of direction", my own conclusion is that maintaining motivation is often more frustrating than being lost.
Yours wearily,
JANET WHITBY,
London N6. December 11

From Mrs Dorothy Drake

Sir, Perhaps men do learn to pay attention to direction more than women.

My husband has no use for road maps. When finding his way in this country and in Europe all he needs is the answer to two questions:Where's the sun? Where's the sea?

He's not bad at reaching his destination - except after dark.   *Yours faithfully,*
DOROTHY DRAKE,
Harrogate, West Yorkshire. December 15

COMINGS AND GOINGS

From the Head Master of Westminster School

Sir, This day contains an interesting double bill. Mr Gerry Adams walks into 10 Downing Street for the first time; HM The Queen walks off the Royal Yacht for the last time.   *Yours etc,*
D. M. SUMMERSCALE,
London SW1. December 12

HOME BIRTHS

From Mr P. R. Ridgway

Sir, I was interested in the article promoting the benefits of birth at home, including the greater sense of continuity and family ties.

I too was born at home, in the same house where my mother had been born. Unfortunately the adjoining property has since expanded, and when I now point out to my children my birthplace, it is located in the saloon bar of the Fox and Goose.

Yours sincerely,
PHIL RIDGWAY,
Woodbridge, Suffolk. December 16

From Mrs Anne Scott

Sir, I often remind my son, at present out celebrating the festive season, that his birthplace, on Hyde Terrace, Leeds, is now a Detoxification Unit.   *Yours faithfully,*
ANNE SCOTT,
Sale, Cheshire. December 22

From Mr Paul Ketteridge

Sir, The nursing home I was born in is now an old people's home. No doubt they will have me back.   *Yours faithfully,*
PAUL KETTERIDGE,
North Marston, Buckinghamshire.
December 31

STOCKING FILLERS

From Mr Alasdair Maclean

Sir, Some years ago, when I left home, my mother gave me a list of what she believed to be the contents of a traditional Christmas stocking, together with a brief explanation as to why each item should be included.

It went as follows:

Socks, pants, hanky, toothbrush: the emergency kit.

Pencil, notebook: to use later to record who sent what.

Book/toy, food: to keep the child quiet for another few minutes.

Chocolate money: reminder of the gold.

Shiny money: St Nick's first gift.

Smelly: the frankincense.

Spicy: the myrrh.

Candle/torch: the light of the world.

Round thing, ball: the world.

Soft toy: the animals and lambs.

Tangerine: gold, round and food.

Nuts: the hard life of the Christ child.

Mouse: traditional, but why?

Over the years I have found many people who agreed that the stocking ought to contain such a variety of things, without necessarily sharing the reasons, but no one has ever been able to supply an explanation for the mouse.   *Yours faithfully,*
ALASDAIR MACLEAN,
Sutton, Surrey. December 20

From Mrs Sue Catt

Sir, Mr Alasdair Maclean asks why the mouse in the Christmas stocking? – perhaps the answer lies in

'Twas the night before Christmas, when all through the house
Not a creature was stirring, not even a mouse;

As the mouse was made of hard sugar and took longer to consume, it was just buying a few more minutes of precious peace in the morning.   *Yours faithfully,*
SUE CATT,
Blakeney, Norfolk. December 24

From Mrs Ann Hughes

Sir, I suggest that, in the days when there were holes in the wainscot, the original mouse put himself in the Christmas stocking, attracted by the nuts, fruit, food and chocolate (much better than cheese for baiting a mousetrap).   *Yours faithfully,*
ANN HUGHES,
Sevenoaks, Kent. December 24

From Dr Tom Tate

Sir, The presence of mice is inevitable. Last year, they polished off Santa's mince pie and carrot, had a go at his whisky, and I have no doubt, investigated the stockings. Not a creature was stirring - excepting the mice.   *Yours faithfully,*
TOM TATE,
Bearsted Green, Kent. December 24

From Mr Richard Carlyon

Sir, The presence of the mouse is easily explained: it is to assist in the production of personalised, word-processed, thank-you letters.   *Yours faithfully,*
R. J. CARLYON,
Somerton, Somerset. December 24

From Dr J. Caroe

Sir, What a delightful present Mrs Catt gave us on Christmas Eve. She quotes the mouse poem, "'Twas the night before Christmas . . .", thus neatly providing the answers to five clues in today's Times Two crossword. Thank you!   *Yours etc,*
JOHN CAROE,
Eastbourne, East Sussex. December 26

HEAVENLY GIFT

From Mr Charles Ottaway

Sir, Browsing through a well-known firm's Christmas brochure recently, I was startled to come across the following: "Christmas angels playing cards in a tin."

Imagine one's joy on opening that present on Christmas morning.   *Yours truly,*
                          CHARLES OTTAWAY,
                              Luton. December 20

From Mrs Elizabeth Elliot

Sir, Mr Charles Ottaway's discovery raises a new and interesting philosophical point, namely: how many angels can play cards in a tin; and have they room to dance?
                          Yours faithfully,
                          ELIZABETH ELLIOT,
Chorleywood, Hertfordshire. December 22

REALLY USEFUL NAMES

From Mr David R. Wright

Sir, Your analysis of the choice of boys' names omits one key factor: three of the five most popular names come from the *Thomas the Tank Engine* books.
          I remain, Sir, your obedient namespotter,
                          DAVID R. WRIGHT,
              Mulbarton, Norfolk. December 27

1998

EXTRA SPICE

From Mr Raymond Wergan

Sir, In order to differentiate between grandparents, our latest granddaughter has started calling my wife "Granny Spice".

I find this charming, but it has the drawback that I am now known as "Old Spice".
                          Yours faithfully,
                          RAYMOND WERGAN,
          Newton Ferrers, Devon. January 2

SO THERE

From Mr James S. Barnett

Sir, Today you report Ms Vivienne Parry ("Diana trustees defend law firm in fees furore") as saying: "You can't expect to pop into a local high street solicitors and ask them to do international copyright law."

Well, you can, in Hungerford.
                          Yours sincerely,
                          JAMES S. BARNETT
          (Solicitor), Hungerford, Berkshire
                              January 17

THE RIGHT STUFF

From Professor Emeritus Michael Bond

Sir, At last something in your columns on which I am a real expert (report, January 13). What you do is this. Turn the duvet cover inside out. Clasp in each hand the two inside far corners of the cover, and (through them) the two top corners of the duvet. Go to the top of the stairs, and firmly holding these two points, throw the bulk of the duvet and the cover over the banisters. The cover will fall neatly and squarely, right way out, over the duvet. Haul it back up, and do the poppers.

Not much use to those in flats or bungalows, I'm afraid, but there you are.
                          Yours sincerely,
                          MICHAEL BOND,
                  Colyton, Devon. January 19

From Mr Andrew Wood

Sir, 1. Start by washing duvet cover inside out. 2. Reach inside and grasp two "top" corners of duvet through cover. 3. Shake arms as in "Mexican wave" - cover will un-roll itself over duvet. 4. Put clothes pegs on corners and position closed end at head of bed. 5. Tuck bottom corners into cover and close. 6. Remove clothes pegs. 7. (optional) Assume "what a good/clever boy I am" look, and pour congratulatory whisky.

It's all so easy my wife lets me do it every week.   *Yours faithfully,*
ANDREW WOOD,
London N2. January 19

From Mr Alexander Donald

Sir, Take a tip from a lazy bachelor. Open the bottom seam in two places to make six-inch hand-holes; reach through and pull the duvet into the cover.   *Yours faithfully,*
ALEXANDER DONALD,
Ramsey, Isle of Man. January 19

From Mr R. D. Parkinson

Sir, The course in duvet handling in North Yorkshire received blanket media coverage. If you fail, do you get sent down?
Yours etc,
R. D. PARKINSON,
London SW17. January 19

From Major John FitzGerald

Sir, It is obvious from today's letters that all that is needed for successful duvet stuffing is ingenuity and common sense - I person-ally find having a German wife to be an additional and possibly unfair advantage.

I am distressed to think that we in North Yorkshire are to be deemed to be so lacking in any of these attributes that special school-ing has to be laid on.   *Yours etc,*
JOHN FitzGERALD,
York. January 24

From Sir Rowland Whitehead

Sir, Married to a Norwegian for 44 years I have had a pretty good time. Till, that is, one comes to duvet-changing. Mockery fills the air.

I think it is in the genes. *Yours helplessly,*
ROWLAND WHITEHEAD,
London W4. January 24

From Mr David Tribe

Sir, Three cheers for Derwent May ("Du-vets mean sleeping with the enemy"). No one would expect a summer guest to arrive in a winter coat, but many a hotelier will provide a 12-tog duvet for the warmest of nights. A campaign to bring back the flex-ible comfort of the British blanket and end the tyranny of the universal duvet is long overdue.   *Yours faithfully,*
DAVID TRIBE,
London SW19. January 24

From Mr Paul Colgrave

Sir, What a mess Derwent May's bedroom must be, with blankets strewn everywhere.

Duvets are a great solution to numerous problems. I sleep in a king-size bed with my partner, and we both have single quilts of different tog values to sort out tempera-tures. Their main advantage though is re-moval of the possession problem – the con-stant tug-of-war which results in lack of sleep, stiff necks/backs from draughts (in mid-battle a double duvet or sheet/blanket combo pulled tight opens a huge hole that lets cold air in) and bad moods in the morn-ing.   *Yours etc,*
PAUL COLGRAVE,
Altrincham, Cheshire. January 24

From Mr John R. Sharp

Sir, Having got the wretched thing in, how do I prevent the duvet migrating laterally within the cover so that I am not left insu-lated with only the thickness of the cover while the wife is double lagged?
Yours faithfully,
JOHN R. SHARP,
Cheadle, Cheshire. January 24

From Mr Michael Banister

Sir, My wife and I endorse the advice given by Professor Bond. We throw our duvet over the Banisters every night.

Yours eponymously,
MICHAEL BANISTER,
Solihull, West Midlands. January 24

UPWARDLY MOBILE

From Mr Alan Millard

Sir, Mobile phone companies' aerial masts on church spires (article, Weekend, January 17)? What next?

Stands the Church clock at ten to three? And is that mast AT&T?

Yours faithfully,
ALAN MILLARD,
Lee-on-the-Solent, Hampshire. January 21

FACE TO FACE

From Mr David S. Cole

Sir, Transatlantic communication regularly brings to light new expressions. An e-mail I received recently from a colleague in the San Francisco office of my company contained the expression "face time". On asking, this turned out to mean a personal meeting between two people.

As voicemail, telecommuting and similar expressions seem to have been absorbed into English, I suppose this one will follow?

Yours sincerely,
DAVID COLE,
Knebworth, Hertfordshire. February 5

From Mr John Murray

Sir, Mr David Cole should brace himself for further unpleasant transatlantic expressions.

When I raised an objection by e-mail to a US-based colleague's proposal, I received the message: "No prob. Re-up at next skull-session" (translation: No problem. Bring it up next time we meet).   *Yours faithfully,*
JOHN MURRAY,
London SW10. February 7

From Mr D. Goldie-Scot

Sir, Mr David Cole can expect worse than "face time".

I've been told that a problem needs to be discussed in "meatspace" (translation: an encounter in the flesh, as opposed to cyberspace).

Occasionally I am asked for a "3D" (the same thing).   *Yours faithfully,*
DUNCAN GOLDIE-SCOT,
London SW1. February 7

COLLISION COURSE

From Rear-Admiral J. F. Perowne

Sir, Having just watched the film *Titanic*, I was amused to note that when the officer of the watch ordered "full starboard rudder" on sighting the iceberg right ahead, the helmsman put the wheel smartly to port. Perhaps this confusion was because all the officers were wearing their shoulder boards back to front, which is known in the Royal Navy as "going astern".

Yours faithfully,
JAMES PEROWNE,
HMS *Warrior*, Middlesex. February 7

FOOTBALL FRENCH

From Mr P. M. Demetriadi

Sir, You report that *Ici, mon fils, sur ma tete* is the translation given by Bilston Community College, in its course on football supporters' French, for "Over 'ere, son, on me 'ead". This sentence could only have been uttered by a Frenchman who was a cleric and probably of a certain age.

The correct translation would be *Ici, fiston, a la tete!* but a French person would be more likely to say *Fais-moi une tete*. This would normally be accompanied by a gesture, obbligato but in any event untranslatable, with the second rather than the index finger; the latter might be misconstrued as putting a pistol to one's head or referring to the sanity of the addressee.   *Yours faithfully,*
PETER DEMETRIADI,
Alcester, Warwickshire. February 21

From Mr Robert Hill

Sir, I commend Bilston Community College's enterprise and hope they will not have overlooked basic everyday phrases, such as:

Any spare tickets, guv? (*Est-ce qu'on a quelques tickets de trop, chef?*)

You're nicked, mate. (*Vous etes pincé, mon vieux.*)

Where's my brief? (*Où est mon dossier?*)

Got legal aid? (*Est-ce qu'on offre une système d'aide juridique?*)

I need my social worker/probation officer. (*Je demande ma travailleuse sociale/deleguée a la liberté surveillée.*) Yours etc,

ROBERT HILL,
Harpenden, Hertfordshire. February 21

AN EXTRA TINCTURE

From Dr J. R. O'Brien

Sir, Dr Edward Wilson, explorer and artist with Captain Scott in the Antarctic, had to sketch his paintings in pencil and take notes of the colours. Returning to the ship or camp – and comparative warmth – he could only then apply his watercolours.

If he had known that watercolours are gin-soluble, life would have been easier. The freezing point of gin is about −80C, depending on the amount of tonic.

I can just see the pencil outlines on my Mt Erebus, which is, typically Wilson, unsigned. *Yours faithfully,*

J. R. O'BRIEN,
Droxford, Hampshire. February 23

From Professor Robert Spence, FEng

Sir, While my scientific career has, to my knowledge, not suffered unduly from being unable to remember such fundamental quantities as Avogadro's Number and the charge on an electron, Dr O'Brien's mention of the freezing point of gin did recall my extreme embarrassment following failure to remember such a fundamental constant of nature when attempting to manufacture gin-and-tonic lollies. *Yours etc,*

ROBERT SPENCE,
Whyteleafe, Surrey. March 7

A1 ANGEL

From Mr Patrick Whitworth

Sir, You report controversy over the sculpture *Angel of the North.* Were the angel to flap its wings and make environmentally clean electricity the number of objectors would double. *Yours faithfully,*

PATRICK WHITWORTH,
Nairn, Inverness-shire. February 24

ALL THE DUCHESS'S MEN

From Mr Garth ap Rees

Sir, Ernest Simpson was not the first husband of Wallis Warfield (Diary, February 27). From 1916 to 1927 she was married to E. W. Spencer Jnr. She divorced him and married Simpson in 1928.

This led to the explanation at the time of the abdication that Spencer was the First Mate; Simpson, the Second Mate; Edward, the Third Mate; Cosmo Gordon Lang, the Primate; and Stanley Baldwin the Checkmate. *Yours sincerely,*

GARTH ap REES,
Shepton Mallet, Somerset. March 4

From Admiral Sir William O'Brien

Sir, A less kind observation about the Duchess of Windsor's men recorded the Duke's demotion "from Admiral of the Fleet to Third Mate of an American tramp". *Yours sincerely,*

W. D. O'BRIEN,
Trowbridge, Wiltshire. March 7

PILE-UP IN THE PARK

From Mr Gerard Stamp

Sir, For the past four years, my journey to work has taken me across Hyde Park. In all that time I had no idea the Serpentine Gallery was being refurbished. I thought the mixture of scaffolding, Portakabins and tarpaulin were all part of a particularly long-running exhibit. *Yours faithfully,*

GERARD STAMP (Executive Creative Director), Leo Burnett Limited,
London SW3. March 6

SHEEP'S CLOTHING

From Mr Rob Pratt

Sir, I read with interest that Dolly, the cloned sheep, has had her first fleece knitted up into a jumper which is to be displayed at the Science Museum.

Can we now expect to find many hundreds of identical jumpers, possibly on sale in the museum shop?   *Regards*,
ROB PRATT,
Southampton. March 13

INTERNET ADDICTION

From The Dean of Lichfield
Sir, Logging on to a website to seek help with Internet addiction (report, March 16) is like going into a pub to cure one's alcoholism.

Perhaps we should give up the Internet for Lent, before it gets the better of us: from sins of body, mind and modem, Good Lord deliver us.   *Yours etc*,
TOM WRIGHT,
Lichfield, Staffordshire. March 18

From Mr John O'Byrne
Sir, Can Internet addiction be cured by going on the www.agon ?   *Yours etc*,
JOHN O'BYRNE,
Harold's Cross, Dublin. March 19

GENDER BENDING

From Rear-Admiral J. A. Bell (retd)
Sir, I believe that all words in French ending in "ance" and "ence" are feminine, except one: *le silence*. No comment.

Yours faithfully,
JOHN BELL,
Wellington, Somerset. March 21

From Mr R. Q. Drayson
Sir, During 35 years of teaching French at a modest level in four schools, I, too, found the suggestion that *le silence* was masculine because of the ladies' inability to keep it, whether true or not, was certainly an aid to memory.

Along the same line, when asked to distinguish between *le poisson* and *le poison*, one bright boy deemed them to mean fish and school fish.   *Yours faithfully*,
ROBERT DRAYSON,
Cranbrook, Kent. March 28

A LIGHT LUNCH?

From Mr David Edwards
Sir, In explaining the new crackdown on ministerial leaks to journalists over lunch, a spokesman said: "Everyone's been warned off lunches, but if they must, they have been told to keep their mouths shut" (report, March 13).

This sounds pretty drastic.

Yours sincerely,
DAVID EDWARDS,
Southsea, Hampshire. March 23

PAYMENT OF DOCTORS

From Dr I. A. McCoubrey
Sir, John McNicholas asks if the idea of payment by results might spread to doctors, with their being paid when patients recover.

Many years ago an even better practice existed in China. Patients paid their doctor a monthly retainer, but stopped paying it if they were ill. Among other benefits, this encouraged the practice of preventive rather than curative medicine.   *Yours faithfully*,
I. A. McCOUBREY,
Wantage, Oxfordshire. March 30

SHIPS' NAMES ALL AT SEA

From Mr Martyn Compton
Sir, Today's sailors should spare a thought for their predecessors in the 1960s, some of whom had to go ashore with *Gay Charger* or *Gay Fencer* emblazoned above their foreheads (report March 28).

Yours faithfully,
M. T. COMPTON
(Royal Navy, 1961-70),
Farnborough, Hampshire. March 31

From the Venerable R. J. D. Newhouse
Sir, Sailors are traditionally concerned with the names of their ships and ready to invent alternatives if the official title seems inadequate. So HMS *Vanguard* became *The Guard's Van*, not inappropriately for the very last in a long train of British battleships.

One of the best such stories concerns a 1940 frigate named HMS *Weston*. Everyone then venerated the memory of Dame Agnes Weston (also affectionately known as "Aggie") who devoted her life to the welfare of sailors; and the ship was soon known as HMS *Aggie*.

Official attempts to counter this by lengthening the name were not successful; HMS *Weston-super-Mare* became simply *Aggie-on-Horseback*.   *Yours faithfully,*
R. J. D. NEWHOUSE,
Okehampton, Devon. April 6

From Captain P. A. C. Harland, RN (retd)
Sir, I served in an Algerine-class minesweeper, HMS *Truelove* (not a particularly macho name), from 1951 to 1953, when the ship invariably received a warm reception in foreign ports. Perhaps it was not surprising that many a sailor used to return onboard after a good run ashore minus his cap ribbon.

On the other hand, my son was serving in HMS *Battleaxe* at the time when Wrens started going to sea. I wonder how they enjoyed having that name emblazoned on their cap ribbon.   *Yours sincerely,*
PATRICK HARLAND,
East Lydford, Somerset. April 6

From Mr H. Knox
Sir, In the late 1950s I worked on a Navy guided missile project. It was known internally as CF211, but a suitable name was sought for its release to the Navy.

The Admiralty did not accept our suggestion of "Sea Lord". Perhaps the thought of attending the firing of the first Sea Lord was too much to contemplate.

Yours faithfully,
H. KNOX,
Beaconsfield, Buckinghamshire. April 6

From Mr P. S. H. Lawrence
Sir, It is hard to understand this anxiety about macho names for HM ships (letters, March 31, April 6). Are they not properly referred to as "she"?   *Yours faithfully,*

PETER LAWRENCE,
Little Milton, Oxford. April 7

SPRING MIGRATION

From Mr A. J. Saunders
Sir, On my travels this weekend I could not help but notice that there were hundreds of caravans on the move, presumably to their summer spawning grounds of the countryside and coastline.

This is the earliest migration I have seen; is this another manifestation of the El Niño effect?   *Yours etc,*
A. J. SAUNDERS,
Swindon, Wiltshire. March 31

POETS' CORNER

From Mr W. S. Becket
Sir, When mentioning Keats and Bob Dylan in the same breath (leading article, "Blowin' in the wind", March 28) should you not start by drawing a distinction between art and entertainment?

Yours faithfully,
W. S. BECKET,
Deiniolen, Gwynedd. April 1

From Mr Matthew Stephenson
Sir, Mr W. S. Becket assumes – apropos of Keats and Bob Dylan – that there is a distinction between art and entertainment.

Surely the best art entertains and the best entertainment is an art.

I am, Sir, Yours faithfully,
R. M. STEPHENSON,
London N1. April 6

SALES DRIVE

From Mr Roger Morton
Sir, There has been a recent proliferation of home-made signs in this area exhorting us to "Buy British beef". I was particularly interested to note two examples on the rear of R-registration four-wheel-drive vehicles – an Isuzu Trooper and a Jeep Cherokee.

Yours,
ROGER MORTON,
Shrewsbury, Shropshire. April 3

WISH LIST

From Mr Michael R. Taylor

Sir, I saw your headline "Teenagers want lottery win instead of a job" and thought how grown-up and mature of them. I am 63 and want exactly the same.

Yours faithfully,
MICHAEL R. TAYLOR,
Broadford, Isle of Skye. April 3

CHEERS!

From Mr Tony Wilmot

Sir, Ben Reed, reviewing *The Martini Companion*, says he keeps the Martini glass and the vodka or gin in the freezer ready for mixing.

My copy of Lawrence Blochman's round-the-world bar guide, *Here's How!* (Signet Key Books, New York, 1957), says that a Martini cocktail is always made with gin. Aficionados, he says, prefer it very dry, at least eight to one, gin to vermouth.

Indeed, Hemingway readers will recall that Colonel Cantwell, hero of *Across the River and Into the Trees*, drank a dry Martini with 15 parts Gordon's gin to one part vermouth.

Yours soberly,
TONY WILMOT,
London SW20. April 7

From Sir Humphry Wakefield

Sir, Hemingway readers may well recall his manly Martini 15/1 mix. Noel Coward's was more manly still.

I was lucky enough to stay in the Master's New York apartment for a few months long ago and his Martini directions were very clear: Chill the gin and shake it, lemon peel routine, incline towards Italy and serve.

Yours &c,
HUMPHRY WAKEFIELD,
Chillingham, Northumberland. April 11

From Miss Deborah Lane

Sir, According to Salvatore Calabrese, in *Classic Cocktails* (Prion, 1997), Sir Winston Churchill would make his Martinis by "pouring gin into a pitcher and 'glancing briefly at a bottle of Vermouth' across the room".

Kind regards,
D. J. LANE,
Kenninghall, Norfolk. April 11

From Mr David Politi

Sir, I was taught four parts gin to no parts vermouth.

Yours,
D. POLITI,
London SW5. April 11

From Miss Mary P. Johnston

Sir, My father used to tell the following story: If you are lost in a jungle, just pour a measure of gin and a measure of Vermouth into a glass (letters, April 7 and 11). As if by magic a man will jump out from behind a tree and say: "That's not how you make a dry Martini."

Yours faithfully,
MARY P. JOHNSTON,
London SW4. April 15

From Mr Allen Keep

Sir, Miss Mary Johnston's letter demonstrating the inevitability of criticism of one's dry Martini reminds me of the story of the Australian long-distance lorry driver.

He said if you're ever stranded in the Outback, simply get out of the vehicle, produce a pack of cards and start playing Patience. Within seconds someone will appear at your shoulder and say: "That six goes on the seven."

Yours faithfully,
A. E. KEEP,
South Gloucester. April 20

LANE DISCIPLINE

From Mr David Green

Sir, Owners of four-wheel-drive off-road vehicles force other vehicles off narrow country lanes because they don't want to get their own muddy.

Yours faithfully,
DAVID GREEN,
Castle Morris, Pembrokeshire. April 21

CHANCING THEIR LUCK?

From Mr Peter Tandy

Sir, I have thought for many years that I had a reasonable idea of how actuaries performed their complex and highly responsible tasks. Having read today that they were joined for their annual dinner by the Makers of Playing Cards, I am no longer sure.

Yours,
PETER TANDY,
Stratford-upon-Avon, Warwickshire. April 23

From the Master of the Worshipful Company of Actuaries

Sir, Mr Peter Tandy spotted the supposed close relationship between the Actuaries and the Makers of Playing Cards.

He could perhaps also have noted from the Court and Social page announcement the presence at the same dinner of the Company of Glass Sellers, from whom one might just be able to buy a crystal ball.   Yours,
RICHARD HAWKES,
Twyford, Winchester, Hampshire. April 25

JUNK IN THE POST

From Mrs Catherine Bradshaw

Sir, Dr Georges Ware wonders what to do with a steadily increasing pile of unwanted CD-Rom discs.

We put a similarly unwanted collection to good use last December by gluing them together in pairs (printed sides together), drilling a hole near the rim, putting thread through the hole and hanging them on the church Christmas tree, where they caught the light most effectively and attractively, particularly during candle-lit services.

A friend is using her CDs to the same effect in a sensory stimulation room for children with special needs.   Yours,
CATHERINE BRADSHAW,
Bushey, Hertfordshire. April 24

From Mr Simon M. Westcott

Sir, Hung by threads in the vegetable garden, unwanted CDs make effective and highly reflective bird-scarers.

Yours faithfully,
SIMON WESTCOTT,
Guildford, Surrey. April 24

From Susannah Gibbs

Sir, Freebie CDs lit up my family's Christmas table as candleholders.   Yours faithfully,
SUSANNAH GIBBS (age 12),
Kelvedon, Essex. April 24

From Mr John O'Byrne

Sir, I find that CD-Rom compact discs make excellent Frisbees, and this opinion is shared by our dog, which is an expert Rom-catcher.   Yours truly,
JOHN O'BYRNE,
Harold's Cross, Dublin. April 24

A WORLD OF BOOKS

From Mrs Sue Ogden

Sir, I note that Valerie Grove (World Book Day supplement) prefers to have her bookshelves "organised". I cannot agree with her. I find that not having them arranged in any sort of order means that in finding a particular title, I come across all sorts of interesting books I had forgotten about.

Ms Grove's preference for order prompted me to look at my own shelves again, with a view to reorganisation. However, when I spotted that Silence of the Lambs by Thomas Harris had managed to get itself sandwiched in between Ethics by P. H. Nowell-Smith and Malcolm Bradbury's Eating People is Wrong, I left them as they were.

Yours faithfully,
SUE OGDEN,
Bearsden, Glasgow. April 28

LEARNING FROM INDIA

From Mrs Christine Jowett

Sir, Last week I was much taken by a huge slogan on the wall of a school in southern India: "There is no school equal to a decent home and no teachers equal to honest, virtuous parents."

Close inspection revealed that it was credited, not to David Blunkett, but to Mahatma Gandhi. This week a similar poster appeared on my classroom door for parents' night.

Yours faithfully,

C. JOWETT,
Dunlop, Ayrshire. April 28

UNSOUGHT HONOUR

From Mr Tony Wilmot

Sir, Since you published my letter about the Martini cocktail, I've received an unsolicited offer to

reproduce (it) digitally and present it mounted and framed. The finished product (ideal for the smallest room) will be A4 size (landscape or portrait as appropriate) with non-reflective glass... Your opinion on a subject about which you feel strongly enough to write, and be published in a national newspaper, can now be preserved for posterity ... for £16.50 (£2 p&p).

Have other *Times* readers had similarly bizarre responses to letters they've had published?   *Yours faithfully*,
TONY WILMOT,
London SW20. May 1

From Canon John Oates

Sir, Flattered though I was that an earlier letter of mine had evoked the offer of encouragement and rather expensive help in compiling my autobiography, I had to make clear that any agreement on my part would be entirely conditional on the guarantee of the Editor of *The Times* that he would serialise the masterpiece.

Yours faithfully,
JOHN OATES,
London EC4. May 15

From Mr David Edwards

Sir, A letter you published from me some seven years ago, on the subject of my mother boiling her alarm clock to make it work, caught the eye of CNN Television, who promptly featured *The Times* letters page, co-starring my letter and myself.

I also received an unsolicited copy of the *Church Times*.   *Yours sincerely*,
D. J. EDWARDS,
Southsea, Hampshire. May 15

From Major John FitzGerald

Sir, The first response to my light-hearted letter about the Cross of St Patrick (May 27, 1997) said: "No wonder St Patrick's cross, with all those snakes to chase off the island" (a reference to my reason for the saint not looking for martyrdom).

The second letter, from a publishing company, invited me to spend good money on a creative writing course.   *Yours etc*,
JOHN FitzGERALD,
York. May 11

From Mr Alan Millard

Sir, Soon after you published a letter of mine (April 5, 1997) on the subject of Rutland's motto, *Multum in parvo* – a lot in a little – which, in view of my stature, I chose to adopt for myself, I received a response from a short person in Roseville, California. He had read my letter on the Internet and asked if he could share the motto with me.

My reply marked the beginning of a delightful correspondence which culminated this year with his visit to England and our first meeting at a local inn.

Needless to say, as founder members of the *Multum in parvo* Society, we had no difficulty in recognising each other. I have high hopes for the society's future growth.

Yours faithfully,
ALAN MILLARD,
Lee-on-the-Solent, Hampshire. May 11

From the Reverend Canon Charles Taylor

Sir, If my experience is anything to go by, the company which offers to mount and frame published letters to the Editor would be able to target a far wider market by offering to provide the same enhancement for letters purporting to be from the Editor expressing his alleged interest in the correspondence but regretting his inability to publish it.   *Yours faithfully*,
CHARLES TAYLOR,
Lichfield, Staffordshire. May 11

MARATHON WINNERS

From Mr Jim Moyes and Mr Iain Smith

Sir, Having completed the London marathon last weekend we hailed a taxi back to our hotel. Chatting to the cabbie we told him that we had run to raise funds for Whizz Kidz, the charity that provides mobility for non-mobile children.

Arriving at our destination he refused to take our fare and told us to put the money into our fund – as the notice in his cab states: "the best taxis in the world!" Thanks, London. *Yours etc,*

JIM MOYES, IAIN SMITH,
Perth. May 2

From Mr Patrick Howarth

Sir, The two London Marathon runners collecting on behalf of Whizz Kidz are right in their assessment of London taxi drivers.

A few years ago I asked a cab driver to take me to the Special Forces Club. He asked me some questions about the club and who was eligible to join. After I had explained he refused to accept payment.

As my only real distinction acquired during several years of service in SOE was to have had my hotel bedroom invaded in the middle of the night by a beautiful foreign spy, I thought this excessively generous.

Yours faithfully,
PATRICK HOWARTH,
Sherborne, Dorset. May 11

FELLOW FEELING

From Mrs Rory Peck

Sir, Canvassing for the Tadcaster West ward in a Selby District Council by-election, I struck up a conversation with a local pensioner. She asked me which party I was standing for and when I told her the Conservatives she replied: "Oh my dear, I know just how you feel. I'm a Jehovah's Witness."

Yours sincerely,
JULIET PECK,
Healaugh, North Yorkshire. May 6

SHADES OF DIFFERENCE

From Mr L. P. Rowley

Sir, The Government's concern over the high price of sun-protection creams (report, May 12) may be good news for southern baskers, but here in Leeds we'd appreciate cheaper umbrellas.

Yours faithfully,
L. P. ROWLEY,
Leeds. May 15

BROKEN DREAMS

From Mr C. J. Vollers

Sir, Policemen have, of course, been getting younger for years, but I was reminded that I was no longer in the first flush of youth when I read "The opening concert . . . by the Rolling Stones has been put back after the guitarist Keith Richards broke a rib falling off a ladder in the library of his Connecticut home" (News in brief, May 19).

Yours sincerely,
C. J. VOLLERS,
Godalming, Surrey. May 26

THE CASE FOR CASH

From Mrs Patricia P. Duncan

Sir, Jane Shilling's article on being a "hopeless packer" (features, May 22) reminds me of the wise advice given by my mother many years ago, and not always followed: "Take half the clothes, and twice the money." *Yours faithfully,*

PATRICIA P. DUNCAN,
Landican, Birkenhead. May 26

A WISE SAW

From Mr John Raybould

Sir, As well as my mother's good advice (letter, "The case for cash"), the exhortation by Mr Smith, my woodwork master at Westminster City School some fifty ago, has always stuck in my mind.

"Measure twice, cut once," he bellowed. This principle has served me well, not just when attempting do-it-yourself handiwork

but also when making decisions in business or in my family.   *Yours sincerely,*
JOHN RAYBOULD,
Sawbridgeworth, Hertfordshire. June 2

From the Reverend Roger Combes

Sir, In my occasional forays into DIY, the words of my builders-merchant father invariably return to me:"Two checks are better than one mistake."

Then I am distracted by wondering if he meant "cheques".   *Yours faithfully,*
ROGER COMBES,
St Leonards-on-Sea, East Sussex. June 9

USES FOR ECONOMISTS

From Mr Eddie Kent

Sir, I would add to Philip Howard's entertaining account of economics and economists (May 29) the aphorism of which my maths tutor was most fond: "An economist is someone who, if you have forgotten your telephone number, will estimate it for you."   *Yours faithfully*
EDDIE KENT,
Norwich, Norfolk. June 3

From Mr Arthur S. Hoffman

Sir, Further to Mr Eddie Kent's letter, my preferred definition of an economist is someone who knows more about money than people who have got it.   *Yours,*
ARTHUR S. HOFFMAN,
Bexhill-on-Sea, East Sussex. June 10

From Mr Clive R. Wismayer

Sir, I have always understood an economist to be someone who, by looking out of the rear window of a car, can tell the driver where he is going.   *Yours faithfully,*
CLIVE WISMAYER,
London SW19. June 17

CHURCH CHALLENGE

From Mr Julian Washington

Sir, You reported on June 5 plans to sell Lambeth Conference souvenirs – including ties – to the bishops of the Anglican Communion at their gathering next month. Now there's a challenge: selling ties to bishops!   *I am, Sir, yours faithfully,*
JULIAN WASHINGTON,
London E2. June 9

A HELPING HAND

From Sir Robert Sanders

Sir, Budding authors and playwrights may be interested in a notice by the Glenalmond to Gilmerton road in Perthshire. It reads: "Plots for sale".   *Yours faithfully,*
ROBERT SANDERS,
Crieff, Perthshire. June 10

AND THE LOSERS?

From Professor Alec Eden

Sir, I was saddened to read today that Ola, the chimpanzee who beat a team of international stockbrokers in a share-tipping contest in Sweden, has been found "downcast" in a 12ft by 12ft cage in Thailand.

Your report omits to say what happened to the stockbrokers.   *Yours faithfully,*
ALEC EDEN,
Torquay, Devon. June 19

NO MONEY GO ROUND

From Dr Jonathan Tuliani

Sir, The Royal Mint should be praised for its choice of a scientific theme for the design of the new two-pound coin (photograph, June 15). However, the 19 cogs depicted on the reverse are configured in such a manner that they cannot turn.

Perhaps the euro will work a little better?
Yours faithfully,
J. TULIANI,
Department of Mathematics, Royal Holloway (University of London), Egham, Surrey. June 22

SMOOTH MEN

From Mr Allen Brown

Sir, Gentlemen having difficulty ironing their shirts ("Science proves men can't iron", June 16) may care to be guided by the following, which I recall from my naval days:

First the collar, then the cuff, Then the front, and that's enough.

Yours faithfully,
ALLEN BROWN,
Headcorn, Kent. June 22

From Mrs Sara Mason

Sir, I totally disagree with Jason Cowley that men are unable to iron properly. My man certainly can. Before he retired from the bench, he used to iron his shirts and starch his bands. The Old Bailey never had a smarter nor more crease-free judge.

Yours thankfully,
SARA MASON,
Stroud, Gloucestershire. June 22

From Major T. A. E. Gibson, RA (retd)

Sir, Forgive my poor handwriting: I'm laughing too much!

Men can't iron? Twice a week I complete a voluntary morning stint in the back of a local charity shop, when I do the ironing which the ladies (the majority of the voluntary staff) prefer not to do. They like the glamour of the cash till, selling and chatting.

I spent some of 1941 in the Infantry as a batman and as a latrine orderly. Perhaps that's why I do the ironing at the shop, and at home, where I also do the Hoovering and the washing-up, and other chores.

My wife (and Commanding Officer) does not know I've written to you.

I am, Sir, your, and others', obedient servant,
T. A. E. GIBSON,
Ivybridge, Devon. June 22

From Mrs Shirley Kirby

Sir, I wash my husband's shirts. I iron them badly. Result: misery.

I wash my husband's shirts. He irons them. Result: happiness.   *Yours faithfully,*
SHIRLEY KIRBY,
Lewes, East Sussex. June 22

From Mrs S. C. Bain

Sir, Ah, but can men iron and watch the World Cup at the same time?

Yours faithfully
BETH BAIN,
Solihull, West Midlands. June 23

From Mrs Jane Cooper

Sir, The answer to Mrs Beth Bain's query about whether men can iron and watch the World Cup is – most certainly.

My husband reckons that American football is best for ironing with lots of boring bits between the bursts of action. However, during yesterday's England match he managed to get through all three loads of washing which the day's breezy sunshine had allowed me to dry.

I am not sure if this is a reliable indicator of the quality of the match or merely a demonstration of speed increasing with practice.

Yours faithfully,
JANE COOPER,
Newcastle upon Tyne. June 26

From Mr Richard Wrigley

Sir, The answer to Mrs Bain's question is yes. The offer and completion of the ironing during World Cup games is a successful tactic in gaining full access to the TV without argument. One word of warning – ball watching can have dire consequences.

Regards,
RICHARD WRIGLEY,
Goring-on-Thames, Oxfordshire. June 23

From Mr James R. Hooke

Sir, Scotland 0, Morocco 3, shirts 4, sheets 2, pillowcases 2, shorts 1. One yellow card for ungentlemanly conduct refusing to press female underwear.   *Yours faithfully,*
JAMES R. HOOKE,
London SW18. June 26

From Mr Gregor Macaulay

Sir, The continuing correspondence on the ironing of shirts amazes me. Why do otherwise sensible people buy shirts made of drip-dry, no-iron fabrics and then proceed to iron them?

Wash your shirts using a gentle washing cycle, hang them immediately on plastic hangers to dry, and they will give years of unwrinkled and low-maintenance wear. Polyester-cotton fabrics are a boon and a blessing, and ironing is folly.

Yours faithfully,
G. A. MACAULAY,
Dunedin, New Zealand. June 26

From Mr Colin Gordon

Sir, Men ironing shirts? Sir, in 1949 as National Service recruits at Catterick we ironed our boots!   *Your obedient servant,*
COLIN GORDON (847 Tpr Gordon, C.),
London NW6. June 26

KORENS KEYBOARD

From Dr Susan Milligan

Sir, I read with interest and amusement Alan Corens article (June 24) about the non-functioning letter c on his obsolete Apple Mac!

I have a similar problem with mine, but in this case it is the full stop I have lost! Fortunately the problem only arose after I had completed the text of my forthcoming book, but I am not sure how I am going to punctuate my next piece of writing! The apostrophe has also gone!   *Yours sincerely,*
SUSAN MILLIGAN,
Glasgow G11! June 30

From Ms Maria Cope

Sir, Single sentence paragraphs would be my answer to Dr Susan Milligan. For more than 40 years I have abandoned full stops at the ends of paragraphs. I cannot see the necessity for them

Or she could emulate a friend of mine who enthusiastically adopted the idea and used no full stops at all. She relied on sufficient space at the end of each sentence to make the point   *Yours faithfully,*
MARIA COPE,
London NW1. July 7

From Mr Andrew Gardner

SIR COMMA DR SUSAN MILLIGAN COULD RESORT TO TELEGRAMS STOP *YOURS FAITHFULLY* COMMA ANDREW GARDNER COMMA
Islington, London N1. July 7

FIRST POOHSTICKS

From Lord Kilbracken

Sir, In weighing up the rival claims of bridges in Sussex and Devon to be the site where Poohsticks was invented (article, "Put yourself in Pooh's corner", Weekend, July 4), Rachel Kelly doesn't mention the vital fact that the Milnes' country house, Cotchford Farm, where Christopher Robin spent most of his school holidays, was in Hartfield, within a short walk of the Sussex bridge.

Besides, it was here that I played Poohsticks with him in our boyhood.

Yours faithfully,
JOHN KILBRACKEN,
House of Lords. July 8

ULSTER MARCHES

From Mr Cyril Bryan

Sir, William of Orange was reminded by the first Duke of Devonshire that "he had come to England to protect Protestants, not to persecute Papists" (*Georgiana*, Brian Masters, Hamish Hamilton, 1981).

How can the marching by today's supporters of that King achieve this laudable aim?

Yours faithfully,
C. BRYAN,
London SW10. July 9

MOVIE MISHAPS

From Mr J. K. West

Sir, Thank you for publishing the picture of Julie Andrews and the von Trapp children paraded above an orange box marked "Produce of Israel" in Salzburg market. This is one of the best known cinematic anachronisms and is always well worth seeing.

How about a photo of the 1952 rubber

dinghy in *South Pacific* to illustrate a travel piece on the South Seas? *Yours sincerely,*
J. K. WEST,
Wimborne, Dorset. July 17

BIBLICAL ORIGINS

From Mr M. B. Simons

Sir, Now that scientists have established a direct-line genetic link from Aaron of the tribe of Levi down through the ages to present-day Cohanim (Jewish priests), cannot we of this priestly sect now state without fear of contradiction that we are possessors of Levi genes? *Yours etc,*
M. B. SIMONS,
Edgware, Middlesex. July 23

STAGE DIRECTIONS

From Mr P. R. Davis

Sir, In the 20 minutes I spent on the steps of Wyndham's Theatre (dressed in a smart new blazer with shiny brass buttons) awaiting an unpunctual companion, I was approached no fewer than 14 times by bewildered tourists asking for directions. The inquiries were as follows:

    The Coliseum (four times),
    The Palace Theatre (three times),
    The Garrick Theatre (twice),
    The Prince Edward (twice),
    The Apollo, Shaftesbury Avenue,
    St Martin's,
    Her Majesty's.

Is this representative of the relative popularity of London's entertainment? And what should I wear next time to avoid being mistaken for the doorman? *Yours etc,*
PAUL R. DAVIS,
Forest Hill, London SE23. July 23

From Miss Mary E. Jelley

Sir, If Mr P. R. Davies should again have a fancy for standing on the steps of a London theatre dressed in his sporting new brass-buttoned blazer, he will be quite safe from being mistaken for a doorman if he unbuttons his smart blazer, thus at least helping

to hide the buttons that played him false.

If that does not work he can tie a knot in all four corners of his handkerchief and wear it on his head to complete the picture of a holiday spirit. *Yours sincerely,*
MARY E. JELLEY,
Chute, via Andover, Hampshire. July 27

From Mr Amir Shivji

Sir, What Mr Davis needs if he wishes not to be accosted by the London tourists is not so much a change of "dress", but more a change of disposition.

"What should he wear?" he asks. Wear a frown. *Yours faithfully,*
AMIR SHIVJI,
Kingston upon Thames. July 27

From Mr D. G. Bevan

Sir, I do understand Mr Davis's experience. About thirty years ago I awaited the arrival of a guest at the Royal Opera House, Covent Garden. Dressed in dinner jacket (many if not all did in those days), I stood in the foyer holding two copies of the programme; within just a few minutes a number of people tried to purchase them from me. *Yours etc,*
D. G. BEVAN,
Ingatestone, Essex. July 27

From Captain C. P. R. Belton, RN

Sir, May I suggest to Mr Davis that he dress in a pair of dirty jeans and a T-shirt, in which he could only be mistaken for a theatregoer.

I have the honour to be, Sir, your obedient servant,
CHRISTOPHER BELTON,
Midhurst, West Sussex. July 27

From Mr John S. Price

Sir, I write to commiserate with the sartorially induced confusion experienced by your correspondents. When appearing in court, I wear the traditional barrister's outfit of black jacket, waistcoat and striped trousers. Whilst travelling to and from, I have been variously mistaken for an under-

taker, a master at Eton College, a head waiter, a station master (several times) and, on one happy occasion while riding on the platform of a Number 23 from the Strand, as a bus conductor.   *Yours faithfully,*
JOHN S. PRICE,
Caversham, Reading, Berkshire August 1

From Mr Rodney B. Spokes

Sir, At least Mr P. R. Davis, standing on the steps of a London theatre, was only asked for directions.

In the early Sixties I was in the foyer of a Monaco hotel at the end of the Monte Carlo Rally, proudly wearing my new racing overalls, which were just starting to be worn for international rallies.

A guest asked me to collect his cases from his room.   *Yours faithfully,*
RODNEY SPOKES
(Vice-Chairman, International Rally Drivers Club),
Leicester. August 1

From Mr Martin R. Davies

Sir, About 20 years ago, in the foyer of the Opera House in Budapest, I found I could read the figures but not the wording on my ticket. I approached a doorman in his imposing uniform and sought directions. He looked none too pleased at first but did show me towards my seat with a smile.

I was truly glad that I had not offered him a tip when, a few moments later, I observed him taking his seat in what I imagine had once been the Royal Box, in company with a number of other high-ranking officers of the Hungarian Army.   *Yours faithfully,*
MARTIN R. DAVIES,
Leigh Woods, Bristol. August 1

From Mr Michael Horne

Sir, Early in 1947 I was waiting outside the Academy cinema in Oxford Street on a rainy evening for a girl who in fact never turned up.

I was wearing my recently acquired "demob suit" (tweed jacket, grey flannels) underneath an ill-fitting raincoat that had also been provided by a grateful King and country. The trilby hat issued had blown away the previous week and I'd taken to wearing a black beret.

Because I'd run from Tottenham Court Road Tube to be on time and was hot, I was holding the beret in my hand. The girl was already 15 minutes late and my facial expression was probably beseeching of fate.

In any case, a passer-by suddenly tossed a sixpenny piece into the beret. Somewhat bemused I left it there, and by the time I finally gave the girl up 25 minutes later and went into the cinema alone I'd gained a full half-crown – more than enough to pay for my customary seat in the front stalls.

Yours sincerely,
MICHAEL HORNE,
Morston near Holt, Norfolk. August 3

BUS SERVICE

From Mrs J. M. Lockett

Sir, The Government would like me to dispense with my car and use public transport. Can they also recommend a bus company that would be prepared to loan a vehicle at weekends for my husband to dismantle, polish and rebuild?

Would they also mind if there were a few nuts and bolts left over?   *Yours sincerely,*
JOHANNA LOCKETT,
Hyde, Cheshire. July 29

From the Managing Director of Buffalo Travel

Sir, Whilst I do not think that the Department of Transport would approve of us allowing Johanna Lockett's husband to dismantle and rebuild our buses and coaches at weekends, polishing is a different matter.

Yours faithfully,
TIM CECIL,
Flitwick, Bedfordshire. August 3

SCHOOL UNIFORM

From Ms Patricia Leon

Sir, An eerie transformation occurred when my daughter, 13, moved from an inner-city Pimlico comprehensive (no uniform) to a smart Surrey village comprehensive (uniform) of similar size.

From androgynous attire of baggy pants or jeans, puffa jacket and trainers (Sporty Spice), she suddenly went into tart-mode with skirt hoisted thigh high, white shirt spilling out, eye make-up and tottering off to the school coach on platforms (Ginger Spice).

She said this was her way of fitting in.

Yours faithfully,
PATRICIA LEON,
East Horsley, Surrey. July 31

From Mr Nick Elsley

Sir, I remember arguing with a friend and rival who attended a nearby public school and telling him that he and his mates looked like proper little swots in their distinctive smart blue uniforms.

"Well, you wear uniforms at your school, too", he retorted. "Yes", I replied, "but at least we take care to keep ours dirty".

Yours sincerely,
N. J. ELSLEY,
London N20. August 10

From Mrs R. L. Henson

Sir, I went to Cheltenham Ladies College in September 1924. Until that term home clothes had been worn by the girls on Sundays.

There had been some competition, not only between the girls within the houses, but also, I believe, between the various houses, as to the smartest outfits. The end came in January 1923, when someone arrived in a fur coat.   *Yours faithfully,*
MARY HENSON,
Banbury, Oxfordshire. August 10

From Mrs Moira Kleissner

Sir, I'm all for school uniforms. Sensible, late 20th-century uniforms, that is. Let those who advocate ties change a class of 30 infants for PE!   *Yours sincerely,*
MOIRA KLEISSNER,
London W12. August 10

From Mrs Mona Clark

Sir, My (just) five-year-old grandson's school tie is fully formed and attached to an elastic cord which is hidden by his collar. I took this to be because the traditional tie could be used to cause harm to himself or others.

However, his father has been heard to boast that when he was five he was able to tie his own tie, and that was then a measure of being a "big boy".

Obviously I had more patience with him than he has with his son.   *Yours sincerely,*
MONA CLARK,
Dundee. August 13

From Mrs Philippa Parker

Sir, When my middle son had to learn to tie his school uniform tie, at the age of four, my husband made up the following mnemonic to help him: "Around the tree, up through the rabbit hole and down the chute."

It worked very well for him, but is not as easy for my left-handed, youngest son, currently struggling before this autumn's term.

Yours faithfully,
PHILIPPA PARKER,
St Albans, Hertfordshire. August 13

From Lieutenant-Colonel Tom Gibbon, Royal Tank Regiment (retd)

Sir, More years ago than I care to remember my second son, having observed his one-armed father dealing daily with his neckwear, proceeded to tie his school tie with one hand and his teeth.

He seemed surprised when I told him he could use both hands.   *Yours faithfully,*
T. H. GIBBON,
Pulborough, West Sussex. August 21

DRINKING TIME

From Mr Frederic Cassin

Sir, Your report about the proposal to reform the licensing laws and extend public house hours reminded me of an anecdote about the great American humorist, Will Rogers.

In 1933, after the repeal of Prohibition in America, the New York city fathers, in their wisdom, set the bar closing hours at 4am. Citizens, who had been able to drink around the clock when liquor was illegal, complained about this. But Rogers said: "If you can't get drunk by 4am, you ain't really trying."

Yours faithfully,
F. CASSIN,
Belfast. August 3

NEVER A LENDER

From Dr Brian Chadwick

Sir, Regarding the loan of books, *The Brains Trust* may well have referred to Richard Heber, bibliophile to some, bibliomaniac to others, 1773–1833, who opined that "No gentleman can be without three copies of a book, one for show, one for use, and one for borrowers." (*Left Hand, Right Hand!* by Osbert Sitwell, Macmillan, 1945, p43).

Yours sincerely,
BRIAN CHADWICK,
Exeter, Devon. August 4

MODELS OF THEIR KIND

From Mr Richard Russell

Sir, My mother remembered from her childhood a London surgeon at the turn of the century called Arthur Reckless whose brass plate was inscribed:

A. Reckless Surgeon.

Yours faithfully,
RICHARD RUSSELL,
Shipston-on-Stour, Warwickshire. August 4

From Mr Colin F. Smith

Sir, When my great-uncle retired in the 1930s from business life in India to the peace of a country home in Argyll, he recalled that in the main street of his nearest town, Lochgilphead, was the firm Kilbairn & Kilbride – Registrars of Births, Deaths and Marriages.   *Yours faithfully,*
COLIN F. SMITH,
Edgbaston, Birmingham. August 4

TESTING TIMES

From Mrs Sylvia Crookes

Sir, Who says that Yorkshiremen put money before everything? The noisy machines at our local ropeworks were all switched off at 11am today so that the employees (and the boss) could listen unhindered to the final moments of the Test match.   Yours,
S. CROOKES,
Bainbridge, North Yorkshire. August 11

PREJUDICE AND AN AGEING WORKFORCE

From Mr Charles Quant

Sir, There is, I believe, a West Indies saying that "New broom sweeps clean, but the old broom knows the corners."

Yours faithfully,
CHARLES QUANT,
Gwernymynydd, Flintshire. August 17

LIFE ON THE OCEAN WAVE

From Mr P. J. K. Tither

Sir, As an ex-seafarer, my experience was that sufferers from seasickness ("Travel blues", Body and Mind, August 13) fell into two distinct groups: those who felt better by being able to see the horizon (presumably as a fixed reference point) and those for whom comfort was found by being able to see only the confines of the vessel (which had no relative motion to them).

For all categories of sufferer, however, there was but one sure cure: all that was required was to sit down under a tree.

Yours faithfully,
P. J. K. TITHER,
Cydweli, Carmarthenshire. August 18

GARRICK COLOURS

From Mrs Giles Playfair

Sir, The late departed senior member of the Garrick Club, Giles Playfair, would have been surprised to learn (report, August 15) that the club's "bilious" tie is connected to anything as tame as salmon and cucumber.

A member for 62 years and both the father and son of a member, Playfair always stoutly maintained that the slightly "raffish" tie is meant to provoke thoughts of oysters and pink champagne.   *Yours etc,*

ANN PLAYFAIR,
London W4. August 19

END OF FO TELEGRAMS

From Sir Horace Phillips

Sir, Using e-mail for messages to the FO will not, I hope, make embassy staff more prolix. They should perhaps be reminded of the injunction to us in my day: Draft telegrams as if they were to be read by an idiot and paid for by yourself.

Yours briefly,
HORACE PHILLIPS
(Diplomatic Service, 1947–77),
London SW19. August 20

TO BOLDLY SPLIT/GO

From Air Commodore Iain McCoubrey

Sir, I wouldn't dare challenge Simon Jenkins's grammar, but surely it is the SAS ("Who Dares Wins"), not the Royal Marines, that uses "dare" as their equivalent of "boldly go".   *Yours faithfully,*

IAIN McCOUBREY,
Letcombe Regis, Oxfordshire. August 20

From the Reverend Francis Gardom

Sir, Splitting infinitives is akin to burping: a habit disdained in some company, tolerated in others, and highly esteemed in a few. It's all a matter of upbringing.

Yours sincerely,
FRANCIS GARDOM,
London SE10. August 20

From Professor John Bowker

Sir, Before you abandon the split infinitive for another season it is surely right that you should recall the letter written to you by Bernard Shaw, plagued by the corrections being made to his prose by someone on your staff. It comes about as close as anything can to a final word:

There is a pedant on your staff who spends far too much of his time searching for split infinitives. Every good literary craftsman uses a split infinitive if he thinks the sense demands it. I call for this man's instant dismissal; it matters not whether he decides to quickly go or to go quickly or quickly to go. Go he must and at once.

(Quoted in *The Times,* July 7, 1972.) *Yours,*
JOHN BOWKER,
Cambridge. August 27

From Major-General G. B. Fawcus (retd)

Sir, Whilst I heartily applaud the attitude of Simon Jenkins towards the split infinitive, I cannot agree with the blame he apportions to Dr Spock.

If a Spock were to blame for the infamous *Star Trek* split infinitive it was surely not Dr Spock, the Earthman child-rearing guru, but Mr Spock, the Vulcan space warrior. And can we not find it in our hearts to boldly forgive the grammatical error of a Vulcan speaking one of the languages of Earth?

Yours faithfully,
GRAHAM FAWCUS,
Flowton, Ipswich, Suffolk. August 27

From Mr A. C. Record

Sir, That much discussed creature, the split infinitive, can be a source of great pleasure. In quiet moments I still enjoy reflecting on a plaintive sentiment popular with my family many years ago, which runs: "I wish I'd learnt to never play the cello."

Yours faithfully,
TONY RECORD,
Bristol. August 27

From Miss Judith-Anne MacKenzie

Sir, It was Captain Kirk who boldly went. Mr Spock's English grammar approached perfection, of course.   *Yours faithfully,*
JUDITH-ANNE MacKENZIE,
London SW19. September 1

SALES PRESSURE

From Mr Philip H. Stunt

Sir, I am puzzled why sell-by dates always seem to be expressed as, for example, "Best before end August", rather than simply, "Best before September".   *Yours faithfully*,
PHILIP H. STUNT,
Chelmsford, Essex. August 25

From the Reverend P. M. Hickley

Sir, What annoys me about "best before" dates is insufficient information.

What I need to know is, "best before September; very nice before November; quite good before March; gone off by May".
Yours faithfully,
MICHAEL HICKLEY,
Lowestoft, Suffolk. August 27

From Mr Simon Le Couteur

Sir, Surely the main purpose of " best before " dates is that one may spend a happy hour ceremoniously examining every packet and tin in the kitchen cupboards condemning approximately one quarter to the bin, whilst simultaneously feigning disgust that this would not happen if you were in charge of the kitchen.

Products with labels offering the chance to win a Sinclair C5 or tickets for the World Cup in Mexico should be used immediately or thrown away.   *Yours,*
SIMON Le COUTEUR,
Frodsham, Cheshire. September 2

From Mrs Penelope J. Power

Sir, One should simply draw the line when the price is shown in shillings and pence.
Yours faithfully,
PENELOPE J. POWER,
Upper Swanmore, Hampshire. September 2

From Mrs Jenifer Hudson

Sir, Our family owns (but does not now use) a bottle of Worcestershire sauce which once belonged to my mother.

It has no sell-by date but instead states: "Temporary label. This is owing to damage to our factory by enemy action."

Yours faithfully,
JENIFER HUDSON,
Middleton Stoney, Oxfordshire
September 4

DON'T SAY CHEESE

From Mr Adrian Linger

Sir, Your back-page photograph today records Mr Kevin McCarthy and his world not-smiling record of 2hr 25mins.

Whilst not wishing to tempt fate, may I suggest that should it rain this Bank Holiday weekend the researchers of the Guinness Book of Records may care to observe one of our ritual traffic jams. I am sure they will find Mr McCarthy's record smashed by many potential champions glumly returning home.   *Yours faithfully*,
ADRIAN LINGER,
Elstow, Bedfordshire. August 28

From Mr Colin Bailey

Sir, I am amazed that the not-smiling record was broken with a 2hr 25min glare. Last Friday I started a tooth infection and have not smiled since. I make that 120 hours.   *Yours faithfully*,
COLIN BAILEY,
Coddenham Green, Suffolk. August 28

MARCO'S HOME

From Mr John Milligan

Sir, Reading Richard Owen's nicely rounded and easily consumed report on the house discovered during restoration work in Venice, I am pleased that even the "oral tradition" of Venice supports the assertion by the architect concerned that a house with a well in its centre is that of a Polo.   *I am, yours faithfully*,
JOHN MILLIGAN,
Galashiels, Selkirkshire. September 4

REPELLING THE BEASTIES

From Mr Nick Alexander

Sir, "Midge" or "midgie" (report, "Scots get the bug after a record midge season", August 29)? Surely an academic point, since they never appear in the singular? As with Visigoths, the smallest known grouping is the horde. In the plural the words are near enough the same.   *Yours sincerely,*

NICK ALEXANDER,
Kirknewton, Midlothian. September 5

From Mr Frank Day

Sir, The midges at Lake M\010vatn (pronounced Mevat) in northeast Iceland may well be closely related to those found in Scotland; but in general they do not bite, nor do they buzz like the mosquito, and they are usually only a problem for a short time during the summer months.

They tend to swarm about the head and face, and trying to fan them away with one's hand seems only to attract more of them. The secret is to raise the arm high into the air and to extend one's fingers, as the midges are attracted to the highest part of the body.

Yours sincerely,
FRANK DAY
(Accountant), Arctic Experience Ltd,
Banstead, Surrey. September 11

From Mr Joseph Fitton

Sir, It is particularly unpleasant to have M010vatn midges blocking up one's facial orifices, and fortunate indeed that they don't bite.

However, there was a wee local shop where one could buy an elongated Chinese lantern-like cage, covered by fine white mesh, to put over one's head.

I have the honour to be, Sir, your obedient servant,

JOSEPH FITTON (RAFVR meteorologist, Reykjavik airfield, 1945),
Rochdale, Lancashire. September 15

From Miss Helen Rigby

Sir, I can confirm Mr Frank Day's advice to raise one's arm when trying to distract midges.

My father, with whom I have walked on several warm days over the past years through the Wyre Forest, always advocated holding a large sprig of fern above the head, rather like an umbrella. Flies and midges would always circle around that, instead of buzzing into your face.

It does, admittedly, make you look as if you are taking part in some animist procession, but it works.   *Yours faithfully,*
HELEN RIGBY,
Battersea, London SW11. September 15

From Mr F. E. Hobbs

Sir, I, too, have long been an advocate of a trefoil of bracken, balanced on the head, as an effective midge and fly-repellent when out walking. I wear it to the embarrassment of my daughters.

On one occasion we were accompanied by a boyfriend, attired in a floor-length greatcoat and dangling scarf, with his shoulder-length hair topped by a multicoloured knitted hat of generous proportions.

He declined my offer of a suitable sprig of bracken as he did not wish to look silly.

Yours faithfully,
F. E. HOBBS,
Wolverhampton, West Midlands.
September 23

RAINED OFF

From Mr Rupert Godfrey

Sir, What a wet excuse, for clothing company Monsoon to blame poor trading on "dire weather conditions" (Business, September 3).   *Yours faithfully,*
R. D. GODFREY,
Blandford Forum, Dorset. September 5

CALMING RURAL DRIVERS

From Wing Commander T. F. H. Hudson, RAF (retd)

Sir, The answer to speeding on country roads is simple – save money and don't maintain them to our ridiculously high standards. There's nothing like pot holes to slow up irresponsible drivers.

Yours faithfully,
T. F. H. HUDSON,
Buckingham. September 12

BALANCED VIEW

From Mr Anthony Brindle

Sir, I was delighted to read that the findings of research at the Max Planck Institute into the connection between mental decline and the ability to balance confirm the instruction from my father in the 1930s: "Stand up my boy, it's the first sign of old age when you sit to put on your socks."

Yours vertically,
ANTHONY BRINDLE,
Cowes, Isle of Wight. September 16

HONORARY CATS

From Mrs John Peake

Sir, Your report on Sprite the dog being transmogrified into a "college cat" to circumvent an entry ban reminds me of the time, after the war, when several undergraduates at Cambridge were married men.

Learning that many of their wives were lonely, Launcelot Fleming, then Dean of Trinity Hall, arranged a tea party in his rooms so that they could meet each other. However, several had to decline as prams and their occupants were not allowed in college.

To overcome this problem for the afternoon concerned the college authorities arranged that babies should be deemed "honorary college cats". The Dean was then left wondering whether to tell the mothers.

Yours faithfully,
ELIZABETH PEAKE,
as from Stibbington, Cambridgeshire.
September 21

From Mrs Muriel G. Foster

Sir, To settle the question of women's membership of the MCC, could not the applicants be registered as "honorary men"? *Yours sincerely,*
MURIEL G. FOSTER,
Folkestone, Kent. September 24

From Mr Ronald Balaam

Sir, Animals have long been whatever a man says they are. Charles Keene's *Punch* drawing of March 6, 1869, is captioned:

Railway Porter (to Old Lady travelling with a Menagerie of Pets). "Station Master say, Mum, as cats is 'dogs', and rabbits is 'dogs', and so's parrots; but this ere 'tortis' is a insect, so there ain't no charge for it!" *Yours sincerely,*
RONALD BALAAM,
Ashstead, Surrey. September 25

NEAR MISS

From Mrs J. Morris

Sir, I was delighted to read that help is on the way for us "technophobe parents".

Reading through my daughter's information technology class notes I gleaned the information that "secondary units attached to a computer network are known as profiteroles".

I was delighted with this image-friendly term and used it a lot to show off my new-found knowledge, until it was pointed out that my daughter's spelling was at fault and the correct term was in fact "peripherals".

Yours faithfully,
JUDY MORRIS,
Radnage, Buckinghamshire. September 22

A KEY WORD?

From Mr Dean Bailey

Sir, Why are absent musicians at a performance always described as "indisposed" rather than being ill, dead or sitting at home because their watch has stopped?

Yours, alive and kicking,
DEAN BAILEY,
Ryde, Isle of Wight. October 5

From Mr Christopher Nourse

Sir, When in the 1980s my job as general manager of Sadler's Wells Royal Ballet required me to announce changes of cast before a performance, I made a point of not using the word "indisposed" and always explained exactly why X, Y or Z (and sometimes more) couldn't appear.

Not only did members of the audience come up to me afterwards to thank me for such honesty but, since I often used the opportunity to "warm up" the audience by making it into a good story, on several occasions I was even reviewed in the arts columns of this and other newspapers.

Yours faithfully,
CHRISTOPHER NOURSE (Executive Director) Rambert Dance Company, London W4. October 15

IN A TWIST

From Mr Nicholas Wibberley

Sir, One trusts that the instruction in Ranulph Fiennes's fitness programme (This Life, October 3) to "revolve your neck through 360 degrees" is not widely adopted by readers.

It could have a most unfortunate effect on your circulation.   *Yours etc,*
NICHOLAS WIBBERLEY, Barnstaple, Devon. October 13

SOFT TOUCH?

From Ms Tei Williams

Sir, I have been carefully moisturising my face for over 30 years, in the hope I will maintain a youthful skin. I use my right hand to apply the elixir of hope. Given that, why, when examining both palms, can I see no difference in skin quality?

Yours faithfully,
TEI WILLIAMS, Eynsham, Oxfordshire. October 15

ANXIOUS TIME

From the Reverend Kieran Conry

Sir, This new so-called shyness pill is fine, but how do you ask for it? *Yours faithfully,*
KIERAN CONRY, Wandsworth, London SW18. October 15

SCHOOL FOR SOCIALITES

From Mr Nigel R. MacNicol

Sir, When I was a child, my father (a war-time RAF officer) taught me why "socialites" should never say "pleased to meet you" (article, October 14).

His station had been honoured by a royal visit (the Duke of Gloucester, I think). At the following reception in the Mess a long line of senior officers and civic dignitaries were introduced. One bigwig fatuously blurted out "pleased to meet you" and the startled Duke, after looking him up and down, cheerfully replied: "So you jolly well should be!"   *Yours faithfully,*
NIGEL MacNICOL, Oakham, Rutland. October 16

NO CONKER CRISIS

From Mr J. A. Hadman

Sir, The members of Ashton Conker Club, the organising body for the World Conker Championship, are far from despondent about the men's title going to Germany. In fact we are proud that this has shown ours to be an authentic international event.

Over the past 34 years, during which time we have raised more than £150,000 for the visually handicapped, the number of overseas entries has grown and now stands at 13 per cent, with 46 players representing ten nationalities.

The day of the Euroconker is here.

Yours etc,
J. A. HADMAN
(Secretary, Ashton Conker Club), Oundle, Northamptonshire. October 17

CREDIT WHERE DUE

From Mr H. Neel

Sir, I wonder if anyone else has noticed that when the garden looks good it is due to the season, and when it doesn't it is due to the gardener.   *Yours faithfully,*
H. NEEL, Exeter, Devon. October 17

From Mrs Wendy Evans

Sir, When I was the fortunate co-owner of a small garden, I happily accepted any praise that came my way. Failures could always be blamed on adverse conditions.

Perhaps this is the difference between an optimist and a pessimist.   *Yours faithfully*,
WENDY EVANS,
Exeter, Devon. October 26

VITAL SIGN

From Mr Peter Jones

Sir, I have just been informed whilst job-hunting that a major company in the UK is looking for "vitality hires". Dare one suspect that there might be a correlation between "vitality" and age measured in years?
Yours etc,
PETER JONES,
Andover, Hampshire. October 17

FOILED OVER WRAPPING

From Mr Frank Gilbert

Sir, If KitKat is no longer foil-wrapped I shall have to find a substitute for it in my car's tool kit. Years ago I was advised to include this item, as the foil could be - and on one occasion was - used to pack out a loose battery terminal connection, or cover a failed fuse to make a temporary repair. The contents make a satisfactory snack if I am pondering more intractable problems.
Yours faithfully,
FRANK GILBERT,
Derby. October 17

From Mr Justin Marsh

Sir, While I can think of no secondary use for the new KitKat wrapping, I can, somewhat belatedly, advise on a further use for the old-style foil.

I fish with a cheap fly rod and, after having eaten the contents, KitKat foil has, in the past, proved sufficient to hold the two sections of rod together.

On a recent fishing trip, with no KitKat foil now available, the rod parted company mid-cast and I spent some 20 minutes in the gloaming fishing for half a rod in a Lakeland tarn. Now I secure the rod with insulating tape, but this solution, better for my waistline, is nowhere near as pleasing.
Yours faithfully,
JUSTIN MARSH,
Ambleside, Cumbria. October 22

From Mr J. R. Knight

Sir, Like Mr Edgley, I have reason to deplore KitKat's change of wrapping. The very thin aluminium, for which kitchen foil is no possible substitute, forms a vital part of equipment which we have built for electrostatic measurements of atmospheric phenomena.

We were forced to consider a bulk-purchase of the original bars – purely in the cause of science, naturally.   *Yours bloatedly*,
JEY ROGER KNIGHT,
Department of Meteorology,
University of Reading
October 22

From Mr Mike Lewis

Sir, How can I persuade my two border collies to come in from the garden when the irresistible rustle made by KitKat foil is no more? The dogs are far too intelligent to be duped by any other foil.   *Yours faithfully,*
MIKE LEWIS,
Hinstock, Shropshire. October 22

BITING BACK

From Dr Ian Gosney

Sir, Bedbugs may not carry disease but their irritating bites (report and photograph, October 20) recalled to me overnight stays in the poorer of Kabul's hotels during the Sixties.

An ex-Indian Army officer showed me that a bar of damp, sticky soap, applied quickly to bugs on the undersheet of a bed at the very moment the light was switched on would trap the beasts. Pain-free longer stays followed the placing of cans containing a little kerosene under each leg of the bed.
Yours faithfully,
IAN GOSNEY,
Edinburgh. October 23

PERIOD PIECES

From Dr Emma Coleman

Sir, Whilst shopping at a DIY store I was interested to note the availability of "Georgian Style" light switches.   *Yours sincerely,*
EMMA COLEMAN,
Watford, Hertfordshire. October 26

From Dr Martyn Green

Sir, Dr Emma Coleman's letter rekindles my interest in the "Jacobean Steam-Train" which runs each year on the Fort William to Mallaig line. I enjoy the notion of Bonnie Prince Charlie raising the clans on a whistle-stop tour of the Highlands.
Yours faithfully,
MARTYN GREEN,
Didcot, Oxfordshire. October 29

From Mr Andrew Ammerlaan

Sir, The DIY store I used to work for sold "Tudor Style" electric door-bell pushes.
Yours faithfully,
ANDREW AMMERLAAN,
Kensal Rise, London NW10. October 29

From Mr Raymund Dring

Sir, My favourite "period piece" was seen advertised by the local DIY store. The flat-pack item of furniture was described as "Heirloom Style".   *Yours faithfully,*
RAYMUND DRING,
London SW1. November 4

From Mr Richard Pollard

Sir, I live in a modern housing development in California. Last year when a neighbouring house was put on the market, it was described as "English Country Style". This same, unaltered, property is now on the market again. This time there is a new agent and its styling is now listed as "French Chateau".   *Yours faithfully,*
RICHARD POLLARD,
San Luis Obispo, California. November 4

From Mrs Margaret Grint

Sir, I was recently shown round a country mansion during a holiday in Vermont. The guide announced that its style was "Queen Anne Tudor".   *Yours sincerely,*
MARGARET GRINT,
Harrogate, North Yorkshire. November 6

From Mr James Bogle

Sir, I never did divine the significance of "semi-contemporary dwellings", seen some time ago on a housing development in Yorkshire. Anyhow, they weren't "semis".
Yours faithfully,
JAMES BOGLE,
London SE14. November 17

PUTTING IT MILDLY

From Mr J. P. Henderson

Sir, In your article today on Monica Lewinski you quote Lucianne Goldberg: "(Monica was) very very angry with the President, called him lots of four-letter words, the mildest of which was the Big Creep."
What about a recount?   *Yours faithfully,*
JOE HENDERSON,
Edinburgh. October 29

QITE USEFUL

From Mr Brian Seager

Sir, Your spelling of "debaqle" (first leader, October 28) will give hope to all those Scrabble players left with a "q" and no "u".
Yours faithfully,
B. D. SEAGER,
Mickleover, Derby. October 30

TOO SHORT FOR COURT?

From Mr Benjamyn Damazer, JP

Sir, Lisa Armstrong asks, in relation to the television series *Ally McBeal* (Ins and Outs, Fashion, November 2), "Since when did attorneys wear micro minis in court?". In the magistrates' court where I sit as a JP, one lady solicitor regularly wears micro-minis, lowering the hemline to mini in winter. As I recall last year, the winter lasted about two weeks.   *Yours faithfully,*

BENJAMYN DAMAZER,
Crowland, Lincolnshire. November 4

RULE OF THUMB FOR FLU

From Mrs Simon Wainman
Sir, Dr Thomas Stuttaford explains (Body and Mind, November 3) how to tell the difference between a cold and flu. I was told years ago: if there's a £50 note in the middle of a field and you can reach it, you haven't got flu.   *Yours faithfully,*
DIANA WAINMAN,
Basingstoke, Hampshire. November 6

From Mrs A. J. Wilcock
Sir, I have no difficulty in differentiating between a cold and flu: mothers have colds, fathers have flu.   *Yours faithfully,*
A. J. WILCOCK,
Farnham, Surrey. November 18

SECOND CHAMBER

From Professor Graham Zellick
Sir, Mr Frank Wintle suggests Echo Chamber as a name for the revamped Upper House. I prefer Wind Tunnel.
Yours faithfully,
GRAHAM ZELLICK,
London WC1. November 6

BATTLE OF WATERLOO

From Lieutenant-Colonel David Sievwright
Sir, As an ardent Francophile I am rather astonished by the suggestion of the Paris councillor M Longuepee to rename Waterloo station (report and leading article, November 6). I wonder if he has considered the confusion and cost that his suggestion would entail for the citizens of Paris if it was taken as a precedent.

Few cities can be as endowed with victorious nomenclature as Paris; the Gare d'Austerlitz, Place de Iena and Avenue Wagram immediately spring to mind, and what do the Russians make of Place d'Alma and Boulevard de Sevastopol?
Yours faithfully,

DAVID SIEVWRIGHT
The Cavalry and Guards Club,
London W1. November 7

From Mr Mark Lomas
Sir, Our response to Councillor Longuepée should be simple. We will rename successive London stations Sluys, Crecy, Poitiers, Harfleur, Agincourt, Verneuil, Blenheim, Ramillies, Oudenarde, Malplaquet, Dettingen, Quiberon Bay, Quebec, Cape St Vincent, Aboukir Bay, Trafalgar, Vimiero, Talavera, Busaco, Albuera, Ciudad Rodrigo, Badajoz, Salamanca, Vitoria, Toulouse . . .

The difficulty is that we do not have enough stations.

I am, Sir, your obedient servant,
MARK LOMAS,
Oakham, Rutland. November 7

From Mr David Davies
Sir, The Gare du Nord has indeed been renamed, albeit unofficially. On account of the arrival and departure of several thousand Eurostar passengers daily between Paris and London, it has become known as the Gare de Londres.

Parisians, always so cosmopolitan, have a way of taking such matters out of the hands of their elected representatives.

Yours faithfully,
DAVID DAVIES,
London SW1. November 13

From Mr A. R. Titchener
Sir, The French have always been valiant fighters – opposite or at our side. They are noble friends and worthy colleagues. They have been ill-used by the widespread publicity about the suggestion to rename Waterloo station, which has the appearance of having been made by a minority with an unnecessary guilt complex.

It is all an irrelevant storm in a *demitasse*.
Yours faithfully,
A. R. TITCHENER,
Windsor, Berkshire. November 13

From Mr Alan Magrath

Sir, The French do not have to worry about past battles. What matters is the present and future. They can be proud that, while they hurtle at 180mph on Eurostar through northern France, they have to slow to less than half that speed across the Channel because the English cannot be bothered to invest in their own country.

Yours sincerely,
ALAN MAGRATH,
Croydon. November 18

From Mr Jack Owens

Sir, By jingo! *Quel brouhaha!* Surely the solution to the station-naming spat is for both termini to be renamed after respective national heroes – Wellington for ours in London, and Napoleon for theirs in Paris.

Yours faithfully,
J. M. OWENS,
Eastleigh, Hampshire. November 18

From Mr Robert Wilton

Sir, The indispensable *1066 and all that* reminds us that Richard the Lionheart travelled through France so often on his way to war that he was known as Richard Gare de Lyon.

Would it not avoid all difficulty if we were in future to ensure that all battles were fought at railway stations? *Yours faithfully,*
ROBERT WILTON,
Islington, London N1. November 18

From Mr Gerald Vinestock

Sir, I don't mind if the French want to rename the Gare du Nord, but why "Fontenoy"? Wasn't he that little Lord chappy in the book by someone or another?

Yours faithfully,
GERALD VINESTOCK,
Carnforth, Lancashire. November 18

MANY A SLIP

From Mr Gary Bullard

Sir, I have just tried to book an appointment with my osteopath to treat my slipped disc, only to be informed that he is booked up "back-to-back". *Yours faithfully,*
GARY BULLARD,
Richmond, Surrey. November 7

DRIVING PREFERENCE

From Mr Keith B. Pearson

Sir, At a hotel commandeered for the duration of the war by the RAF for trainee airmen there was an occasion when it seemed that those on the ground floor were required to go upstairs and those upstairs to come down with consequent turmoil on the stairs. A corporal, who today would be defined as having learning difficulties, sought to alleviate the chaos by shouting: "Keep to the left going up; keep to the right coming down." *Yours faithfully,*
KEITH B. PEARSON,
Purley, Surrey. November 17

From the Chief Executive of Dover District Council

Sir, The spirit of the RAF corporal lives on.

This council received presentations from all the competing companies before the Channel Tunnel was selected by the British and French Governments in 1986.

At the end of the Eurobridge presentation someone asked on which side of the road people would drive on the bridge across the Channel. Their spokesman unhesitatingly replied that "Each country will drive on its normal side of the road until it gets to the other side". *Yours faithfully,*
J. P. MOIR,
Dover District Council, Dover, Kent.
November 23

NEW DEPTHS?

From Mr Alan McLoughlin

Sir, I thought that the phrase "to die for" was in an unassailable position as the most irritatingly silly expression of the decade. Now, however, I believe that the description of almost anything which is currently in vogue as "sexy" has cruised into the lead.

The PM's use of the word to describe economic stability clinched it for me.

> Yours faithfully,
> ALAN McLOUGHLIN,
> Helston, Cornwall. November 19

From Mrs M.A. Campbell

Sir, Mr Alan McLoughlin finds that "sexy" has overtaken "to die for" as the most irritatingly silly expression of the decade.

Has he noticed, coming up close behind, the way organisations "get into bed with" each other?

> Yours faithfully,
> ALEXANDRA CAMPBELL,
> London W2. November 24

From Mr Denys Franzini

Sir, Mrs Alexandra Campbell adds organisations that "get into bed with" each other to the list of irritatingly silly expressions.

If two (or more) organisations "get into bed together" following a "sexy" deal and have a relationship "to die for", might they then be "touching base" with each other?

> Yours faithfully,
> DENYS FRANZINI,
> London SW5. November 27

From Sir Bryan Thwaites

Sir, All these ridiculous modern phrases should be put on the back burner.

> Yours faithfully,
> BRYAN THWAITES,
> Milnthorpe, Winchester. November 27

OEUFS EN CONCRETE?

From Mr Eric Davies

Sir, I look forward to Delia Smith explaining how to cook the surfeit of dinosaur eggs that have been discovered (report, November 18).

> Yours etc,
> ERIC DAVIES,
> Buriton, Hampshire. November 20

From Mrs Eileen Craine

Sir, I like Mr Eric Davies's idea of a recipe from Delia Smith using the present glut of dinosaur eggs.

And she wouldn't need to tell us how to test for freshness either.

> Yours faithfully,
> EILEEN CRAINE,
> London W1. November 25

From Dr David Keeling

Sir, No more letters about Delia Smith, please. Un oeuf is un oeuf.

> Yours faithfully,
> DAVID KEELING,
> Oxford. December 7

From Mrs Maureen Harkavy

Sir, In replying to Dr David Keeling's delicious postscript in today's letters, all I can say is "faire un oeuf"!

> Yours faithfully,
> MAUREEN HARKAVY,
> Alvechurch, Worcestershire. December 9

CRY HAVOC

From Mr Bob Gledhill

Sir, Reading your report that the incoming meteor shower could "wreak havoc" reminded me of a linguistic oddity that has always puzzled me.

Is there any other way that havoc can arrive except by way of a wreak, and can anything else except havoc be wreaked?

> Yours sincerely,
> BOB GLEDHILL,
> Cleveleys, Lancashire. November 23

From Mr Robert Maxtone Graham

Sir, The linking of "wreak" with "havoc" is one example of the several dozen "matchwords" collected by my family. What do you gnash, except your teeth? What can be akimbo, apart from arms? When do we hear of a riband that is not blue, or a grail that is not holy? And what palls, except pleasure?

> Yours faithfully,
> ROBERT MAXTONE GRAHAM,
> Sandwich, Kent. December 3

From Professor C.H. Orchard

Sir, I always thought that one could cause havoc and wreak revenge. However, I am at a loss to know whether I can do anything with my troth other than plight it, or if I can plight anything else.

> Yours faithfully,

C. H. ORCHARD,
Leathley, North Yorkshire. December 3

From Mr E. S. Hooper

Sir, Is there somewhere a non-safe haven?
Yours sincerely,
STANLEY HOOPER,
Coroner's Court and Office, Doncaster
December 3

From Mr David Foster

Sir, Can anything but warmth be luke?
Yours faithfully,
DAVID FOSTER,
Ludlow, Shropshire. December 3

CONFUSED DIRECTIONS

From Mr Bernard Dunstan, RA

Sir, I was interested to read that Alan Clark's grandfather commissioned a family portrait from "Labery" (sic).

Sir John Lavery's name did sometimes cause confusion. The old story goes that, at a reception, Lady Lavery gave her name to a flunkey who promptly replied in a whisper: "Yes, madam: down the corridor and the first door on the right." *Yours faithfully,*
BERNARD DUNSTAN,
Kew, London TW9. November 25

SILVER SURFERS

From Mr Thomas Denne

Sir, Some of us silver surfers, who spend an average of ten hours a week on the Internet (report and leading article, November 18), may be driven as much by incompetence as by enthusiasm. I certainly waste an awful lot of time groping my way around the Web. *Yours faithfully,*
THOMAS DENNE,
Nottingham. November 26

From Mrs Pauline M. Atkins

Sir, This granny finds that spending ten hours a week on the keyboard helps to sustain and even improve one's waning powers of concentration, muscular co-ordination, aural attention, critical self-appraisal, finger dexterity and musical appreciation. The instrument in question is called a pianoforte.
Yours sincerely,
PAULINE M. ATKINS,
Kirkby Stephen, Cumbria. November 26

From Dr D. W. Robinson

Sir, I may have the explanation of why the over 60s spend more time at the keyboard than other age groups.

A contemporary of mine (ie, over 60) has recently acquired a home computer. He boasts that, after only three two-hour lessons, he is now capable of writing letters with it.

Unfortunately, one short letter takes him most of the day. *Yours faithfully,*
DAVID ROBINSON,
Shalterford, Bewdley. November 28

From Mr M. A. Lassman

Sir, Dr D. W. Robinson has nom right to denugrate themefforte of us Silver Suyrfetes.

AfTER ONLY THERE YEARS i HAVE MENAGED TO INCREASEDR MY TYOPOING SPEDD THREEFOLD – TO SIX WORDA A MINUTW.

yoUORS, ETC,
M. A. LASSMAN,
London NW11. December 3

From Mrs Georgette Behar

Sir, Last night I telephoned my daughter and told her that I had had a severe breakdown. In view of the fact that I am 80 years old, she expressed great anxiety and concern.

However, I reassured her by saying that fortunately I had sorted the problem out with "Scandisk". *Sincerely,*
GEORGETTE BEHAR,
London NW1. December 10

ESSENTIAL EXPLETIVE

From Mr R. J. White

Sir, I disagree with your leading article that the word "bloody" was ill chosen by the Prince of Wales.

Frankie Howerd, who used very little bad language, used to say that the expletive is sometimes essential to turn an ordinary line into a funny one. He told a joke about an hotel guest who was given a trumpet to play if he wanted to know the time in the night. When he did so another guest shouted: "Who's that playing the trumpet at three o'clock in the bloody morning?"

Yours faithfully,
R. J. WHITE,
La Colle sur Loup, France. November 27

EAT BEFORE READING

From Mr Stanley Armstrong

Sir, Having made some myself recently, I bought a package of tiramisu to see if Tesco's was as good as mine. Thinking that the ingredients might be on the bottom, I turned the package over to find, in small print and in six languages, the instruction: "Do not turn upside down."

I was a little upset, but fortunately the contents were not. *Yours faithfully,*
STAN ARMSTRONG,
Malvern Link, Worcestershire. December 1

COST OF CHRISTMAS

From Mr Alexander T. Murray

Sir, I note with interest that, this year, the average cost of a Christmas gift will be £42.

The mid-Sixties was when it first fell to me to spend my pocket money (6d per week) on family presents rather than rely on parental munificence. The final tally was three bath cubes (3d each), pipe cleaners (9d), a pencil (4d) and a pencil sharpener (7d). The total of 2s 5d now translates into roughly 12p.

Wrapping paper was, of course, in the decorations box and re-used from previous years. *Yours faithfully,*
ALEXANDER T. MURRAY,
Plaxtol, Kent. December 2

From Mr Neil Murray

Sir, My younger brother is indeed correct when he recalls how in our household Christmas wrapping paper was saved and re-used from year to year.

What he omits to mention was the chaos this caused when one received a gift bearing the legend "To Alex from Neil", or "From Mum to Alex", or "From Dad to Gilly", or half a dozen similar dedications, not all of which had been crossed out.

I vividly remember, at the age of eight or thereabouts, opening one such relabelled Christmas present, to be confronted by a packet of pipe cleaners (supposedly destined for Father). *Yours faithfully,*
NEIL MURRAY,
Sutton, Surrey. December 14

From Mrs Kate Wilson

Sir, I can reassure Mr Murray that good value can still be achieved at under £42 per present. My daughter, when aged six in 1994, was able to undertake all her Christmas shopping with her £1 coin.

She bought ballpoint pens for her father (21p), a bath oil for me (17p) and a plastic toy for her brother (26p). She was delighted, as this left her 36p "to get something really good for myself".

You can't say fairer than that.

Yours faithfully,
KATE WILSON,
Le Vesinet, France. December 14

From Mrs Christine Edgar

Sir, A cherished memory for me is hearing my two eldest sons exhorting their younger brother "to buy Mum and Dad a proper present, not a Blue Peter one!"

Ah, but I still have the Blue Peter ones.

Yours sincerely,
CHRISTINE EDGAR,
Stowmarket, Suffolk. December 14

CRUELTY TO MOLES?

From Mrs Denise Dew-Hughes

Sir, I have spent a depressing weekend watching a mole slowly destroy my lawn.

Gardening friends advise me that the most humane way to repel moles is to detach the battery-operated cell from a musical greeting card and drop it into the excavations.

I don't have a singing greeting card, but a recently issued report from a major PR company delivers a short spoken address from the chairman on opening. Would this be an effective alternative? *Yours faithfully,*
DENISE DEW-HUGHES,
Oxford. December 2

From Mr Bert Staddon

Sir, Mrs Denise Dew-Hughes asks if a recorded message from a PR company might repel moles.

It might; but then again the moles might learn how to convince her to put up with them, and she would be worse off.

Yours faithfully,
BERT STADDON,
Langley, British Columbia, Canada.
December 10

From Mr Paul Thomas

Sir, I had a problem with garden moles some three years ago while living in Southend.

I fitted an extension from my mega bass CD system to the lawn and piped music to the miscreant's lair. As I recall, The Beatles, Rachmaninov and George Melly were hopelessly ineffective, but Lulu worked.

Yours faithfully,
PAUL THOMAS,
St Edmund's College, Cambridge.
December 10

HEARD BUT NOT SEEN

From Mr G. M. N. Whiting

Sir, When I asked our three-year-old son Harry what he thought his mother wanted for Christmas I was impressed when he replied "Lorjesus". When he repeated this later, my wife (the better interpreter) confirmed that he was right, but identified the word as "Mortesas". *Yours etc,*
GILES WHITING,
Taunton, Somerset. December 8

SEASONAL STRESS

From Mrs Ingrid Ransome

Sir, I see that shopping "damages men's health" (report, later editions, December 2). My husband's accompanying me Christmas shopping once a year doesn't do much for my health either. I've now found a cure – I leave him at home. *Yours faithfully,*
INGRID RANSOME,
Colchester, Essex. December 10

From Mr Julian M. Marks

Sir, At this season of the year, I add to the traditional Jewish morning prayer for men, thanking God for not creating me a woman (with the benefit of not having to do the everyday shopping), an extra prayer thanking Him for not making me a Christian (so that I don't have the added burden of Christmas shopping). *Yours faithfully,*
JULIAN M. MARKS,
Wallingford, Oxfordshire. December 15

From Mr David Powell

Sir, "How many things I can do without!" was the response of Socrates when looking at the multitude of items exposed for sale in the Athenian market. This is the sort of positive attitude to adopt when we are indulging in Christmas shopping.

Yours sincerely,
DAVID POWELL,
Northampton. December 23

IT GIRLS

From Mrs P. Forster

Sir, I was told by someone recently that he had been to a club where the girls did "laptop dancing".

Is this an example of the way in which IT will affect people's lives? *Yours faithfully,*
PAULA M. FORSTER,
Oswestry, Shropshire. December 11

BONES OF TRUTH

From Mr Daniel Weltman

Sir, Your front-page headline, "Three-mil-

lion-year-old skeleton may rewrite man's history" (December 9), was wonderful news for anthropologists and literary fans alike.   *Yours sincerely,*
DANIEL WELTMAN,
Chesham, Buckinghamshire. December 11

STILL ARGUING

From Mr Peter Clark

Sir, You began your report on the Queen's visit to the cast of *Aladdin* at the Harrogate Theatre by saying: "Fifty-five years on, the jokes are as bad as ever."

Oh no they're not.   *Yours faithfully,*
PETER CLARK,
Sawbridgeworth, Hertfordshire.
December 15

A SINGULAR FEAT

From Mr Patrick Fisher

Sir, I feel increasingly left behind by today's youngsters.

How will one in seven manage to have unsafe sex over Christmas? (report, December 7).   *Yours faithfully,*
PATRICK FISHER,
Bromsgrove, Worcester. December 16

From Mr Lorne Mackillop

Sir, Your report "Government to tell teenagers all they need to know" demonstrates that the Government continues to waste its time and taxpayers' money. It is a well-established fact that teenagers already know everything.   *Yours faithfully,*
LORNE MACKILLOP,
Eastbourne, East Sussex. December 18

PREPARING FOR THE BUG

From Mr Geoff Bliss

Sir, Action 2000 advises us to have a fortnight's rations in hand for next new year. This seems positively frugal. From observations in my local supermarket most people appear to get in two months' supplies at this time of year.   *Yours faithfully,*
GEOFF BLISS,
St Albans, Hertfordshire. December 21

From Mrs Kate Brookman

Sir, Like Libby Purves, I too enjoy my computer; but in a year when my roses had greenfly, the children nits and the cat had fleas, it is with a sense of the inevitable that I assume my computer is saving the best bug for last.   *Yours sincerely,*
KATE BROOKMAN,
Montacute, Somerset. December 21

DRESSING THE PART

From Mr David Shamash

Sir, A note from my granddaughter's school was pinned up in my daughter's kitchen a few days ago, which read: "Alice is an angel. Please can she wear white knickers on Tuesday."   *Yours faithfully,*
DAVID SHAMASH,
Wantage, Oxfordshire. December 24

IRAQ DIPLOMACY

From Miss Sarah Wildy

Sir, If Operation Desert Fox had to be initiated before Ramadan (reports, December 22), why does it not matter that it was happening during Advent?   *Yours sincerely,*
SARAH WILDY,
Weobley, Herefordshire. December 29

WINTER CLEAN-UP

From Mrs Jose Fernandez

Sir, Coming late to the table for several meals my husband said he was busy defragmenting his computer. When asked to explain, he said he was tidying up his hard disk and rearranging the bits and pieces in a more orderly state.

I have asked him to defragment the garage after Christmas.   *Yours,*
ROSEMARY FERNANDEZ,
Kenley, Surrey. December 29

From Mrs G. R. Ely

Sir, Rosemary Fernandez has given us her husband's invaluable word "Defragmenting". I do not know how I have managed without it.

I can offer him, in exchange, a word from my French mother-in-law's private collection of Franglais – to "demantipulate". It means to take to pieces such items as the vacuum cleaner. It might help him while defragmenting his garage.   *Yours faithfully*,
M. L. ELY,
Shaftesbury, Dorset. January 7

TIME WARP?

From Mr Edward A. Russell

Sir, Surely it is not correct to refer to the years in the new millennium as two thousand and odd, as seems to be the current trend?

Is not the correct phrase twenty and odd, or am I to understand that the Battle of Hastings was in one thousand and sixty-six, the war ended in one thousand, nine hundred and forty-five, or indeed that I am writing this letter in one thousand, nine hundred and ninety-eight?   *Yours faithfully*,
E. A. RUSSELL,
South Shields. December 30

From Mr David T. Staples

Sir, Mr Edward Russell (queries the correct naming of years in the next century. Two thousand and odd or twenty and odd.

In 1968 Arthur C. Clarke and Stanley Kubrick made the definitive science fiction film *2001* (pronounced two thousand and one). They seem to have set a precedent.
Yours sincerely,
DAVID T. STAPLES,
London N8. January 13

From Mr Gerard Farrell

Sir, Mr David T. Staples is correct in his assertion that Arthur C. Clarke and Stanley Kubrick established a precedent for the new millennium by pronouncing their film *2001* as two thousand and one.

May I remind him, however, that the film's sequel, *2010*, was pronounced twenty-ten.
Yours faithfully,
GERARD FARRELL,
Fallowfield, Manchester. January 19

From Mr Ivan K. Rowland

Sir, I seem to recall that the esteemed film critic Mr Barry Norman referred to the film *2010* as "ten past eight".
Yours faithfully,
IVAN K. ROWLAND,
London SE23. January 26

THE 51ST STATE

From Dr Philip F. Roberts

Sir, Now that Puerto Rico has voted against being America's 51st state (report, December 15) why not give the British people a chance?

Consider the advantages. We would join the most powerful country, one of English-speaking peoples with a modern, vibrant democracy providing superb defence arrangements.

Lying as we do at the front door of Europe we would be the recipients of massive industrial development by the US to promote (our) American goods in Europe.

We would abolish the House of Lords at a stroke and have relative independence as a self-governing state with low taxes.

Distance would not be a problem as we are closer to Washington than is Hawaii.
Yours faithfully,
PHILIP F. ROBERTS,
Norwich, Norfolk. December 30

From Mr Graham Bate

Sir, Although the abolition of the House of Lords is a strong temptation, the rest of Dr Philip Roberts's list of benefits of the UK becoming the 51st state of the US is heavily outweighed by the crosses we would have to bear.

Baseball caps, worn in both directions, would proliferate, television would be interrupted by advertisements every three minutes, our spelling would become non-U, lawyers would increase tenfold in number to cope with the litigation and Lord's would be levelled in order to play rounders. Worst of all, every day would become "nice".

On balance, becoming a *departement* of the old enemy would seem preferable.

Yours faithfully,
GRAHAM BATE,
Oundle, Peterborough. January 7

OUTLOOK UNSETTLED

From Mr Geoffrey N. Dence

Sir, Yesterday evening I watched an ITV news bulletin which reported that the weather had caused many thousands of unfortunate people in the North to be deprived of electricity. Immediately following this bulletin was the weather forecast sponsored by PowerGen with the slogan "Power whatever the weather".

Does this constitute a prima facie case of misleading advertising?   Yours faithfully,
GEOFFREY N. DENCE,
Salisbury, Wiltshire. December 31

1999

ADDRESSING POSTCODES

From Mr Reg Gale

Sir, Many of us have the habit of putting our own addresses on the backs of letters we send to families and friends abroad.

I always put simply:"GALE FORCE TEN CV35 0AQ UK", which is sufficient worldwide, I am sure.   *I have the honour to be,*
Sir, your obedient servant,
REG GALE,
Lighthorne, Warwickshire. January 1

From Mr Barrie Jenks

Sir, Sir Francis Beaufort would request that Reg Gale should either change his surname to Storm, or move next door to number eight so that his postcode address would be "meteorologically" correct, ie, Gale Force Eight or Storm Force Ten.

Yours faithfully,
BARRIE JENKS,
Worcester. January 6

From Mr Christopher Y. Nutt

Sir, In 1929, when my late father was working at the Cavendish Laboratories in Cambridge, he received a letter from the US in regular time addressed simply, "Mr Nutt, physicist, England".

In modern times I have lived in an area of Pimlico postcoded SW1V. Naturally I, and no doubt many others, found our mail was redirected via Clapham SW4, as the result of the efforts of some redundant classicist in the employ of the Post Office.

So much for technological progress.

Yours faithfully,
CHRISTOPHER Y. NUTT,
Little Abington, Cambridge. January 12

ROMANCE OF THE ROAD

From Mr Richard Need

Sir, I have often thought that it would be fun to have roadside notices on the M25, where the meridian crosses it near Waltham Abbey to the north and Limpsfield to the south, announcing to motorists: "You are now entering the eastern (western) hemisphere."   Yours faithfully,
RICHARD NEED,
Cheam, Surrey. January 8

PROBLEM SHELVED

From Mr R. F. J. Slade

Sir, Has continental drift reversed without me noticing?

I found that a local supermarket stocks

Worcestershire sauce in the section headed "Mexico".

Yours faithfully,
R. F. J. SLADE,
Ipswich, Suffolk. January 18

From Major-General I. S. Harrison, Royal Marines (retd)

Sir, Mr R. J. Slade reports finding Worcestershire sauce in a supermarket food section headed "Mexico".

In my post-retirement capacity as Director General of the British Food Export Council, I visited a supermarket in southern Italy, where I found Birds Custard on shelves reserved for petfoods.

Yours sincerely,
I. S. HARRISON,
Chichester, West Sussex. January 20

From Mr M. J. J. Tanner

Sir, Whilst in Normandy last summer, I found Bisto gravy powder in a hardware shop on the same shelf as colouring for tile grout.

And in a small town near Oslo, a number of years ago, I saw Findus fish fingers in a freezer selling frozen cat food.

Yours sincerely,
M. J. J. TANNER,
Worthing, West Sussex. January 26

From Mrs Imogen Mottram\

Sir, Unable to find any tins of tomatoes in the canned vegetables section of a supermarket in Aberdeen I was directed to the Italian section, marked "Foreign Foods".

Yours sincerely,
IMOGEN MOTTRAM,
Ickleford, Nr Hitchin, Hertfordshire.
January 26

MILLENNIUM BART

From Dr Morley Halse

Sir, Seeing the Simpsons featured in Saturday's meg@ section of *The Times* serves to remind us that the year 2000 is significant only as a result of a long process of evolution that has given us four fingers and a thumb on each hand.

If, like Bart Simpson, we had four digits per hand, base eight arithmetic would be universal.

Next year would then be 3720 and so nothing particularly special.

Yours sincerely,
MORLEY HALSE,
Herne Bay, Kent. January 20

WIGS FOR JUDGES

From His Honour Anthony Tibber

Sir, I have just retired from the circuit bench. For many years I wore a wig when entering court (that was my concession to convention) but removed it in the early stages of the proceedings and sat for most of the day bareheaded. Some counsel glared and kept their wigs on, others, with a sigh of (I think) relief, took them off.

I know of no power and no authority which can tell a judge that he or she must wear a wig. If those judges who wish to get rid of the wig simply ceased to wear them, most of the remaining judges would probably follow suit.

Yours faithfully,
ANTHONY TIBBER,
London N3. January 20

From His Honour Patrick Halnan

Sir, A wig is wonderfully warm in a cold court.

Yours truly,
PATRICK HALNAN,
Cambridge. January 28

From Lord Millett

Sir, English judges are an eccentric lot.

When I had a full head of hair, I wore a wig. Now I have no hair, I have dispensed with my wig.

Yours sincerely,
MILLETT,
House of Lords. February 2

THE RIGHT STUFF?

From Mr Brian Butcher

Sir, I was delighted to read of Irish schoolgirl Sarah Flannery's award-winning data-protection code. I was particularly pleased that she "had to go through lots of stuff" before achieving success.

When quizzed on the content of their school day, my own teenage children regularly admit to doing "just stuff".

Is it too late, or can I fill the gap in my own education by taking up this subject now? *Yours faithfully,*
BRIAN BUTCHER,
Cholsey, Oxfordshire. January 25

BRIDE FOR THE NINETIES

From Mr Brian Parker
Sir, The success of the 98-year-old Chinese man in attracting 11 replies to his "marry me" advertisement (World in brief, January 19) reminds me of the story of a 70-year-old who sought similar good fortune.

He asked for advice: "Should I subtract 20 years from my age?"

"No," was the reply, "you would do better if you add 20." *Yours sincerely,*
B. H. PARKER,
Dartmouth, Devon. January 25

ONLINE MPS

From Mr Nicolas Owen
Sir, The problem with e-mail in general and publicising e-mail addresses of Members of Parliament in particular is that anyone with five minutes spare and nothing to do can create needless work and expense for others by sending trivial messages that require acknowledgement.

This being a classic case in point.
Yours faithfully,
NICOLAS OWEN,
Orpington, Kent. January 29

MI5'S GERMAN MOLE

From Mr Dillwyn Miles
Sir, Your report on Klop Ustinov recalls to mind the story told, I believe, by his son, Sir Peter Ustinov.

While still working at the German Em-

bassy, Klop Ustinov secretly applied for British nationality by printing his intention in Welsh in the *Carmarthen Journal*, which defied the expertise of the German Intelligence. *Yours faithfully,*
DILLWYN MILES,
Haverfordwest, Pembrokeshire. February 2

EXPLORING MARS

From Dr Patrick Moore
Sir, Your report on plans for a robot aircraft, Kitty Hawk, to fly over the Red Planet takes me back to the only conversation I ever had with Orville Wright at the very start of the Second World War, when I was an (admittedly under-age) teenager learning how to fly.

I had about ten minutes' talk and I well remember saying: "Will we ever fly to the Moon?" He paused, and said: "Well, they said we couldn't fly over the Earth, but we did."

Neil Armstrong, the first man on the Moon, and Orville Wright, the first airman, could have met. I am sure they didn't, but their lives overlapped.

Where is the first man on Mars?
Yours faithfully,
PATRICK MOORE,
Selsey, Sussex. February 10

MUMMIES AND DADDIES

From Mrs Tamsin Woolsey-Brown
Sir, A study by Care for Education tells us (report, February 4) that nursery school children are abandoning traditional games of "Mummies and Daddies" in favour of those featuring mothers only.

I am pleased to say that the children at my nursery school in Norwich delight in playing "Mummies and Daddies", even discussing at length whose turn it is to be Daddy or Mummy, and sometimes agreeing to having at least two of one or the other.

Yours faithfully,
TAMSIN WOOLSEY-BROWN,
Sunningdale Nursery, Norwich. February 11

POCKET PEVSNERS?

From Mr Graeme Woolaston

Sir, I am delighted to learn from "Diary and Letters" that Nikolaus Pevsner's wonderful guides to English architecture are being put online, so enabling anyone with a laptop, a modem, and a mobile phone to gain instant access to information about any country church or building they happen to be visiting.

Nonetheless, the equipment involved is a tad cumbersome. Couldn't technology come up with a more portable means of conveying the information, which might even fit into one's pocket? *Yours faithfully,*
GRAEME WOOLASTON,
Stepps, Glasgow. February 16

TOKEN GESTURE

From Mr Dean Bailey

Sir, At dawn this morning I observed a well-dressed gentleman examining the contents of the public litter-bins on the seafront. His strange behaviour was explained when he produced a pair of nail scissors from his waistcoat pocket and began cutting out the Books for Schools tokens from discarded crisp packets

When I commended him on his initiative, he explained to me that if he began his search any later someone had usually been there before him. *Yours faithfully,*
DEAN BAILEY,
Ryde, Isle of Wight. February 16

From Miss Lizzie Broughton

Sir, I saw Mr Bailey's letter in *The Times* today. On Sunday my mother made ME go round all the tables and bins in the cafe at the Science Museum to look for Free Books for Schools tokens.

They were not even for my school, but the school where she teaches.
Yours faithfully,
LIZZIE BROUGHTON (aged 10),
Twickenham, Middlesex. February 18

SCATTERED RELICS

From Mr Christopher Y. Nutt

Sir, As a lawyer of some thirty years' standing, I can assure your correspondents that the relics of Saint Valentine are not in Dublin, Glasgow or Edgbaston.

No Sir, they are scattered all over the divorce courts of southern England.
Yours faithfully,
CHRISTOPHER Y. NUTT,
Little Abington, Cambridge. February 17

OVER BUT NOT OUT

From Mr Alan J. Moorse

Sir, I fear that those who state that Morse has now ceased to have relevance as a means of communication are a little premature in their pronouncements.

I seem to recall that Morse was used in an emergency situation in at least one of the *Star Trek* episodes; the exact date escapes me, but it was/will be some time in the 23rd century. *Yours, but with no connection,*
ALAN MOORSE,
Salisbury, Wiltshire. February 18

FOX IN DISTRESS

From Mr Clifford Chatterton

Sir, Now we are provided with information that foxes can have stress when hunted, should we not also be advised what chickens feel like when foxes raid their pens? *Yours faithfully,*
CLIFFORD CHATTERTON,
Naples, Florida. February 19

TRUE ENOUGH

From Mr Bryan Marson-Smith

Sir, A small piece of social history: my grandson, aged just four, pointed to a red roadside telephone kiosk and observed: "That's where you go if you don't have a mobile." *Yours faithfully,*
B. MARSON-SMITH,
Sevenoaks, Kent. February 19

CHRISTENING A COMPUTER

From Father Robert Henshaw

Sir, It is the custom in our religious community for new members to adopt new names. This week we are installing our first computer.

Is there an appropriate religious name for our new electronic recruit?

Yours faithfully,
ROBERT HENSHAW,
Our Lady Immaculate & St Andrew,
Hitchin, Hertfordshire. February 27

From Mr John Peter Horsam

Sir, May I suggest that Father Henshaw name his silicon novitiate Dunstan: Digital Unit Noting Sacred Text And Novenas? My professional advice would be to install (stained glass) Windows 98 and to rename the find facility Anthony. Modesty forbids me to add any lines about icons and the like.   *Yours faithfully,*
JOHN PETER HORSAM,
Brussels, Belgium. March 6

From Mr Keith Spragg

Sir, Father Henshaw might take inspiration from the Irish, who are ever resourceful when incorporating modern technology into their culture.

The national airline, Aer Lingus, names each of its jet aircraft after a different saint. While working at the flying training centre in Dublin in the 1980s, I was amused to note that the flying training simulators were painted in the same, smart airline livery, complete with saint's name on the nose. Closer inspection revealed that each of the several models of simulator bore the same name: St Thetic.   *Yours faithfully,*
K. F. SPRAGG,
Stanton, nr Ashbourne, Derbyshire.
March 6

From Mr Alan Bird

Sir, It depends, of course, on what sort of computer Father Henshaw has. A while ago the people at the Met Office at Brack-nell were said to have named their two Crays Reggie and Ronnie.

Yours faithfully,
ALAN BIRD,
Richmond, Surrey. March 6

From Mr Keith Jowett

Sir, Since, no doubt, the computer will have many fonts, how about "The Baptist"?

Yours faithfully,
KEITH F. JOWETT,
Barnsley, South Yorkshire. March 6

From Mr George Royce

Sir, If Father Henshaw has purchased his computer from a certain manufacturer it will already be a "Brother".

Yours faithfully,
GEORGE ROYCE,
London SW17. March 6

From Mr Michael Lavelle

Sir, May I suggest one of the following: St Surf the Internet or the Ram of God.

Yours faithfully,
MICHAEL LAVELLE,
Birmingham. March 6

From Mr Callan Dick

Sir, Adam or Eve may fit the bill - it rather depends on whether Father Henshaw picked an Apple.   *Yours faithfully,*
CALLAN DICK,
Larkhall, Lanarkshire. March 6

From Mr E. C. Entecott

Sir, Because my computer has proved to be pretentious, fickle, unreliable, and irrational, I have long called her Jezebel.

I write this in longhand because, yet again, she has deserted me.   *Yours faithfully,*
EDWIN ENTECOTT,
Nuneaton, Warwickshire. March 6

SPICE BABY

From Mr Colin O'Donnell

Sir, I see from your report today that David Beckham and Victoria Adams have named their son Brooklyn after the district in

New York where they discovered she was pregnant.

I suppose it is a blessing that they were not visiting Pratt's Bottom in Kent at the time.

With all good wishes to them.

Yours faithfully,
COLIN O'DONNELL,
Bromley, Kent. March 6

From Mr R. Fell

Sir, Is it true that Mr Alex Ferguson has already taken an option on Brooklyn Joseph?

Yours faithfully,
R. FELL,
Bognor Regis, West Sussex. March 6

From Mrs Pam Tull

Sir, Nearly 27 years ago my son was born in a Nottingham hospital. I shared a room with a lady who also had a son.

She named the boy Clint because he had been conceived in the Nottingham suburb of Eastwood.   *Yours sincerely,*
PAM TULL,
Brockenhurst, Hampshire. March 6

From Mrs Felicity Luke

Sir, David Beckham and Victoria Adams are following a literary example. In *Bleak House* the Bagnet children are called Woolwich, Quebec and Malta, after the military barracks in which each was born.

Yours faithfully,
FELICITY LUKE,
London NW1. March 10

ITV'S PUBLIC SERVICE

From Mr Ronald Williams

Sir, I cannot but admire the verbal ingenuity of Richard Eyre in striving to defend ITV against charges of dumbing down; particularly in his phrase "that whilst ITV does not try to flatter an intellectual elite ...".

This reminds me of the story (which I like to believe is true) of a conscientious, though somewhat obsequious, biographer of Edward VII who, when faced with the necessity of confronting the sheer gluttony of

that monarch, recorded that His Majesty was not given to toying with his food.

Yours sincerely,
R. W. WILLIAMS,
Poole, Dorset. March 8

COURT NAPPING

From His Honour Judge Barrington Black

Sir, The new series of *Kavanagh QC* is so true to life (Television review, March 9) that I fell fast asleep during the last ten minutes of counsel's speech to the jury.

Yours faithfully,
BARRINGTON BLACK,
Harrow. March 10

WOMEN PRIESTS

From the Reverend John Papworth

Sir, Why all this fuss about women priests? With the house on fire have people no other preoccupations than to worry about the gender of the fire brigade?

With respect,
JOHN PAPWORTH
(Editor), *Fourth World Review,*
London NW8. March 12

INCREASED INCENTIVE?

From Mr John O'Byrne

Sir, Would a National No Smoking Month offer more encouragement to those who want to give up the habit for good (report, March 11)?   *Yours truly,*
JOHN O'BYRNE,
Harold's Cross, Dublin. March 12

AWASH WITH WINE

From Mr F. C. Peacock

Sir, Is it an absolute journalistic requirement that food, however delectable, must be "washed down with" wine, however noble (leading article, March 12)?

Even specialist "foodie" writers almost invariably use this barbaric imagery.

Yours faithfully,
F. C. PEACOCK,
Newlyn, Penzance, Cornwall. March 16

PHANTOM DINER

From Lieutenant-Colonel D. P. Earlam

Sir, I am worried. I note from your Court Page announcements that the Chairman of British Invisibles attended dinner with the Navy Board on March 11. Does this predict another, even more stringent, defence review?   *I am, Sir, Your obedient servant,*
DAVID EARLAM,
Canterbury, Kent. March 16

From Mr Barry Pixton

Sir, So the Chairman of British Invisibles attended dinner with the Royal Navy Board, did he? How do you know?
Yours faithfully,
BARRY PIXTON,
Burnley, Lancashire. March 16

From Mr Danny Davis

Sir, Of course one would know if one were at dinner with the Chairman of the Invisibles. His title would be on the name card at the seat that appears to be empty. However, I would not wish to be seated on his right.   *Yours faithfully,*
DANNY DAVIS,
Bath. March 19

WEDDING GIFTS

From Monsignor Graham P. M. Adams

Sir, When I am invited as a guest to a wedding, I send every couple the same gift (feature, "Every wedding list tells a story", March 16). They receive bathroom scales with the message, "May your way in life be happy and blessed."   *Yours sincerely,*
GRAHAM P. M. ADAMS,
Daventry, Northamptonshire. March 18

From Mr James Lancelot

Sir, Perhaps the most unusual wedding present my wife and I received was a pair of books, *The Oxford Dictionary of Quotations* and *The Oxford Dictionary of the Christian Church*. They were not on our list; yet 16 years on they remain among the most valued and most used of our presents.

They have not suffered breakage, they do not require washing or polishing, but they do solve many an argument.
Yours faithfully,
JAMES LANCELOT,
Durham. March 24

From Mr J. M. Cockram

Sir, Having an interest in antique English silver I have for years always given a Georgian or Victorian silver butter knife as a wedding present.

Such a historical gift is usually well received, although I was worried by one young bride who, some time after the event, did query the receipt of only one fish knife.
Yours sincerely,
JOHN COCKRAM,
Brockenhurst, Hampshire. March 24

From Mr Geoffrey Robinson

Sir, Many years ago, as a practising stained-glass artist, I made as a gift when an old school friend of mine got married a leaded-up stained glass roundel of coloured pieces, about 8 inches in diameter, complete with attached loop, that he could hang in a window for, I hoped, pleasing decorative effect.

Visiting them a couple of years later, I found that, not knowing what it was for, they were using it as a teapot stand.
Yours faithfully,
GEOFFREY ROBINSON,
Clifton, Bristol. March 30

From His Honour Judge William Rose

Sir, Monsignor Graham P. M. Adams would presumably not wish his gift of bathroom scales to carry the message (or even the interpretation): "Thou art weighed in the balance, and found wanting."
Yours faithfully,
WILLIAM ROSE,
Putney, London SW15. March 30

From Mr Maurice D. Stanton

Sir, About two years ago my wife and I were invited to the wedding of a friend's daughter. We selected a gift from the wedding list included with invitation; bride notified by store; father of bride disinvites us from wedding.

Why? Because he stated the value of the gift had to relate to the number of years we had known him.

Was it our present or our presence that was required at the wedding?   *Yours etc,*
MAURICE D. STANTON,
Wembley, Middlesex. March 30

From Mr Neil Kennedy

Sir, At my only experience of an Irish wedding, I gave the happy couple a rather expensive set of glassware from Thos. Goode.

The wedding started half an hour late. The bridegroom did not appear in any of the wedding photographs, as he was in the bar (with me); and the reception lasted three days, covering three different towns.

Six months later I received a letter thanking me for the charming coffee mugs.

Yours faithfully,
NEIL KENNEDY,
Althorne, Essex. April 2

From Mrs Alison Musker

Sir, As a wedding present I gave Georgian silver grape-scissors to a schoolfriend.

She wrote back thanking me for the "beautiful candle snuffers".   *Yours faithfully,*
ALISON MUSKER,
Reading, Berkshire. April 5

From Mr Henry Button

Sir, Mr John Cockram tells us that he has for years given a silver butter knife as a wedding present. He may have had in mind the old definition of a gentleman as someone who always used a butter knife even if he was dining by himself.   *Yours faithfully,*
HENRY BUTTON,
Cambridge. April 5

From Mr Peter Hudson

Sir, As the knife was given as a wedding present, it should have been obvious it was intended "for butter or worse".

Yours faithfully,
PETER HUDSON,
Ufford, Nr Stamford, Lincolnshire. April 5

From Mrs Elizabeth Bridger

Sir, The most original wedding gift we received was from a saintly retired clergyman. It was a little booklet, entitled *Words of Comfort.*   *Yours truly,*
ELIZABETH BRIDGER,
Sheringham, Norfolk. April 5

From Mrs C. M. McLean

Sir, My most appreciated wedding present – in 1948 – was the small collection of clothing coupons given me by colleagues in the publishing office where I worked at the time.

Clothes rationing was still in force, but these precious extra coupons enabled me to buy the material for my wedding dress.

Yours sincerely,
MOLLY McLEAN,
Rickmansworth, Hertfordshire. April 12

SIGN OF SPRING

From Mr H. Sutherland Pilch

Sir, I was walking down King William Street in the City yesterday and I saw a bare navel for the first time this year. Surely these days this is a better harbinger of spring than the cuckoo?   *Yours faithfully,*
H. SUTHERLAND PILCH,
Pulborough, West Sussex. March 19

From Mr Alan Sloan

Sir, Mr H. Sutherland Pilch reports an early sighting of a bare navel in the City on March 17.

Such sights are commonplace in Sheffield city centre on Friday nights throughout November to March.

Are the citizens of that place proudly claiming their home a land of perpetual summer? Or is there a hardy, non-migratory northern sub-species of navel?

Yours faithfully,
ALAN SLOAN,
Buxton, Derbyshire. March 23

From Mr J. Sanderson

Sir, Mr Alan Sloan's zoology needs amending.

There is a resident sub-arctic species of navel. It can be seen every Friday and Saturday night, all year round, in Newcastle, Sunderland and Hartlepool.

It appears to prefer hard frosts, sleet, pouring rain and a howling gale.   *Yours faithfully,*
J. SANDERSON,
Peterlee, Co Durham. March 29

From Mr David Edwards

Sir, I am ashamed to have to say that my navel has been "migrating" southwards for quite some time now.   *Yours sincerely,*
DAVID EDWARDS,
Southsea, Hampshire. March 29

From Mrs Olwen Davis

Sir, Observing the migratory habits of the navel would seem to be rather more scientific a study than I had first appreciated. The one I spotted in Fishguard this afternoon had been ringed.   *Yours faithfully,*
OLWEN DAVIS,
Castlemorris, Pembrokeshire. April 1

WORTH A DRINK?

From Mr Steve Wedd

Sir, Given the apparent success of the Guinness marketing effort for St Patrick's Day, will the English Tourist Board be pushing St George's Day this year; and, if so, with which liquid product?
Yours faithfully,
STEVE WEDD,
Brighton. March 23

From Mr Nick Gooblar

Sir, Mr Steve Wedd must be aware that on St George's Day we will be partaking of that traditional English dish, Chicken Tikka Masala, washed down by the old favourites, Foster's, XXXX or, for the more delicate palate, Lambrusco.   *Yours faithfully,*
NICK GOOBLAR,
Leeds, West Yorkshire. March 26

FINE FEATHERS

From Mr David Renshaw

Sir, From the the Congregation of Regent House, University of Cambridge, March 20, 1999:

Academical Dress – Bachelor of Veterinary Medicine: similar to the hood for Bachelor of Medicine, but with more fur.
Yours faithfully,
DAVID RENSHAW,
Stalybridge, Cheshire. March 26

CLASSICAL CONFUSION

From Mr Andrew Wilson

Sir, I was interested to read that Sainsbury's is transferring £300 million of its pension fund from Mercury (Asset Management) to Hermes (Liberty).

I wonder whether its next move will be to withdraw the Mars bar in favour of an Ares bar.   *Yours faithfully,*
ANDREW WILSON,
Christ's College, Cambridge. March 27

SICK LEAVE

From Mr Ian H. G. Wilson

Sir, Half a century ago one might have got a heavy cold in the head, felt run-down after it and then tried to wangle a day or two off.

Nowadays one catches a virus, then suffers from post-viral syndrome and has a holiday prescribed.

Perhaps the modern technocratic language sounds better, elicits more sympathy and (for the naughty ones) provides cover for latent malingeringitis.   *Faithfully,*
IAN WILSON,
Yelverton, Devon. March 29

THE BEST MEDICINE

From Dr Andrew Severn

Sir, Our local Nuffield hospital recently asked the opinion of the nursing staff about the renaming of its two wards.

Local beauty spots and historic monuments

were predictable choices, but the obvious winner in my view is the choice of one of the theatre nursing staff who suggested "Morecambe" and "Wise"   *Yours faithfully*,
ANDREW M. SEVERN,
Bolton-le-Sands, Lancashire. March 31

SEX APPEAL

From Mrs S. Millington

Sir, A sign of the times? A local charity shop has a black beret for sale in its window: "As worn by Monica Lewinsky".

Yours faithfully,
SHEILA D. MILLINGTON,
Weybridge, Surrey. April 3

SIGNS OF THE TIMES

From Mr Stephen Walker

Sir, A sign on a table in a local furniture shop states: "This item is not currently available due to its desirability".

Whatever happened to "sold out"?

Yours faithfully,
STEPHEN WALKER,
Brighton, East Sussex. April 5

COMING AND GOING

From Dr Patrick Harris

Sir, Recently I find that the news programmes spend most of the time forecasting future events while the weather reports spend their time telling me about the weather I have just had.   *Yours*,
PATRICK HARRIS,
Cannock, Staffordshire. April 6

CLARIFICATION SOUGHT

From Mr Anthony P. Moran

Sir, Driving past the main gate of a military establishment recently, I noticed a guard who appeared to be wearing a you-can't-see-me camouflage uniform superimposed upon which was a you-can't-miss-me fluorescent yellow waistcoat.

I wonder if there is an appropriate word or expression for this odd conflict of purpose?   *Yours faithfully,*

ANTHONY P. MORAN,
Gosport, Hampshire. April 6

From Mr Peter Wade

Sir, To assist Mr Anthony P. Moran's search for an expression to describe Service personnel wearing fluorescent waistcoats over camouflage uniforms, I feel that the word "stealth" should be in there somewhere.

Yours faithfully,
PETER WADE,
Colchester, Essex. April 7

From Mr John Humphries

Sir, Anthony Moran will have to provide more details of the military establishment he passed in order to assist identification of the unusual guard on duty.

If it were a branch of the Royal Tank Regiment, then "ironic" would identify the person. If it were The Parachute Regiment, it could have been a paradox. The Intelligence Corps' sentry might be an enigma.

Yours etc,
JOHN HUMPHRIES
(Registrar), Culford School,
Bury St Edmunds, Suffolk. April 10

From Mr Michael Howarth

Sir, A clear case of sartorial oxymoron.

Yours etc,
MICHAEL HOWARTH,
Exeter, Devon. April 10

From Mr J. M. Cockram

Sir, I would extend Mr Peter Wade's description of fluorescent vests over combat kit from "stealth" to "Stealth and Safety".

Yours faithfully,
JOHN COCKRAM,
Brockenhurst, Hampshire. April 10

HAPPY ENDING

From Dr John Pease

Sir, Green string used in the garden never seems to have a free end: a frustrating and time-wasting situation. Threading the string through a half cork and moving it along the string as required will ensure no lost ends and happier gardening.

Yours faithfully,
JOHN PEASE,
Wells-next-the-Sea, Norfolk. April 9

SO THAT'S ALL RIGHT

From Mr Nicholas Wibberley

Sir, I have to hand a plastic bottle which bears the legend "Carbonated spring water. Suitable for vegetarians."   *Yours etc,*
NICHOLAS WIBBERLEY,
Barnstaple, Devon. April 9

DICTATING BRANDS

From Mr J. G. Peacock

Sir, *Tea with Mussolini* (PG). Has product placement in films gone too far?   *Yours,*
J. G. PEACOCK,
Headington, Oxford. April 10

MOBILE PHONES

From Mr Christopher Balkwill

Sir, "Mobile phones 'quicken the brain'", headline, April 8).

At last I know how my student son manages to do nothing much but still gets results.   *Yours sincerely,*
CHRISTOPHER BALKWILL,
Abingdon, Oxfordshire. April 13

DEVOLUTION LICENCE

From Dr Iain A. McCoubrey

Sir, The Driver and Vehicle Licensing Agency is clearly preparing for devolution. My recently issued photocard driving licence gives my place of birth as "Untied Kingdom"!   *Yours faithfully,*
IAIN McCOUBREY,
Letcombe Regis, Oxfordshire. April 13

MAKING A PACKET

From Mrs Eira Harris

Sir, I see that the country's richest businessman makes packaging for the food industry ("Britain's top 10", April 12). Am I right to believe that many of the country's poorest businessmen produce the food that's placed inside this packaging?   *Yours faithfully,*

EIRA HARRIS,
Abercych, Pembrokeshire. April 16

From Mr Jeremy Burrows

Sir, I have not the slightest idea how much I pay Britain's richest businessman to make the packaging in which most of the food I buy is wrapped, but would willingly pay him twice as much not to.
Yours faithfully,
JEREMY BURROWS,
Elstow, Bedford. April 20

HIGH ROMANCE

From Mr Frederick O. Marsh

Sir, Who says that romance and chivalry are dead?

I have just heard of a pilot who proposed to his future wife in a glider, over the top of a loop. He lowered a wing, so that he was down on one knee.   *Yours sincerely,*
FREDERICK O. MARSH
(Vice-President, The Royal Aero Club),
London W8. April 16

From Sir Rowland Whitehead

Sir, Frederick Marsh's glider pilot didn't give his lady a chance. She was strapped in.

Our skydiving girls are free to escape.
Yours in freefall,
ROWLAND WHITEHEAD
(Member, British Parachute Association),
London W4. April 17

From Mr R. N. Pittman

Sir, I liked my acquaintance's proposal of marriage: he set up his camera with delayed action for a photo of him and his girlfriend, pressed the button, ran to her side and popped the question.   *Yours faithfully,*
ROBIN PITTMAN,
St Peter, Jersey. April 23

From Mr Richard Green

Sir, It was my intention to propose on a high peak to the Australian woman who is now my wife, during the three-week visit to the UK of her sprightly father in 1988.

I lost my nerve the first weekend atop

Snowdon and was thwarted by adverse weather the following weekend at Ben Nevis.

Weather and nerve were overcome on the final weekend of his visit when I handed him the camera and asked him to take a photo of Kym and me at the top of Scafell Pike on St George's Day. I shouted "Now!", popped the question and the rest, as they say, is history. *Yours faithfully*,
RICHARD GREEN,
Bowdon, Cheshire. April 27

WEATHER REPORT

From Mr David L. Pugh

Sir, When I mowed my front lawn (which it badly needed) in bright sunshine today, it was necessary to break the continuity of the stripes to go around the snowman and snowlady built yesterday by my grandchildren. *Yours faithfully*,
DAVID L. PUGH,
Toller Porcorum, Dorset. April 22

MILLENNIUM BABIES

From Mrs Sue Wright

I agree with Mr Douglas Bugler (letter, April 19) that the best things in life are often unplanned. My daughter will be nine years old on 9.9.1999 which, in the words of any self-respecting eight-year-old, is "really cool". *Yours faithfully*,
SUE WRIGHT,
Chippenham, Wiltshire. April 23

A LONG TIME IN POLITICS

From Mr Andrew McClintock

Sir, I have recently been reading *A Handbook to Political Questions of the Day*. They include Ireland, Church and State, House of Lords (Ending or Mending?) and London Municipal Reform, but not a reference to the Balkans. The author? Sydney Buxton, MP. The date? 1892. *Yours etc*,
ANDREW McCLINTOCK,
Brincliffe, South Yorkshire. April 23

MARITIME HEROES

From Dr Stanley Solomons

Sir, Captain P. M. Adams states that Christopher Columbus and Amerigo Vespucci "crossed unknown oceans when the English were just able to ship wine up the coast from Bordeaux".

Got their priorities right, these old English navigators, it seems. *Yours sincerely*,
S. SOLOMONS,
London NW3. April 26

FIT TO READ?

From Miss Susan Pease

Sir, There appears to have been a bad infestation by an elusive creature that eats newsprint, the evidence being a number of small, rectangular holes throughout *The Times*.

Would it not be a good idea to put all the useful offers for books, cottages, CDs, etc, on one page? We then might be able to trap and identify this animal. *Yours faithfully*,
SUSAN PEASE,
London NW6. April 27

NAME OF THE GAME

From Mrs Angela Callaghan

Sir, You provided today two wonderful examples of people's names eminently fitting the jobs they do. In the Dr Stuttaford article on obesity we had a Professor Michael Lean pronouncing on weight management; and in Birthdays today, the Surveyor of the Fabric of Westminster Abbey has the charming name of Mr Donald Buttress.

This makes a lovely start to the day.

Yours faithfully,
ANGELA CALLAGHAN,
Blackheath London. April 29

From Mr A. K. Wareham

Sir, Reading Angela Callaghan's letter today about matching names to jobs, I am reminded of a personal experience.

My signature may be somewhat illegible, but having warned a school that I was com-

ing to inspect them, I received a reply starting "Dear Mr Watchem".   *Yours faithfully*,
KEN WAREHAM,
Darley Dale, Derbyshire. May 3

A MIR WELSHMAN?

From Mr Anthony Moorman

Sir, Peter Llewelyn, who is said to have agreed to pay for a week-long flight on the Mir space station (report, April 28), is described as a "space-mad Welshman" and as a successful "British businessman".

I wonder whether he will be "successful British businessman who buys trip to space" or "a Welshman who failed to buy space holiday"?   *Yours faithfully*,
ANTHONY MOORMAN,
Otley, West Yorkshire. April 29

RISKS OF DEVOLUTION

From Mr A. W. Glanville

Sir, The suggestion is being put about that the English Parliament should be located in York.

Surely one Shambles in that fair city is enough?   *Yours sceptically*,
A. W. GLANVILLE,
Haslemere, Surrey, St George's Day.
April 30

THE ROYAL LUNCH

From Mr Dean R. Pope

Sir, I am staggered to hear that, after careful examination of Van Dyck's painting *The Five Eldest Children of Charles I*, an expert has identified the item shown adjacent to the bowl in the top right of the picture as a pawpaw.

Anyone living west of the River Tamar will be able to identify the item as a Cornish pasty and not an exotic fruit.

Clearly, the affinity between Cornwall and the Royal Family did not start with the current Prince Charles but originated when King Charles had these pasties delivered to the palace.   *Yours sincerely*,
D. R. POPE,
Blazey, Par, Cornwall. April 30

From Dr Arnold Freedman

Sir, I suspect that the only pawpaws in the *The Five Eldest Children of Charles I* belong to the mastiff.

The fruit beside the bowl is much more likely to be a quince.

The autumnal trees in the background are just right for the time when quinces would be ripe.   *Yours truly*,
ARNOLD FREEDMAN,
Oxford. May 4

From Mr Leslie Cockerham

Sir, Pawpaw, citron, coconut, Cornish pasty, and whatever else . . . one thing is pretty obvious to me: if you can't tell what he's drawn, then this Van Dyck fellow can't have been much of an artist.

Mind you, I thought he was excellent in *Mary Poppins*.   *Yours faithfully*,
L. S. COCKERHAM,
Harrogate, North Yorkshire. May 6

NON-U

From Mr Ralph Hardy

Sir, May I propose a millennium marker that will cost next to nothing, save a few trees and pints of ink, and modestly advance the claims of English to be the world language of the next millennium? From January 1, 2000, let us stop putting the letter u after every q. It is silly.

The change will also help Scrabble players and enhance *Countdown*.

Yours qerulously,
RALPH HARDY,
Wokingham, Berkshire. May 5

From Mr Adrian Brodkin

Sir, While it's difficult to qibble with the logic of Ralph Hardy's argument that omitting the letter u after every q may indeed save trees and ink, surely, when it comes to the Qeen's English, it is qality rather than qantity which counts.

Yours faithfully,
ADRIAN BRODKIN,
London N2. May 11

From Professor Emeritus R. E. Asher

Sir, Mr Ralph Hardy's tree-saving proposal would probably not find ready acceptance with most people, given that the sequence "qu" represents two distinct segments of sound (as indicated by popular spellings such as "Kwik-Fit".) Why, in any case, make things easier for Scrabble players and Countdown contestants?

Much more to many people's taste would be one of George Bernard Shaw's many suggestions for saving space on the printed page, namely doing away with the apostrophe.

The placing of the apostrophe gives many people problems and it probably occurs with greater frequency than q. It's likely that its disappearance would be lamented only by pedants and perhaps a few professional linguists.   *Yours etc,*
R. E. ASHER
(Professor Emeritus of Linguistics),
Edinburgh. May 11

From Mr Alan Webster

Sir, I agree with the proposal to drop the letter u after every q. However, I have one qestion - how will I know how to pronounce Qatar?   *Yours faithfully,*
ALAN WEBSTER,
Hightown, Merseyside. May 11

DISTANT EARLY WARNING

From Mr Anthony Wilcox

Sir, My new university library card bears simply my name, my photograph, and in large print the words "Expires 31/12/03".

Should I take out life insurance?

Yours faithfully,
ANTHONY WILCOX,
Ipswich, Suffolk. May 6

HAPPY LANDINGS

From Mr Anthony Gordon

Sir, On your front page today you report the charming story of a stewardess who ran half-naked round a Boeing 737 as result of a bet with the captain on the plane arriving half an hour early at Genoa.

"We take this very seriously," said a disapproving BA official.

Unfortunately I do not know the stewardess (or for that matter the captain) but I hope BA will recognise this bit of fun as the best publicity they have had for years.

Yours truly,
ANTHONY GORDON,
London SW8. May 6

From Mr Alec Seton

Sir, No wonder the poor girl is in trouble. BA cabin crew are not meant to give pleasure to passengers. It's a sackable offence.

Yours,
ALEC SETON,
Sevenoaks, Kent. May 6

LOST COINAGE

From Mr Paul Bryant

Sir, Whither have they gone? In the last eight months I have received but one £2 coin in my change.   *Yours faithfully,*
PAUL BRYANT,
Cobham, Kent. May 17

From Mr Roger May

Sir, The rarely sighted £2 coin is very useful, but much more so would be a 99p piece.   *Yours faithfully,*
ROGER MAY,
Brimscombe, Stroud. May 20

From Mr Martyn Stevens

Sir, £2 coins are like omnibuses. I had not seen one for several months and then yesterday I received three in my change in two hours.   *Yours faithfully,*
MARTYN STEVENS,
Southampton. May 20

From Mr Chris Jeffrey

Sir, My young daughter disposed of my £2 coins in the dustbin because they had no chocolate inside.   *Yours faithfully,*
CHRIS JEFFREY,
Petts Wood, Kent. May 20

From Mr Allan Reid

Sir, I, too, wondered where all the £2 coins had gone until I started to read medicine at the University of St Andrews last September, where I discovered the answer. They are all in Fife.   *Yours faithfully,*
ALLAN REID,
St Andrews, Fife. May 22

From Mrs John Kerr

Sir, It's very simple. The "lost" £2 coins are the hoards of the future.

A friend of mine travels with a stack of £1 coins, two of which she exchanges for any £2 coin she catches sight of. (She is saving up for that special something.) I thought this such a good idea that I am thinking of doing the same.

Attractive, desirable – and heavy – metal objects have always been hoarded. We hardworking, financially challenged housewives are just continuing our Bronze Age habits.
Yours faithfully,
CAMILLA KERR,
Salisbury, Wiltshire. May 22

SERVICE FIRST CLASS

From Mr John Foley

Sir, Things must be improving at the National Rail Enquiries line. Wanting to find out about travel to Selhurst, I got through immediately. The man on the phone was more than helpful - not only did he divine the purpose of my trip (the relegation clash between Wimbledon and Southampton) but as a "Scummer" (Southampton supporter) - he correctly predicted the outcome of the game.

If I had taken his advice I should have spared myself the trip.   *Yours etc,*
JOHN FOLEY,
Kingston Vale, London SW15. May 17

PAY THROUGH THE NOSE

From Mr Tom Rayfield

Sir, Your report today says that the white powder of the coca plant is "snorted up the nose, usually through a rolled-up £10 or £20 note". As one inexpert in these things, I am left to assume that £5 notes are ineffective and £50 notes must be better.
Yours faithfully,
TOM RAYFIELD,
London W4. May 19

HOMING SNAILS

From Mr M. I. L. Roberts

Sir, For ten days I have tried to banish a large snail which threatens soon-to-emerge seedlings. Each day the snail gets lobbed into long grass of a nearby paddock and each night it quits the paddock, crosses a concrete driveway and returns to lurk under its favourite rock. There is no question of mistaken identity because its shell was marked with white paint after the first return trip.

Are homing molluscs widespread?
Yours faithfully,
M. I. L. ROBERTS,
Bury St Edmunds, Suffolk. May 21

From Mr Gerry Orme

Sir, If I were to lead Mr Roberts from his garden, daub him with white paint and lob him into his paddock, I suspect that (shock permitting) he would still find his way home.

Has he not considered moving the rock rather than the snail?   *Yours etc,*
GERRY ORME,
Ashby de la Zouch, Leicestershire. May 29

From Mr P. John O'Neill

Sir, Can it be that Mr Roberts's snail so enjoys the sensation of flight that it keeps coming back for more?
Yours faithfully,
P. J. O'NEILL,
Totton, Southampton. May 29

From Mrs Kym Wheeler

Sir, Stamping on snails is a waste and a mess. I put them on the bird table, where the blackbirds recycle them.   *Yours faithfully,*
KYM WHEELER,
Corby, Northamptonshire. June 12

FAT CHANCE

From Mr Tony Donnelly

Sir, Your report about the auction of Billy Bunter first editions had me wondering whether the auctioneers would accept telephone bids from callers promising to send postal orders by return.   *Yours faithfully,*
TONY DONNELLY,
Knowle, Solihull. May 24

COLD CALLING

From Mr P. A. L. Vine

Sir, Some years ago, on the morning following a memorial service for my father who was a barrister-at-law in the Temple, a middle-aged man called at my Fleet Street flat to say he had come from Chambers. As my leg was in plaster I was most grateful for the offer of assistance from someone who had presumably been sent to see if help was required. So off we went in his car to collect a copy of the death certificate.

Only on our return did he reveal that he thought it was perhaps not a good time to sell me a set of encyclopaedias.

Yours faithfully,
P. A. L. VINE,
Pulborough, Sussex. May 25

BRIEF BUT EFFECTIVE

From Mr Noel Flannery

Sir, Following Manchester United's astonishing two goals in extra time (reports, May 26), Alex Ferguson's post-match comment, "Football – bloody hell!", surely ranks with "Veni, vidi, vici" (J. Caesar) and "Cogito, ergo sum" (R. Descartes) as among the pithiest three-word position statements in recorded history.   *Yours faithfully,*
NOEL FLANNERY,
Richmond, Surrey. May 28

From the Reverend Dr Thomas Cooper

Sir, If A. Ferguson, J. Caesar and R. Descartes have made the pithiest three-word statements in history, what about "Quod scripsi scripsi" (P. Pilate)?

Yours faithfully,
THOMAS COOPER,
Llandaff North, Cardiff. June 2

NOT BACK TO BASICS

From Lord Janner of Braunstone, QC

Sir, Please would you join me in a campaign to ban the words "basically", "essentially" and "actually" from media and everyday speech?

Basically, if we could remove those words, it would actually add to the time that is essentially available for meaningful language by anything up to a third. And you would remove what is actually, basically and essentially an irritating substitute for "um" - which at least has the virtue of brevity.

Yours sincerely,
GREVILLE JANNER,
House of Lords. June 2

From Mr Michael Hayes

Sir, Lord Janner of Braunstone asks us to join him in a campaign to ban certain words from everyday speech.

Gladly, but will he please add the meaningless "I mean" to his list. This phrase now permeates much of conversation and broadcasting.

However, Lord Janner has hit the nail on the head - it is, like "well", simply another form of "um".   *Yours faithfully,*
M. HAYES,
Stratford-upon-Avon, Warwickshire. June 8

From Mr John Braun

Sir, Lord Janner's list of adverbs which should be banned has missed the prime target, "absolutely".

His letter does, however, include an adjective which is due for banishment. I mean "meaningful".   *Yours faithfully,*
JOHN BRAUN,
London EC1. June 8

From Mr Graham R. Dunn

Sir, It is vitally important that we, as a nation, make an especial effort to do as Lord

Janner advised: get back to the fundamental foundations of our written, and indeed spoken, language.

I feel sure that, at the end of the day, this mutual course of action will result inevitably in an intrinsically greater and deeper understanding of the finer points of English.

I remain, Sir, Your obedient servant,
GRAHAM R. DUNN,
North Walsham, Norfolk. June 8

From Mr Peter Tandy

Sir, I will join Lord Janner's campaign, but only if he allows two additional words.

I would ban "devastated" in news reports relating to problems of a minor personal nature, and "quintessential" in articles discussing anything with even a remote air of English traditionalism.   Yours faithfully,
PETER TANDY,
Stratford-upon-Avon, Warwickshire. June 8

From Dr D. B. Peacock

Sir, (Basically) I would love to join Lord Janner's campaign if only I wasn't so bothered about being unable to "meet" anyone nowadays without having to explain that I am "with" them at the time. Yours sincerely,
DAVID PEACOCK,
Almondsbury, Bristol. June 8

From Mrs John Haines

Sir, Hopefully, "hopefully" will be added to the list of words that should be exterminated.   Yours sincerely,
JOCELYN HAINES,
Stebbing, Nr Dunmow, Essex. June 8

From Mr Robert Twyford

Sir, "Er", like other superfluous words, is often a substitute for plain old unpretentious "um", but it is objectionable when it gets into the middle of words.

"Atherletics" is a well known example. On Radio 4's Farming Today I recently heard "berlood", which made mine curdle.
Yours faithfully,
ROBERT TWYFORD,
Craster, Northumberland. June 12

From Mr Alistair Young

Sir, I hope that Lord Janner of Braunstone will be able to report that "report back" will be banned.   Yours faithfully,
ALISTAIR YOUNG,
Sevenoaks, Kent. June 12

From Mr W. M. Forrest

Sir, We should cease to address anything except envelopes.   Yours faithfully,
W. M. FORREST,
London SW19. June 12

From Mr Adrian Brodkin

Sir, Could we please get rid of "at this moment in time", preferably now.
Yours faithfully,
ADRIAN BRODKIN,
London N2. June 12

From Professor David Robertson Smith

Sir, "Unmissable" would not be missed.
Yours sincerely,
DAVID ROBERTSON SMITH,
Cuddesdon, Oxford. June 12

TITANIA'S TRIAL

From Mr Robin S. Howard

Sir, Your diarist (June 1) quotes Michelle Pfeiffer as saying, apropos her scant costume for her part as Titania in *A Midsummer Night's Dream*: "So my whole performance became about keeping my ass covered."

Perhaps, for the benefit of your readers not conversant with the American language, he might have amended this to: "So my whole performance became about keeping my Bottom covered".   Yours faithfully,
ROBIN S. HOWARD,
Fareham, Hampshire. June 3

EASY MISTAKE TO MAKE?

From Mr A. J. Colbert

Sir, The American evangelist Pat Robertson thinks that homosexuality is exceptionally common in Scotland.

This preacher lives across the sea, over the hills and far away in another land. Perhaps he suffers from a fundamental and potentially deadly misunderstanding of the kilt.

Yours faithfully,
A. J. COLBERT,
Walsall, West Midlands. June 5

FLAMING JUNE

From Mrs Alfred Goldstein

Sir, High winds, torrential rain and squalls in the Channel (reports, June 3) is not "freak weather" for June.

It is D-Day weather. *Yours truly,*
ANNA GOLDSTEIN,
Edenbridge, Kent. June 5

SPACED OUT?

From Mr Robert D. Tucker

Sir, David Hockney (report, May 27) confesses: "I've smoked a lot of marijuana, it hasn't harmed me." He then describes his new work of art, a panorama of the Grand Canyon, by explaining: "You feel the space that can be defined by its edge."

Pass the matches? *Yours faithfully,*
ROBERT D. TUCKER,
Addlestone, Surrey. June 5

READERS' WRITING

From Mr Anthony Franklin

Sir, There are occasions when I wonder if the letters have been drawn from a hat.

Perplexedly Yours,
ANTHONY FRANKLIN,
Pangbourne, Berkshire. June 9

From Mr T. R. Hawker

Sir, Mr Anthony Franklin wondered on this page if letters for publication were chosen from a hat, whereas I have always felt that correspondents with named properties have the edge.

That day was a good example, yielding The Curate's Egg, Heritage Field, Perama, the houses of Hyde, Basing and Hill, together with Silton Cottage. *Yours faithfully,*
T. R. HAWKER,
Barry, Vale of Glamorgan. June 15

From Mr Mike Corser

Sir, Mr T. R. Hawker's theory that readers with named properties have a greater chance of having letters published has not helped me in the past. Perhaps, however, it has something to do with the translation of my address: Little Hill of Rieve, Pig's Place, By the Small Stream, Aberdeenshire.

Yours sincerely,
MIKE CORSER,
Tillyrieve, Pettymuick, Udny,
Aberdeenshire. June 16

From Dr A. Marr

Sir, Mr Mike Corser gives an enlightening translation of his address – Pettymuick, Udny, Aberdeenshire. This is the same small farm on which I was born and brought up, called then, spelt and uncompromisingly pronounced "Pettymuck".

This has enabled me, on the all too infrequent occasions when we have found ourselves at rather posh and exclusive social events, to whisper to my wife: "This is a lang wye frae Pettymuck!" *Yours sincerely,*
A. MARR,
Hildenborough, Kent. June 21

SEEING THE LIGHT

From Mr J. P. Watts

Sir, You seem surprised (picture and caption, May 29) that a lightbulb still worked two months after being swallowed by a snake, but how many of those whose strange tastes you report at length would still be working two months after swallowing a lightbulb? *Yours etc,*
J. P. WATTS,
London SW1. June 9

UK, EURO AND EUROPE

From Mr G. Calderbank

Sir, In view of all the doubt and uncertainty surrounding adoption of the euro, perhaps it would be better if we waited for the globo. *Yours faithfully,*
G. CALDERBANK,
Sedbergh, Cumbria. June 11

BRUSH WITH AUTHORITY

From Mr Geoffrey Planer

Sir, The private view at this year's Royal Academy Summer Exhibition was, as usual, a pleasant occasion where the Friends enjoyed a glass of Pimm's as they viewed the pictures. But not in the room housing the David Hockney canvases. There I was very politely told that "glasses were not allowed in the Hockney room".

Now why do they trust me not to hurl my Pimm's at, say, an Elizabeth Blackadder or an Allen Jones, but feel that I might let fly with a glass of No1 at Hockers?

Yours faithfully,
GEOFFREY PLANER,
Winchester, Hampshire. June 11

BARGAIN OFFERS

From Dr Ian L. Natoff

Sir, I celebrate my 66th birthday on June 20. This has precipitated three proposal offers from Cornhill Direct, inviting me to take out a life-insurance policy before that date.

One offer is addressed to Mr I. Natoff and promises me £10 in Marks & Spencer vouchers if I apply before the closing date (ie, while I am still 65). The other two both offer me £15 of vouchers within the same time limit. Of these, one is addressed to Dr I. Natoff, the other to Dr Ian Natoff.

Working for a PhD so many years ago certainly has paid dividends in life - £5 in this case!   I remain, Sir, with or without title,
IAN L. NATOFF,
Radlett, Hertfordshire. June 16

From Mr D. O. R. Mossman

Sir, At least Dr Ian Natoff is entitled to his title. An American bank's computer imaginatively transformed "First Floor Flat" in our address into "F S T Flr Flight Lieut".

There is, admittedly, a Biggles in the household, but he's a cat.   Yours sincerely,
D. O. R. MOSSMAN
Caterham, Surrey. June 23

ROLE MODEL?

From Ms Helen Grayson

Sir, I see that Mattel has scrapped plans to produce a tattooed Barbie (World in brief, July 15), fearing that impressionable girls will emulate her.

Could I suggest that instead they make Housework Barbie, who has no interest in clothes or make-up, but likes nothing better than tidying her room?   Yours etc,
HELEN GRAYSON
Horsforth, West Yorkshire. June 17

From Mr Rod Burden

Sir, With reference to the scrapping of plans to produce a tattooed Barbie, I wonder if the next product should be "Divorced Barbie".

The most expensive doll yet, it would come complete with Ken's house, Ken's car, Ken's boat . . . .   Yours,
R. A. BURDEN,
Poole, Dorset. June 22

From Mrs Stevie Pattison-Dick

Sir, Mr Rod Burden, who proposes a "Divorced Barbie" may not realise that it is Barbie who has worked for all those years, constantly reinventing herself to pay for the house, the car and the boat. All Ken had to worry about was his Perma-Tan and next tennis lesson.   Yours faithfully,
STEVIE PATTISON-DICK,
London N18. June 25

From Mrs Barbara Eaton

Sir, As Barbie's partner, how about an Action Man who picks up dirty underwear?
Yours faithfully,
BARBARA EATON,
The Lizard, Cornwall. June 25

A WELL–CRAFTED LIKENESS

From the Reverend Ian Gregory

Sir, How much digital reworking would be required on pictures in today's papers of Sir Richard Greenbury to make him look a bit pleased with his reported retirement pension of £465,000 a year and a one-off cash payment of about £112,000 now that he is resigning from Marks & Spencer?

What is it with the super-rich? They rarely look as if life is worth living.   *Yours etc,*
IAN G. GREGORY,
Newcastle, Staffordshire. June 24

From Mr Philip N. Harris

Sir, I was surprised at the Reverend Ian Gregory's inquiry as to why the super-rich rarely look as if life is worth living. His work manual (New International Version) provides the answer in numerous places, for example, Ecclesiastes v,10:

Whoever loves money never has money enough; whoever loves wealth is never satisfied with his income.   *Yours faithfully,*
PHILIP N. HARRIS,
Coldharbour, Nr Dorking, Surrey. July 1

PERU? YAROO!

From Mr Bernard Kaukas

Sir, Philip Howard quotes George Orwell's observation that Billy Bunter's antics "have made him famous wherever the Union Jack waves", but he enlarges the field by adding Peru. This is aptly borne out by Robin Neillands, writing in your newspaper in 1985 of his travels in South America:

Business wasn't brisk; you could see that. The bus was empty, and behind the ticket window the clerk was deep in his comic - *Las Aventuras de Guillermito con el voraz apetito* - or Billy Bunter to you and me.

Yours faithfully,
BERNARD KAUKAS,
Ealing, London W5. June 25

FRIENDS IN HIGH PLACES?

From Mr Henry Howard

Sir, The General Secretary of the National Secular Society has had yet another letter printed by *The Times*. Truly the gods must smile on him.   *Yours faithfully,*
HENRY HOWARD,
London W1. June 25

EARLY 'BUG'

From Mr Nigel Douglas

Sir, I have received a reprimand from the Abbey National for overspending on an account which is in fact healthily in credit. Their letter is dated January 4, 2000. Can the bug be already gnawing at the woodwork?   *Yours sincerely,*
NIGEL DOUGLAS,
Dover, Kent. June 26

From Mr Matthew Flint

Sir, Nigel Douglas wrote that he had received a letter from Abbey National dated January 4, 2000, and wondered if "the bug" was striking six months early.

January 4 is actually the first working day of 2000, and is therefore one of the required test dates in any corporate Y2K program.

I would guess, therefore, that the letter was sent in error during the testing of some of Abbey's systems. Mr Douglas should take this as a sign that the Abbey National takes the Y2K problem seriously.

My only concern would be that to do the job "correctly", all Y2K testing should be performed on a totally isolated computer system, partly to avoid letters like this being sent in error.   *Yours etc,*
MATTHEW FLINT
(IT consultant), Corporate Network Services Ltd, Harrogate. July 2

From Mr R. M. Flaherty

Sir, Pertinent to our apprehension about the Y2K problem, I recently came across this passage in *Harrods: The Store and the Legend* (Pan, 1981):

In 1980 the oldest member of staff was born in the nineteenth century. Thereby hangs a tale. The computer does not recognise any but the twentieth century for the purposes of calculating dates of birth; hence it assumes that anyone born in 1898 was born in 1998 and includes them in a list of employees who are under 18 years of age.

An amendment to the programme has now stopped this charming anachronism.

Would that it were so!   *Yours faithfully,*
BOB FLAHERTY,
Auchterarder, Perthshire. July 2

From Dr John Crosby

Sir, In 1968, when computerised invitations for childhood immunisations were first sent out from County Hall, Taunton, I received a charming letter from an elderly lady suggesting that it was perhaps a little late to have her triple vaccine as she was born in 1868, not 1968. The millennium bug is old hat.   *Yours faithfully,*
JOHN CROSBY,
Taunton, Somerset. July 6

GOODNESS OF GARLIC

From Mr Joseph Sinclair

Sir, I was surprised that in the note on garlic ("Top ten herbs", Weekend, June 26), no mention was made of its other well-known property - the ability to ward off vampires.

I have been taking garlic in capsule form for more than 15 years and have not encountered a single vampire in all that time.
Yours etc,
JOSEPH SINCLAIR,
London NW4. June 29

From Mr Edward Thomas

Sir, Mr Joseph Sinclair reports that, in the 15 years he has been taking garlic, he has not encountered a single vampire. He does not say what happened in the preceding years.

I suggest he has a social duty to advise us at once.   *Yours truly,*
EDWARD THOMAS,
Eastbourne, East Sussex. July 7

PETS IN THE FREEZER

From Mr Ian Macalpine-Leny

Sir, The only time we have had to resort to the freezer (report and photograph, June 23) was when one of the family guinea-pigs was inconsiderate enough to succumb just before we were all due to leave for the US for Christmas. At such a busy time these things are easily forgotten, only to be rediscovered when the unfortunate nanny was cleaning out the freezer some six weeks later.

Had I known at the time that there was even the remotest possibility that this could induce resurrection, then Sarah would have been consigned to the dustbin instead!
Yours faithfully,
IAN MACALPINE-LENY,
London W14. June 30

A PENNY SPENT

From Mr Denys Franzini

Sir, Thames Water, in a commendable attempt to persuade people to use less water, has outlined the cost of various water-using activities (shower, bath, dishwasher, etc). I am informed by its leaflet that the cost of a nine-litre toilet flush is exactly 1p.

Well, well, well – what a coincidence!
Yours faithfully,
DENYS FRANZINI,
London SW5. June 30

WHAT PRICE HISTORY?

From Mr Tony Ashton

Sir, On a recent visit to Sainsbury's my bill came to £10.66. When this came up on the checkout screen, the assistant remarked: "There you go – the Battle of Waterloo."
Yours sincerely,
TONY ASHTON,
Woking, Surrey. June 30

From Mr P. C. Hambleton

Sir, I showed a Sussex University history graduate a copy of Mr Tony Ashton's letter about 1066 and the Battle of Waterloo and asked her what was funny about it.

She replied: "Is it something to do with Oliver Cromwell?"   *Yours faithfully,*
PETER HAMBLETON,
c/o W. T. Jones (solicitors),
London WC1. July 8

MOTORWAY BUS LANES

From Mr Claude Littlejohn

Sir, Where were the buses when Mr Blair, in the reserved bus lane, sped past the fuming voters on the M4 motorway?

Yours faithfully,
C. R. LITTLEJOHN,
London N6. July 1

From Mr R. J. L. Brodrick

Sir, There was a bus in the Prime Minister's lane of the M4 yesterday.   *Yours faithfully,*
R. J. L. BRODRICK,
London SW1. July 1

PEERS' PULLING POWER

From the Chief Executive of Macmillan Cancer Relief

Sir, Mr David Crease's letter, suggesting that the 92 hereditary peers in the reformed House of Lords should be drawn from a pool of peers "large enough" to be representative, is a blatant attempt to rig the next House of Lords v House of Commons tug-of-war match.

In 12 years this annual contest, organised in aid of Macmillan Cancer Relief, has never been won by the Commons. Whether this is due to the innate skills, inbred solidity, or luxurious feeding habits of their lordships has never been determined. But clearly avoirdupois must play a part, and to suggest that only peers who are large enough should have a place in the new chamber can only increase the chances of another ignominious defeat for the Commons next year.

Is this democracy or double standards?

Yours faithfully,
NICHOLAS YOUNG,
London SW3. July 1

MEMORY OVERLOAD

From Mr Masoud Gerami

Sir, I have to remember and use the following every day: a code for setting the alarm system before leaving the house, a password to start my mobile phone, three sets of numbers to get into my office building, two passwords to log in to my computer system, one password to start my personal diary, as well as countless passwords that I need for accessing various websites.

If this is not a valid reason for forgetting my wedding anniversary I don't know what is.   *Yours sincerely,*
MASOUD GERAMI,
Bradville, Milton Keynes. July 10

STRANGE NAMES

From Mrs John Haines

Sir, In 1899 my grandfather was asked to christen a baby girl "Gorilla". He refused, but achieved a tactful compromise with "Corilla".

In 1999 in your columns, along with the Jacks and Olivias, there have appeared a scattering of Indias, an Africa and an Antarctica. Also – sex not disclosed – a Pumpkin.

Perhaps nothing changes?   *Yours faithfully,*
JOCELYN HAINES,
Stebbing, Essex. July 10

From Ms S. E. Sullivan

Sir, I was amused to see that your Diarist found Sir Keith O'Nions surname "silly". For many years I was lucky enough to have two great-grandmothers living, whose surnames were Sage and Onions. I have since married a man whose surname is Bacon.

Yours faithfully,
SUSAN SULLIVAN,
Tatsfield, Surrey. July 17

From Mr Kenneth Cleveland

Sir, A retired teacher friend in Dorset once had a girl in his class called "Pebble". When asked why, she explained that she had been conceived on Chesil beach.

I remain, Sir, your obedient servant,
KENNETH CLEVELAND,
Bedford Park, London W4. July 17

From Miss Prudence Bebb

Sir, At the end of the First World War my grandfather was asked to christen a baby "Zeppelin".

I am happy to say that his persuasive powers saved the unfortunate infant from the appellation.   *Yours faithfully,*
PRUDENCE BEBB,
Upper Poppleton, York. July 17

From Mr Robert Maxtone Graham

Sir, Your correspondent's father, as a clergyman, persuaded a couple not to name their baby "Zeppelin"; but no one dissuaded my kinsman, the Rector of South Witham, Lincolnshire, from naming most of his 14 children in a way which some would have found even more awkward.

After giving his eldest son the family name of Lyonel, he played variations on that theme – Leo, Leone and Lyonulph for some boys; Lyonesse, Lyona, Lyonella and Lyonetta for the last four girls – mostly with a clutch of "historic" middle names.

One son went to live in New Zealand, improbably burdened with 16 forenames. He was my distant cousin, born Lyulph Ydwallo Odin Nestor Egbert Lyonel Toedmag Hugh Erchenwyne Saxon Esa Cromwell Orma Nevill Dysart (which spells out Lyonel the Second) Plantagenet Tollemache-Tollemache (1876–1961).   *Yours faithfully,*
ROBERT MAXTONE GRAHAM,
Sandwich, Kent. July 20

CUP OF CHEER

From Mr David Clifton

Sir, So now we are told that tea drinking reduces the risk of heart failure. Why is it, then, that the Brits, who drink more tea than almost anyone else in the world, suffer so many heart attacks? I think I shall stick to the red wine cure.   *Yours,*
DAVID CLIFTON,
London SE7. July 12

MILLENNIAL BOOST

From the Reverend Malcolm Johnson

Sir, So prayer might "dampen the party atmosphere" in the Millennium Dome on New Year's Eve (report, July 7)?

I am at present Lord Mayor's chaplain and when I say grace before banquets I have not noticed this inhibits conversation or the attack on sea bass and smoked salmon. True prayer whets the appetite, ignites and inflames passions and uplifts body and soul, so watch out on December 31.

Yours faithfully,
MALCOLM JOHNSON,
St Martin-in-the-Fields, London WC2.
July 13

HIGHLAND CLEARANCE?

From Mr R. W. Broadhead

Sir, I understand that since devolution the Scottish midge has been moving south (report, July 9). Is this to torment the English, or does it know something we don't?

Yours faithfully,
BOB BROADHEAD,
Petersfield, Hampshire. July 14

From Mr Iain Macleod

Sir, Some are worried about the spread south of the midge. Maybe they should take the advice I heard in a West Highland church the other day. Rub brown sugar over all exposed areas. It doesn't stop them biting, but it rots their teeth.

Yours faithfully,
IAIN MACLEOD,
Uddingston, South Lanarkshire. July 26

BRITISH MAMMALS

From Mr Oliver Chastney

Sir, Delighted to note that the wood mouse (report, July 6) heads the list of British mammals on the increase, but sad to see the hedgehog tops the list of species in decline.

Despite generations of dedicated effort from the nation's gardeners, it is frustrating that the population of moles remains stable.
Yours faithfully,
OLIVER CHASTNEY,
Cringleford, Norwich. July 15

ASIAN TARTANS

From Mr J. C. S. Mackie

Sir, It was good to see the photograph yesterday of Mr Singh in his new tartan, and to learn that this has been registered with the Scottish Tartans Society.

Tengku Aziz, one of the grandsons of a former Sultan of Johore, told me that Queen Victoria had granted to the Sultan and his family a special tartan. This was based on yellow which was, and still is, the royal colour of Malaysian Sultans. I hope it is still in use, and I wonder if it has been registered.

Yours faithfully,
JAMES MACKIE,
Haslemere, Surrey. July 19

OPEN VICTORY

From Mr William G. Black

Sir, There must be thousands, maybe millions of golfers around the world pontificating about how they could have played the 18th hole at Carnoustie in six strokes to win the Open Championship.

None of them, including the best golfers in the world, could so readily explain how to reach the 18th tee after 71 holes in 283 shots.

Bonne chance, Jean.   *Yours faithfully,*
WILLIAM G. BLACK,
Belfast. July 17

From Mr David M. Morris

Sir, "A blot on the escutcheon of the R & A" (your Golf Correspondent, Sport, July 20)?

How pompous; and what a tonic for sport in its real sense was Jean Van de Velde's magnanimous and realistic reaction to the sad loss of a title which he so richly deserved to win.

Far from being a "blot", it was a delight to see a worthy winner in the Scotsman and a true sportsman of great humour and style in the Frenchman.   *Yours sincerely,*
DAVID M. MORRIS,
Exeter, Devon. July 21

TIME TRAVEL

From Mr Peter Fullerton

Sir, *The Times* today carried an advertisement which offered: ". . . celebrate Millennium in Fiji and next day in W. Samoa crossing Dateline".

Are there others who might join me in reversing the itinerary, thus avoiding the whole silly thing?   *Yours faithfully,*
PETER FULLERTON,
London SE11. July 21

From Mr J. Morse-Brown

Sir, Peter Fullerton's idea of crossing the international dateline in reverse and so missing the millennium celebrations entirely is excellent. To the question, "Where were you on January 1, 2000?" one would be able to give the most memorable of all replies: "I wasn't."   *Yours faithfully,*
JOHN MORSE-BROWN,
Wombourne, Staffordshire. July 23

EARTHLY CARES

From Mr Mark Thakkar

Sir, It would appear that mailshot senders have turned to philosophising.

Today a health insurance offer arrived for my late grandfather, a doctor. Emblazoned on the envelope was: "You spend your life looking after other people. But who's looking after you?"   *Yours sincerely,*
MARK THAKKAR,
Bramhall, Cheshire. July 22

GOODNIGHT LADIES

From Mr Barry Simpson

Sir, I was intrigued to read that the 80 ladies employed by the Mustang Ranch in Nevada entertain some 200,000 customers per year. By my calculation, if they work five days a week and have two weeks' holiday a year, they would be entertaining ten clients a day each.

It is probably just as well that the establishment is likely to close. The poor dears could probably do with a rest.

Yours sincerely,
BARRY SIMPSON,
Oxford. July 26

From Mr Peter Oates

Sir, Mr Barry Simpson bemoans the working conditions of the "ladies" working at the Mustang Ranch brothel who entertain (sic) ten clients a day.

By my calculations this is a working day of only 40 minutes (excluding fag breaks) and so seems to be on a par with that of European MPs, though the latter are no doubt slightly better remunerated for their acts of acquiescence.   *Yours faithfully,*
PETER OATES,
Godmanchester, Cambridgeshire. August 2

STAMP OF APPROVAL?

From the Head Verger of St Clement Danes

Sir, I have just overheard a delightful exchange between two visitors to the church:
"What beautiful carving" (ie, on the pulpit).
"Yes, it's by Stanley Gibbons."

Yours faithfully,
BRIAN M. POAG,
London WC1. July 27

WOMEN PRIESTS

From the Reverend John Camp

Sir, The Bishop of London does not ordain women as priests. The Bishop has recently been elected to the Garrick Club (Anthony Howard's column, July 22). The Garrick does not admit women as members. Are these matters in any way connected?   *Yours faithfully,*
JOHN CAMP,
Great Billing, Northampton. July 28

DEEDS NOT WORDS

From Joan Lady Kings Norton

Sir, The new 19p postage stamp features a woman behind bars and carries the slogans "Votes for Women" and "Deeds not words". Is it not significant that these stamps will now grace second-class mail?

Yours faithfully,
JOAN KINGS NORTON,
Chipping Campden, Gloucestershire. July 28

A WORD FROM THE WISE?

From Mr John Riseley

Sir, The claim of chimpanzees "talking" (report and photograph, July 26) must prompt a reassessment of their intelligence.

It used to be argued that they could speak but have more sense, realising that if they did they would be put to work.

Yours truly,
J. G. RISELEY,
Farnborough, Hampshire. July 28

REFRESHING STEPS

From Mr Anthony Perry

Sir, Your thoughtful and detailed leader on the Government's annual report is, perhaps, a little ungenerous in not giving more weight to its larger achievements.

As a rather dull middle-of-the-road Labour supporter since 1949 I can hardly believe that we have Welsh and Scottish devolution, the House of Lords well on the way to reform and central financial decisions no longer being manipulated by politicians.

I don't remember feeling so refreshed since seeing my first mini-skirt.   *Yours faithfully,*
ANTHONY PERRY,
London N4. August 2

GIFT OF TONGUES

From Mr Bernard Kaukas

Sir, The reluctance of the Finns to provide simultaneous translation services for German at informal EU meetings (article and leading article, July 27) was foreshadowed by Frederick the Great, who never mastered the German language, which he despised to the end of his days: "Only at the end of an entire page," he lamented, "the verb."   *Yours faithfully,*
BERNARD KAUKAS,
Ealing, London W5. August 3

From Mr K. C. E. Ellison Davis

Sir, Dismissive as Frederick the Great was about the German language, the ultimate put-down must surely be that offered by the Emperor Charles V two hundred years earlier, when he observed that to God he spoke Spanish, to women Italian, to men French, and to his horse – German.

Yours sincerely,
KENNETH ELLISON DAVIS,
Amsterdam, The Netherlands. August 6

NOT RIGHT

From Mrs Pamela Morgan

Sir, My husband received a letter this morning addressed to "Leftenant Colonel Morgan" – the best yet! *Yours faithfully*,
PAMELA MORGAN,
Mill Hill, London NW7. August 3

GET AWAY FROM IT ALL

From Mr Peter Hillman

Sir, Surely going abroad and thereby missing the start of the football season by far outweighs Giles Coren's 19 other reasons for staying in Britain for the holidays (August 2). *Yours faithfully*,
PETER HILLMAN,
Horsham, West Sussex. August 3

ALTERNATIVE VIEW

From Mr Richard Thomas

Sir, I am advised not to look at the Sun for fear of damaging my eyes. But is it necessary to wear protective goggles all of the time, or just while reading Page 3?

Yours faithfully,
RICHARD THOMAS,
London N8. August 4

HEART AND SOLE

From Mr Andrew Baines

Sir, My wife works from home as an independent tax adviser. Periodically she receives financial information from a particular company addressed to her as "Soul Practitioner". We have not had the heart to

disillusion the senders, but as she is also a trustee of the Bible Society perhaps they are right for the wrong reason.

Yours faithfully,
ANDREW BAINES,
Speldhurst, Kent. August 5

POLICING ULSTER

From Mr Russell McClelland

Sir, You report that Chris Patten is likely to recommend an increase in the number of Catholic officers in the RUC.

A better strategy would be to recruit atheists, who are more likely to be neutral.

Yours faithfully,
RUSSELL McCLELLAND,
Leicester. August 10

INNOCENT ABROAD

From Mr K. E. J. Henderson

Sir, Your report on the new Tokyo museum that avoids going into detail about Japan's role in the Second World War reminds me of a conversation I once had at a cocktail party with a Japanese lady who was taking an advanced degree at the University of East Anglia.

When I told her that I had fought against her fellow countrymen in Burma, she replied: "Did you win?" *Yours faithfully*,
K. E. J. HENDERSON,
Norwich, Norfolk. August 11

CELLULOID AND PLASTIC

From Mr E. C. Ecroyd

Sir, How gratifying it was to read on today's front page that the US Government appraisers deemed that the JFK assassination movie was merely a strip of celluloid wound around a plastic reel.

The next time I admire a work of art by Gainsborough, Constable, Monet or Pissarro, thinking how handsome it would be hanging above my fireplace, I will console myself in the thought that it is merely stretched canvas daubed with paint.

Yours in exasperation,

CHARLES ECROYD,
Armathwaite, Carlisle, Cumbria. August 11

SAFE ECLIPSE–WATCHING

From Dr A. R. Stanford

Sir, In view of the many warnings regarding adequate safety measures when viewing the eclipse, should we not be sensible and listen to it on the radio?   *Yours faithfully,*
A. R. STANFORD,
Bromham, Bedford. August 11

From Mr B. H. Parker

Sir, A most memorable event, even under eight-eighths cloud.

The sudden onset of deep twilight was sufficient to quieten all species bar one, the Dartmouth seagull. During totality these birds maintained an intense cacophony of complaint, even greater than the noise they generate during the displays of the Red Arrows.   *Yours sincerely,*
BRIAN PARKER,
Dartmouth, Devon. August 12

From Mrs Elizabeth M. Clifton

Sir, "Ninety-five per cent of totality in Oxford", according to *The Times* today. The omens were promising: sun, blue sky and only fluffy white clouds above, so, clutching our home-made pinhole cameras and armed with champagne with which to toast the once-in-a-lifetime spectacle, we trooped outside.

The moment came and went. What happened? Nothing. So we drank the champagne and went back to work.

Now I know why I'm not getting excited about the millennium.   *Yours faithfully,*
ELIZABETH M. CLIFTON,
Oxford. August 12

From Mr A. P. Dearing

Sir, I'm sure the Chief Medical Officer will be relieved to know that the eclipse safety message got through to the public. My mother watched the entire event on television with her sunglasses on.   *Yours faithfully,*
A. DEARING,

Barnet, London. August 12

From the Reverend K. W. Clinch

Sir, I have a parishioner in her middle 80s who watched the last total eclipse of the Sun in 1927, and I have been listening on local radio this morning to a number of people of similar age who did the same. All say that they watched it through a piece of smoked glass prepared by their parents.

It is remarkable that not one of these senior citizens complains of any visual impairment as a result. Could it be that we are being blinded by science?   *Yours faithfully,*
K. W. CLINCH,
Battle, East Sussex. August 13

From Mr P. G. Smith

Sir, What I would like to know about the eclipse is – who would our growing breed of "compensation seekers" have complained to, had it not happened?   *Yours etc,*
P. G. SMITH,
London SW19. August 13

From Mr R. D. Williams

Sir, On holiday on the south side of Lake Geneva, I telephoned a lawyer friend in England. I mentioned in passing that the Mayor of Evian-les-Bains was handing out dark glasses, free, so that the public could safely watch the eclipse.

My friend gasped - in envy. "What liability!", he breathed.   *Yours sincerely,*
R. DEREK WILLIAMS,
Port de Pollenca, Mallorca. August 13

From Mr David P. Lintott

Sir, The end of civilisation as we know it did indeed take place yesterday. This morning, as a direct result of the eclipse, I was forced to open my copy of *The Times* and indeed to fold back a page to get to the crossword.

Disgraceful!   *Sincerely,*
DAVID LINTOTT,
Sheffield. August 13

From Mr D. G. Clark

Sir, I read an extraordinary advertisement

hoarding in Exeter yesterday: "Blackthorn Cider official sponsor to the Eclipse". Is anything sacred?   *Yours sincerely*,
DAVID CLARK,
Sidmouth, Devon. August 13

JUST IN CASE

From Mrs Sue Parkes

Sir, I have recently found further evidence that casts doubt on the permanence of marriage. Pausing to admire the new display in our local bridal shop, I saw, painted on the window, the ubiquitous "Buy one and get one free".   *Yours faithfully*,
SUE PARKES,
Halesowen, West Midlands. August 12

SPREADING DAISIES

From Mrs Jane Pinney Faulkner

Sir, Stephen Anderton (Weekend, August 7) wonders what his *Erigeron karvinskianus* daisies will do next. It's quite simple: they will spread all over the terrace, up the walls of his house, and down through the chimney if he lets them.

In California we call this the "Santa Barbara Daisy". I happen to love it, but it is the bane of many of our gardeners at home.

Sincerely,
JANE P. FAULKNER,
as from: Santa Barbara, California. August 14

BISHOP'S HABITS

From Mr Andrew Stuart

Sir, As British Ambassador in Helsinki (1980-83), I once entertained some distinguished Finns and a visiting British bishop (no names, no pack-drill) to the Finnish social habit of a sauna, where episcopal robes would not have been appropriate.

At supper afterwards the bishop donned a towel before saying grace. He said he did not think God would mind, but he felt more comfortable that way.   *Yours faithfully*,
ANDREW STUART,
Wareham, Dorset. August 14

FOLLOWING A PATTERN

From Mrs Dora Wigg

Sir, After noting the prices, such as £2,025 for a chunky hand-knit cardie, in your fashion article "In praise of the older woman" (August 9), I'd lay bets that, after recovering from shock, the nation's grannies will reach for their knitting needles and set up in business. We've been making them like that for years.   *Yours faithfully*,
D. B. WIGG,
Winchcombe, Cheltenham. August 16

UNJUSTIFIED HYPHENS

From Dr Hugh de Glanville

Sir, As an observer of the inelegant, unintelligent and unhelpful ways in which computers may break (hyphenate) words at line ends – unchecked, it would often seem, by any subeditorial eye – I thought a nadir had been reached recently with "centime-tre" (seen in *The Spectator*).

On August 2, however, you surpassed (underpassed?) this with "w-orker".

Yours faithfully,
HUGH de GLANVILLE,
Weybridge, Surrey. August 16

From Mr D. S. McKie

Sir, My thanks are due to Dr de Glanville. Later in the same issue I read that the model Iman was formerly reputed to be 6ft 2in tall but is in fact "almost half a foot short of her leg-end." The contortions my brain went through to interpret this were torturous, until memory of Dr de Glanville's letter mercifully assisted me to see what was truly *legendum*, to be read.

Yours faithfully,
DAVID McKIE,
Cambridge. August 23

From Mr G. K. Johnston

Sir, On reading Dr H. de Glanville's letter I recalled my own favourite from your paper: "pronoun-cement".   *Yours faithfully*,
GEOFFREY JOHNSTON,
Gloucester. August 25

From Mr T. P. Goldingham

Sir, The prize for ghoulish ineptitude among unintelligent hyphenations that I have come across must go to "brains-canner".

Yours etc,
TIM GOLDINGHAM,
Maidenhead. August 25

From Mr Eric Shackle

Sir, Sometimes the computer improves a word by its placement of the hyphen. My favourite is bed-raggled.   *Yours faithfully,*
ERIC SHACKLE,
Ettalong, NSW, Australia. August 26

From Mr Andrew Bluhm

Sir, A computer hyphenation revealing a new meaning is not-ables, which so well defines a class of persons to be found occupying senior positions in many organisations.   *Yours faithfully,*
ANDREW BLUHM,
Thames Ditton, Surrey. September 1

RIDING TO WAR

From Dr Gerald Danaher

Sir, Friedrich Engels would have agreed with David Hart (article, August 10) that hunting on horseback was good training for war. According to A. J. P. Taylor in his introduction to the Penguin Classics edition of *The Communist Manifesto*, Engels "hunted two days a week with the Cheshire – valuable training, he contended, for a future commander of revolutionary armies".   *Yours sincerely,*
GERALD DANAHER,
Coalville, Leicestershire. August 17

From Mr A. H. Lee

Sir, Friedrich Engels's conception of hunting as good military training effectively consigns the whole business to the last century. Otherwise the foxes would now be chased by tanks after, of course, a suitably protracted period of negotiations followed by sanctions and an air strike.   *Yours faithfully,*
A. H. LEE,
Llandovery, Carmarthenshire. August 21

TESTING TIME FOR MEN

From Mrs Julie Plisner Haines

Sir, If men are unable to do housework because they are "serotonin challenged" and are "more susceptible to boredom", as your article (Weekend, August 14) suggests, how do you explain the vast numbers who sit on riverbanks with rod in hand for hours on end or those who watch 22 men clad in white waiting in vain for England to win a Test match?   *Yours sincerely,*
JULIE PLISNER HAINES,
Radwinter, Essex. August 18

LOADED QUESTION

From Ms Jan Morris

Sir, Brian MacArthur's example of an editor's testy cable to an errant correspondent (Media, August 13) is not as succinct as its obvious inspiration, a famous service message received by the Middle East correspondent of an American journal who happened to be sunning himself on a beach in Beirut when the King of Egypt gave up his throne in Cairo: FAROUK ABDICATED STOP WHAT YOUR PLANS QUERY.   *Yours faithfully,*
JAN MORRIS,
Llanystumdwy, Gwynedd. August 20

LIQUID GOLD

From Mr Brian Bennett

Sir, The recent increase in the price of petrol does not please me at all, but why should beer, an indigenous product whose main constituent is local water, still cost over four times as much?

A gallon of petrol is still less than £4; a gallon of beer costs over £16.

Yours faithfully,
BRIAN BENNETT,
Berkhamsted, Hertfordshire. August 24

From Mr Myles Edge

Sir, Congratulations to Mr Brian Bennett on his comparison of the price of petrol with that of beer. My problem is my inability to understand how the public can be persuaded to pay over £8 per gallon for bottled drinking water, particularly as there is no special tax element in this price.

Yours faithfully,
MYLES EDGE,
Mollington, Chester. August 27

From Mr David Austin

Sir, Whilst wholeheartedly agreeing with Brian Bennett that beer, whose principal ingredient is water, is greatly overpriced when compared to petrol, could I suggest that he move to Yorkshire where he can get 13.67 pints of Samuel Smith's Old Brewery Bitter for his £16 rather than the miserly gallon he would get in Berkhamsted.

Yours sincerely,
DAVID AUSTIN,
Brighouse, West Yorkshire. August 27

CONSULTANTS' ROLE

From Mr David Allison-Beer

Sir, Your correspondents may not be aware of the definition of a consultant: someone who borrows your watch, tells you the time and then charges you for the privilege. *Yours faithfully,*
DAVID ALLISON-BEER,
Uxbridge, Middlesex. August 26

From Mr Robert J. Lewis

Sir, Perhaps Mr David Allison-Beer is unaware of the definition of a consultant's client: someone with a very expensive watch who doesn't know what time it is. *Yours etc,*
ROBERT J. LEWIS,
Isleworth, Middlesex. August 31

IN 75 WORDS . . .

From Mrs Iona O'Connor

Sir, Perhaps all members of the House of Lords, be they there through inheritance or by political patronage, should be required to justify their presence (in 75 words) – maybe annually? *Yours truly,*
IONA O'CONNOR,
Dunkeld, Perthshire. August 27

From Lord Stanley of Alderley

Sir, Do you think that after 28 years in the House of Lords I shall be allowed to give my reasons in 75 words for not wishing to remain there? *Yours faithfully,*
STANLEY of ALDERLEY,
House of Lords. August 27

From Mr H. R. F. Keating

Sir, "Nowhere . . . can anyone write 75 words", Simon Jenkins asseverates today. Wrong. Seventy-five words is the ideal length for a book blurb, long enough to say what's inside, short enough to hold passing attention. I well remember the late Poet Laureate and publisher, Cecil Day Lewis, telling me his two favourite literary forms, challenging in their brevity, were the sonnet and the blurb. *Yours,*
H. R. F. KEATING,
London W2. August 30

From Mr Stuart Sexton

Sir, Would it not be even more interesting if members of the House of Commons had to justify their presence there in 75 words? The current Labour lobby fodder might be hard put to it in any number of words.

Yours faithfully,
STUART SEXTON,
Sanderstead, South Croydon. August 30

From Miss M. Kay Cattell

Sir, Seventy five words smacks of verbosity. "I'm for Tony" or "I holiday in Tuscany" should suffice.   *Yours faithfully,*
M. KAY CATTELL,
Perton, Wolverhampton. August 30

REDEFINING JUNIORS

From Mr Edward J. P. Crawfurd, FRCS

Sir, Frank Dobson would abolish the term "junior doctor". If "juniors" have to go could we not start with "junior ministers"?
Yours truly,
EDWARD J. P. CRAWFURD,
Towcester, Northamptonshire. August 28

From Mr Christopher Elsworth, FRCS

Sir, Unusually I find myself in strong agreement with Frank Dobson when he proposes to abandon the title "junior doctor" in the health service. For the most part these hospital doctors are junior neither in age nor in experience. The term is outdated and belittling.

Whilst on the subject of anachronistic titles, I also think it is high time consultant surgeons like myself stopped calling ourselves "Mr" rather than "Dr", as with the rest of our medical colleagues. The origins of this tiresome affectation date back to some quirk about barbers and doctors over a century ago. The term is confusing for patients, puzzling to surgeons from abroad and portrays an aloof and old-fashioned image.
Yours faithfully,
CHRIS ELSWORTH,
(Consultant orthopaedic surgeon), The Royal Oldham Hospital. August 28

From Mr Peter Mowbray

Sir, Boston Training Agency has also had the difficulty of finding a suitable title for the Junior Director. A parking space is reserved for the Deputy Senior Director.
Yours sincerely,
PETER MOWBRAY,
Boston, Lincolnshire. September 2

From Mr John F. Martin

Sir, Why cannot junior house doctors be called interns, as in the US?

They would doubtless consider it appropriate in view of their long working hours.
Yours truly,
JOHN F. MARTIN,
Loughton, Essex. September 7

BITTER PILL

From Sir William Asscher, FRCP, and Mr F. E. Loeffler, FRCS, FRCOG

Sir, As ageing golfers and former members of the Committee on the Safety of Medicines we are becoming increasingly aware of the use of "mobility pills" such as Ibruprofen and Diclofenac sodium by our arthritic opponents. Are we to attribute our frequent defeats to illegal use of performance-enhancing substances or just poor technique?   *Yours faithfully,*
WILLIAM ASSCHER,
F. E. LOEFFLER,
Aldeburgh, Suffolk. August 28

DEADLY SERIOUS

From Mr A.D.R. Zellick

Sir, I have just received a travel insurance policy with the option to return it within 14 days if I am not satisfied. The policy provides that I MUST inform the insurers in the event of my death.

Will the worry of how to comply with this cast a shadow over my whole holiday?
Yours faithfully,
ADAM ZELLICK,
London WC1. August 30

RISE AND FALL

From Professor Sir Bryan Thwaites

Sir, On being appointed to a university chair in 1959, I bought the house in which I still live for about 1.5 times my starting salary.

It has recently been valued at about 15 times the current salary of a new professor. Something therefore has gone very badly wrong with academic salaries or with house prices – or perhaps with both.

Yours faithfully,
BRYAN THWAITES,
Milnthorpe, Winchester. September 1

From Mr Bob Byrom

Sir, Could I suggest to Professor Sir Bryan Thwaites that a better yardstick than professorial pay to measure the value of his house is the price of a pint of beer. My first house cost me 80,000 pints of beer in 1960. It is still worth the same.

Yours faithfully,
BOB BYROM,
Rowlands Castle, Hampshire. September 3

From Dr R. Gardner

Sir, Professor Sir Bryan Thwaites asks why the value of his house, compared to the pay of a professor, is now ten times what it was when he bought it.

The answer is that houses of the kind he has lived in for 40 years are now relatively scarce, whereas academics have since become plentiful.   Yours etc,
R. GARDNER,
Cambridge. September 6

CRACKING THE CROSSWORD

From Mr D. E. Downs

Sir, Many thanks for your excellent course on how to solve the *Times* crossword.

I now fail to do it with a much greater confidence.   Yours faithfully,
D. E. DOWNS,
Margate, Kent. September 1

GRAVE EXPECTATIONS

From Mrs C. Ann C. Andrews

Sir, "Ten years after his death, Samuel Beckett enjoys a week on Radio Three" (Magazine, August 28). On medium wave, presumably?   Yours faithfully,
C. ANN C. ANDREWS,
Sevenoaks, Kent. September 2

PC FATIGUE?

From Mrs Virginia Childs

Sir, At the end of a long and fraught day my computer has taken to ending my letters sympathetically.   Beset wishes.
VIRGINIA CHILDS,
Newick, East Sussex. September 7

IF PRESSED . . .

From Mr Peter Wade

Sir, Your report, "Bored stiff by ironing" (September 2), claimed that women "would rather spend the time sleeping (than iron) while men would rather have sex".

I never realised that we had the choice.

Yours optimistically,
PETER WADE,
Colchester, Essex. September 7

DATE ORDER

From Professor Howard R. Kirby

Sir, Today's date, 9/9/99, and yesterday's 0–0, 0–0 football scores prompts the reflection that the date 0/0/00 does not exist.

Hence, those who believe that the 20th century ends this year, and those who believe that the century should contain 100 years, can today both celebrate that this day is the last palindromic date of this century, however defined.   Yours faithfully,
HOWARD R. KIRBY,
Edinburgh. September 10

From Mr Peter Louth

Sir, Professor Howard R. Kirby's letter pointing out that 9/9/99 was the last palindromic date of this century reflects common usage on date abbreviation also reflected in your leader of the same day. It prompts the thought that the first palindromic date of both the new century and the new millennium will be not 1/1/11 but 10/02/2001.   Yours faithfully,
PETER LOUTH,
Limehouse, London E14. September 20

INAPPROPRIATE NAMES?

From Mr Peter Hulse

Sir, Philip Howard's comments on Icarus' poor air safety record (article, September 10) remind me that England is not the only place where knowledge of Greek myths is increasingly rare.

While flying to our summer holiday this year, we noticed that the name of the Olympic Airways "frequent-flyer" scheme is also Icarus.

In the next few weeks we discovered a bar called Socrates where fortunately hemlock was not on the menu, and a holiday apartment block named after Clytemnestra - not perhaps the most welcoming of characters from Ancient Greek tragedy.

Yours faithfully,
PETER HULSE,
Sheffield, South Yorkshire. September 13

From Mr Alex Leach

Sir, The holiday apartment block called Clytemnestra that Mr Peter Hulse encountered in Greece could always be renamed.

The Oedipus Complex suggests itself, unless its proprietors are eager to attract family groups.   *Yours faithfully,*
ALEX LEACH,
Shipley, West Yorkshire. September 17

From Mr George R. McGregor

Sir, My favourite inappropriate place name was spotted some years ago, on a bed and breakfast establishment in Plockton, Wester Ross, called "Nessun Dorma".

Yours faithfully,
GEORGE R. McGREGOR,
Haddington, East Lothian. September 22

NO CONTEST

From Mr Michael Wilson

Sir, Why is it that when a heron (30mph, 8lb resident) and a jumbo (600mph, 800,000lb visitor) collide, it is called a birdstrike ("Heathrow heron cripples jumbo", September 9)? Also, your headline overlooks the rather more serious injury caused to the first party.   *Yours faithfully,*
MICHAEL WILSON,
Woking, Surrey. September 10

OFF THE MAINS

From Mr D. Haddon-Reece

Sir, Some winters ago, I "killed" our septic tank – with bubble bath foam, apparently.

For three days running I had counteracted the chill of several hours' organ practice in a freezing church with a long restoring soak. The tank subsequently overflowed and had to be sucked out.

A farmer friend to whom I told this gave me an "o'er-hung" rabbit from his larder to "kick 'er off ageean". I went out on Christmas morning and dropped it down the tank.

It did the trick!   *Yours faithfully,*
D. HADDON-REECE,
Thirsk, North Yorkshire. September 16

CIVIL SERVANTS' ROLE

From Mr Ronald D. Martin

Sir, Peter Riddell asks "whether the present permanent secretaries are the right people to deliver change".

Perhaps removing the word "permanent" from their job title would help focus their minds.   *Your temporary correspondent,*
RON MARTIN,
Maidstone, Kent. September 18

TESTING TIMES

From Mr A. G. Phillips

Sir, Your obituary on Air Vice-Marshal David Dick (September 15) is a reminder of the hazards test pilots constantly face. It reminded me of an entry in a test pilot's report on a certain unpopular aircraft (no doubt still held in the Empire Test Pilots School archives) which included: "Entry to the cockpit is difficult. It should be made impossible."   *Yours faithfully,*
ANTHONY G. PHILLIPS,
Salisbury, Wiltshire. September 20

ACROSS THE POND

From Mrs Angela Barklam

Sir, Your anniversaries column records that on this day in 1620 the Pilgrim Fathers set sail for America on the Mayflower.

On the same day your Diary reported that Hugh Hefner telephoned from Los Angeles to order a curry to be flown out to him by Mr Minar Razza of the Mogul curry house in Manningtree, Essex.

Some progress in 379 years!

Yours faithfully,
ANGELA BARKLAM,
Milton Lilbourne, Wiltshire. September 20

IN A TWIST

From Sir Patrick Salt

Sir, In my youth boxer shorts had their label in the middle of the back so that there was no problem putting them on the right way round. In later years some manufacturers started putting the label on the right-hand side, causing obvious complications.

A new pair just bought have the label on the left-hand side, and so every morning I am faced with the task of working out from which era the underpants emanated.

Why do manufacturers have to add to the problems of old age so needlessly?

Yours faithfully,
P. M. SALT,
Bury St Edmunds, Suffolk. September 21

From Mr W. R. Smeeton

Sir, If Sir Patrick Salt is entirely reliant on the position of the label to put his boxer shorts on the right way round, I hope that he does not have too many designer shirts where the label or maker's logo is on the front. He may be taken for a member of the clergy. *Yours sincerely,*
ROBIN SMEETON,
Bordon, Hampshire. September 25

From Mr C. D. Shann

Sir, Confusingly I have two similarly sized white labels on my boxer shorts (manufacturer's name centre, washing instructions right), and at age 92 there is a limited time in which I can balance on one foot while deciding where to aim the other.

Yours faithfully,
C. D. SHANN,
Blandford Forum, Dorset. September 25

From Mr Geoffrey Shields

Sir, If Sir Patrick Salt cares to visit Gocek (and probably elsewhere) in southwest Turkey he will be able to buy boxer shorts with the label outside, centre of the waistband.

If these are unsuitable for personal use he could always give them to his academic or Sicilian friends – they are labelled "The Don". *Yours faithfully,*
GEOFFREY SHIELDS,
London SW6. September 29

From Mr Jeremy Wheeler

Sir, Whilst sharing in Sir Patrick Salt's confusion, my dilemma is further confounded because the particular nether-region garment I am wearing has its manufacturer's label at the front and on the outside of the supporting band. At least, I hope it does.

Yours faithfully,
JEREMY WHEELER,
Seaford, East Sussex. October 1

From Mr Cyril Wiseman

Sir, I have a Marks & Spencer pair with a label which reads "Authentic Underwear". I have wondered what the alternative is.

Yours faithfully,
CYRIL WISEMAN,
Snaresbrook, London E18. October 1

From Mrs Nicky Bull

Sir, In being unsure whether they should be labelled as centre, right or left, Sir Patrick Salt's boxer shorts may be mirroring British politics. Perhaps to the "wearer" they still feel the same? *Yours faithfully,*
NICKY BULL,
Tring, Hertfordshire. October 1

From Mr Nigel Carn

Sir, In India, in fact close to Jodhpur, we

spotted posters advertising underwear, which probably would have had no label at all, with the slogans "Macro man", "Hang loose", and the favourite, "Bum chums".

Yours faithfully,
NIGEL CARN,
London W7. October 1

From Mrs Melanie Pratt

Sir, How many more column inches concerning men's underwear are we going to have to endure?

Would women's bras get the same level of support? *Yours faithfully,*
MELANIE PRATT,
Tunbridge Wells, Kent. October 5

From Mr Greg Hopkins

Sir, Mrs Melanie Pratt asks if women's bras would get "the same level of support" as underpants in the labelling debate.

While it might, with imagination, be possible to put a bra on upside-down or even inside-out, she would be most unlikely to put it on back-to-front no matter where the label were stitched. *Yours sincerely,*
GREG HOPKINS,
Beaconsfield, Buckinghamshire. October 6

From Mrs Ann Lee

Sir, I find it somewhat disconcerting that the British male needs a signpost to direct him to the front and back of his underpants. *Yours faithfully,*
ANN LEE,
Rumbling Bridge, Kinross. October 7

LOCAL DISH

From Mr Jim McSheehy

Sir, Chalked up on the puddings menu in two of our Exmoor pubs is a local variation on gateau Paris-Brest.

The improved local version, Paris Breast, comes as a generous mound of choux pastry, complete with a strawberry on top.

Yours faithfully,
JIM McSHEEHY,
Porlock, Somerset. September 23

From Mrs Peter Spencer-Smith

Sir, Further to Mr Jim McSheehy's letter, in France I was once offered Supreme de Volaille Duchesse, translated on the menu as The Breast of a Duchess on toast.

Yours sincerely,
PHILIPPA SPENCER-SMITH,
Hitchin, Hertfordshire. September 28

From Mr Raymond C. Sturmer

Sir, Thanks to a lack of comprehension between an American student barman and a chef, customers of The Red Lion in Waverton Street, London W1, were recently offered Corniche Pasta as a bar snack.

Yours faithfully,
RAY STURMER,
Ingatestone, Essex. September 29

From Mr Michael R. Stannard

Sir, A menu in Le Mans once boasted Paté de foie de volaille which was translated as Foul potted meat.

I have the honour to remain, Sir, your obedient servant,
MICHAEL STANNARD,
Hambye, France. September 30

From Baroness Trumpington

Sir, The menu in a French restaurant with its English translation read: "Fruit of the season. Tart of the House".

My male companion's eyes brightened up no end. *Yours faithfully,*
TRUMPINGTON,
House of Lords. October 4

LIB DEM FIREPOWER

From Mr Alun Morris

Sir, If Simon Hughes is known for "his tendency to shoot from the lip" (leading article, September 23) and "speak from the hip" (Adrian Sanders, MP, report, same day) then everyone should take cover when he attempts to shoot himself in the foot.

Yours faithfully,
ALUN MORRIS,
Cambridge. September 24

SPOT ON

From Mr Nicholas Russell

Sir, I was delighted to receive a trade directory this morning with one of the most honest headings I have ever seen, "Direst Mail".   *Yours faithfully*,
N. C. RUSSELL,
Haslingfield, Cambridge. September 27

LONG LIFE

From Mr Simon Howorth

Sir, My greatly esteemed local wine merchant, in encouraging me to stock up with champagne well ahead of New Year's Eve, begins his exhortation, "The dawn of a new millennium is a once in a lifetime event."

What does he drink?   *Yours faithfully*,
SIMON HOWORTH,
London SW14. September 27

UNDERHAND TACTICS

From Mr Brian Lynch

Sir, A quite magnificent picture (September 25) of conkers beginning to burst out of their spiky cases was captioned with the advice to soak them in vinegar, smear them with facecream or bake them.

Such advice on cheating would never have appeared in the pages of *The Wizard* – pity they had to appear in yours.

No wonder the young people of today have no sense of what "being British" means.
Yours,
BRIAN LYNCH (The Stevens Road junior conkerer, 1948–49),
Brentwood, Essex. September 29

From Mr Alan Price-Talbot

Sir, What a load of old conker spikes. Of course we pickled, baked and anointed our conkers. However, casting one in lead and painting it with model-aircraft enamel was not very sporting. But it was unbeatable – until rumbled.   *Yours faithfully*,
ALAN PRICE-TALBOT
(Roath Park junior conkerer, 1950),
Caerphilly. October 2

From Mr James S. Sutherland

Sir, Despite Mr Brian Lynch's assurance that advice on cheating (at conkers) would never have appeared in the pages of *The Wizard*, I must point out that the *Adventure*, *Rover*, *Hotspur*, *Skipper* and *The Wizard* were not averse to giving advice on how to cheat at cricket.

In the mid-Thirties these illustrious boys' papers issued a series of cards entitled "Secrets of cricket". Amongst those still in my possession are "How to raise the seam" (with a coin), "Secret preparations" (pouring buckets of water on the wicket the night before a game) and "The flap flap trap" (leaving one's shirtsleeves unbuttoned when bowling in order to distract the batsman). *The Times* has nothing to be ashamed of!
Yours faithfully,
JAMES S. SUTHERLAND,
Edinburgh. October 2

CRICKET DUO DROPPED

From Mr Peter Nelson

Sir, Although one can share Mr Terence McAllister's frustration at the decision to deprive us of the commentaries of Trevor Bailey and Fred Trueman, we can see why the BBC may consider them too long in the tooth for today's game. After all, they date back to a half-forgotten era when England actually won Test matches.
Yours etc,
PETER NELSON,
Oadby, Leicester. October 1

LIVING NIGHTMARE

From the Reverend Peter Chicken

Sir, Sorry to disillusion your Religion Correspondent, Ruth Gledhill, but many vicars' wives are not dreaming of their husbands being made bishops (report, September 28) – nightmares maybe; dreams never!
Yours faithfully,
PETER CHICKEN,
Cheltenham, Gloucestershire. October 2

GHOST'S CHANCE

From Mr Fraser Riach

Sir, If ghosts walk through solid brick walls, how can the National Gallery ghost (report, September 30) sit on a chair?

Yours faithfully,
FRASER RIACH,
Glasgow. October 2

From Mr Barry Ferguson

Sir, Charles Dickens seems to have the answer to Fraser Riach's question about ghosts sitting.

Scrooge double-locked himself in his room but Marley's Ghost passed through the heavy door.

"Can you – can you sit down?" asked Scrooge, looking doubtfully at him.

"I can."

The Ghost, though transparent, sat down "as if he were used to it".

Humbug?   *Yours faithfully,*
BARRY FERGUSON,
Shaftesbury, Dorset. October 5

From the Reverend P. M. Hickley

Sir, The National Gallery ghost can walk through a brick wall because it wasn't there when he was alive, and can sit on a chair because it was; which is also why his clothes don't fall off.   *Yours faithfully,*
MICHAEL HICKLEY,
Lowestoft, Suffolk. October 8

JOURNALISTIC IGNORANCE

From Mr W. Stephen Gilbert

Sir, I so agree with Brian MacArthur's lament for the loss of a wide frame of reference among journalists (article, Media, October 1), but this is no new phenomenon.

Some 15 years ago, in an article for a distinguished weekly cultural magazine (now defunct), I made passing allusion to "Stinker" Murdoch. (For the benefit of both younger readers and contemporary journalists, the man in question was Richard Murdoch, a radio comic who appeared in two legendary series, *Band Waggon* with Arthur Askey, and *Much-Binding-in-the-Marsh* with Kenneth Horne.)

Sadly, my editor excised the reference. When I taxed him on this, he explained that it was because he had never heard the esteemed proprietor of your newspaper referred to by this name.   *Yours faithfully,*
W. STEPHEN GILBERT,
London N8. October 6

CRIMINAL HASTE

From Mr Douglas Verrall

Sir, The interview by Joanna Coles with the science journalist and author James Gleick on "hurry sickness" was most welcome. To show my appreciation I shall not use fax or e-mail, but will endeavour to post this letter with all convenient speed at a suitable post office either tomorrow or the day after by second-class mail.

On its arrival I would not expect you to feel under any pressure to engage in any undue acceleration to publish it.   *Yours,*
DOUGLAS VERRALL,
St Leonards-on-Sea, East Sussex.
October 6

DEATHBED CONVERSIONS

From Mr Alec Troop

Sir, Shortly before W. C. Fields's death a visiting friend found the great man in bed reading the Bible. The friend expressed astonishment at this, to which Fields is reputed to have replied that he was "simply looking for a loophole".   *Yours faithfully,*
ALEC TROOP,
East Bergholt, Suffolk. October 6

From Mr A. R. Longley

Sir, Voltaire, when asked on his death bed to renounce the Devil, replied: "This is no time for making new enemies."

Yours faithfully,
ADRIAN R. LONGLEY,
Battersea, London SW11. October 6

From Mrs J. G. Jones

Sir, Heinrich Heine did not need a death-bed conversion. He said *Dieu me pardonnera, c'est son metier* ("God will forgive me, it's his job"). *Yours faithfully,*
BETHAN JONES,
Gresford, Wrexham. October 9

ROUGH MEASURE

From Mr David Burrows

Sir, You report Nasa getting its units of force (metric/Imperial) in a muddle, thus unfortunately eradicating the Mars Orbiter mission.

If only they could have been consistent like *The Times*. Both in an illustration on the same page, "German space hotel", and a separate illustration on page 8, "Branson transatlantic catamaran", we are shown that universal unit of comparison, Nelson's Column. *Yours faithfully,*
DAVID BURROWS,
Flitton, Bedfordshire. October 6

From Mr Stephen Axbey

Sir, Actually, Nelson's Column is properly used only for heights; horizontal lengths are measured rather in football pitches.

Another common unit of measurement I have noticed is that used for large areas (such as indicating the size of East Timor): these are typically measured in Waleses.

Yours faithfully,
STEPHEN AXBEY,
Twickenham, Middlesex. October 9

From Mr Ken Broad

Sir, It would of course be extremely foolish to multiply Nelson's Columns by Waleses to arrive at rough volumes when there is a convenient measure still available in Wembley Stadium. A report in *The Sunday Times* (October 3) assured us that the excavations from a proposed Channel road tunnel would fill it no less than nine times.

Yours sincerely,
KEN BROAD,
Church Aston, Shropshire. October 19

From Mr Simon Brock

Sir, I think the one unit of measurement being overlooked is the (always red) dou-ble-decker bus, used for both height and length. *Yours faithfully,*
SIMON BROCK,
Clifton, Bristol. October 19

From Mr M. G. Harman

Sir, Congratulations on your replacement of Nelson's columns, double-decker buses and the like by new eco-friendly organic measures: "The end gallery (of the Tate Modern museum) rises an awesome 12m, the height of two giraffes" (Weekend, Oc-tober 30). *Yours sincerely,*
MICHAEL HARMAN,
Camberley, Surrey. November 2

From Mr Wingfield Martin

Sir, Having just grasped your system of measurement, I find your correspondent reports (November 3) that the Queen will light a beacon "the height of two double-decker buses and as wide as a tennis court".

If you are going to use derivatives please would you be kind enough to inform me what fraction of a Nelson's column a dou-ble-decker is and how many tennis courts are there in a football pitch.

Yours faithfully,
W. WINGFIELD MARTIN,
East Barnet, London. November 10

NOT STARRY-EYED ON EUROPE

From Mr Gwyn ap Thomas Harrison

Sir, For the first time ever I find myself in almost total agreement with Lady Thatcher. I would go somewhat further, however, and say that without doubt all of Britain's prob-lems, not just those faced by her genera-tion, have stemmed from Europe. Specifi-cally – the Angles, the Saxons and the Normans. *Yours faithfully,*
GWYN ap THOMAS HARRISON,
Porthaethwy, Gwynedd. October 7

SPIDERS IN THE BATH

From Mr Richard Lloyd

Sir, There is a much simpler way than using a mini-vacuum cleaner to get spiders out of the bath (report, early editions, September 30).

Hang a bathmat over the side so that one edge reaches the bottom of the bath, and the spiders climb out of their own accord.

Yours sincerely,
RICHARD LLOYD,
Wells-next-the-Sea, Norfolk. October 8

From Mr H. McG. Dunnett

Sir, I, too, have used Richard Lloyd's method to rescue spiders lurking in my bath.

This brings me to two unsolved mysteries: do spiders really emerge from the plug-hole as many believe, and where do they go after they have climbed out of the bath? Mine never seem to hang around.

Yours etc,
H. McG. DUNNETT,
Blackheath, London SE3. October 13

From Mrs Valerie Hanaway

Sir, In case your spider wishes to be uncooperative may I suggest the inner cardboard tube of a toilet roll.

Most spiders, being sensitive creatures, welcome the sanctuary of this dark tube and are easily removed to a safe distance from your bath.   *Yours faithfully,*
VALERIE HANAWAY,
Hertfordshire. October 13

From Mrs Patrick Despard

Sir, Spiders do not emerge from the plug-hole but from the overflow. I have witnessed this twice. I was regaling the story of this to my son, aged five, as he sat in the bath. Almost immediately on cue a huge spider forced its way out of the overflow and fell into the bath. A hasty exit ensued.

Yours faithfully,
EDWINA DESPARD,
London SW1. October 18

From Mr Jon Miller

Sir, The spiders often found in empty baths (genus *Tegenaria*) do not emerge from the plug-hole. They cannot live under water. They get into the bath by climbing in looking for moisture and then are unable to climb out. This happens more frequently in centrally heated houses.

There is only one British spider that can live under water, the water spider (*Argyroneta aquatica*). It spins a silken "diving bell" that, filled with air, is attached to underwater plants enabling it to remain under water in streams and ponds for a considerable time. This species does not venture indoors.

Yours faithfully,
JON MILLER,
Helston, Cornwall. October 20

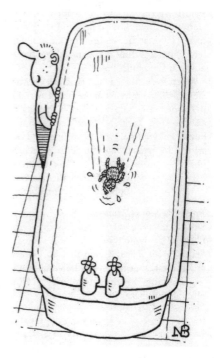

"Mum, there's a spider crawling up the bath!"

GOOD AND BAD NEWS

From Mr Eric Skelding

Sir, Your "A century in photographs" tells us that in 1941 telegraph boys were "regarded with terror because they usually notified families of the missing or the dead".

When I got back from Dunkirk in 1940 I sent my mother a telegram. Some kind person in the GPO wrote "Good news" in pencil on the envelope. I have always been grateful to that unknown person.   *Yours,*
E. C. SKELDING,
Swadlincote, Derbyshire. October 9

DISPLAY OF UNION FLAG

From Commander G. S. Pearson, RN (retd)

Sir, We have seen it all now, pole to pole. A year or two ago, we had photographs of a British adventurer at the North Pole with an upside-down Union Flag and your issue today ("Antarctic rescue for cancer sufferer") has a picture of a Union Flag upside down at the South Pole.

When even the average Brit, far less foreigner, will wonder what on earth I am talking about, is it time to redesign the flag or decree that it really does not matter a bunting toss which way up it flies, and put an end to pedants like me getting steamed up?   *Yours faithfully,*
GEORGE S. PEARSON,
London SW6. October 12

From Mr Simon Mathews

Sir, Commander G. S. Pearson notes the Union Flag flying upside down in a photograph in *The Times*. Given that the photograph is taken at the South Pole, surely the flag is flying the right way up – it's the photograph that is upside down.

Yours faithfully,
SIMON MATHEWS,
Hong Kong. October 13

From Mr R. W. Pullan

Sir, Why not have "This way up" stamped on all Union Flags?   *Yours sincerely,*
R. W. PULLAN,
Hampton, Middlesex. October 18

From Mrs Mary Maddicks

Sir, An upside-down Union Flag signifies distress. The lady doctor marooned in the Antarctic was in distress – QED.
Yours faithfully,
MARY MADDICKS,
Bristol. October 18

LETTER BY LETTER

From Mr Dennis Powell

Sir, What rhymes with Motion, asks your leading article on poetry (October 7). There are five rhyming two-syllable words, including the common noun version of the poet's name, all beginning with the consecutive letters that virtually sit in the middle of the English alphabet.
Yours faithfully,
DENNIS POWELL,
Winchester, Hampshire. October 12

From Mr Gerald Moggridge

Sir, Only five two-syllable words to rhyme with Motion? Seafarers who have served in the Andrew (or Navy) will tell you otherwise.

How do we deal with the motion
Of a heaving, rolling ocean?
Is there a healing lotion?
Or perhaps a secret potion?
But soft, I have a notion.
Why don't we ask the boatswain?

Yours etc,
GERALD MOGGRIDGE,
Sutton, Surrey. October 16

From Mr John Fuller

Sir, Mr Gerald Mottridge introduces a new dimension – that of poetic licence - into the quest for rhymes for Motion, other than lotion, notion, ocean and potion, with the use of "boatswain" as the final rhyme of his sextuplet.

In similar vein, let us finish his poem with a further two lines:

A very bright Nova Scotian
With a high intelligence quotient.

Yours,
JOHN FULLER,
Penmaenmawr, Conwy. October 20

From Mr R. M. White

Sir, Hooray and up she rises! Surely only the drunken sailor would pronounce boatswain like motion. *Yours sincerely,*
RICHARD WHITE,
Tunbridge Wells, Kent. October 20

From Mr K. T. Powell

Sir, Doubtless Mr Gerald Moggridge hoped someone would challenge his rhyming skills and Messrs Fuller and White duly did so. However, the bo'sun will surely have the last laugh. Perhaps I set myself up, but is the last "t" in quotient really silent like the proverbial "p" in ocean? Yours quietly,
KEN POWELL,
Chiswick, London W4. October 22

CHURCHILL'S GENES

From Mr Norman Sanders

Sir, According to his family tree (report, October 13), Sir Winston Churchill had less than 2 per cent Iroquois blood in him. If his genes are the explanation for his fighting spirit the Iroquois must have been a very rough lot indeed. *Yours faithfully,*
NORMAN SANDERS,
Tattingstone Park, Ipswich. October 14

TOPSY-TURVY

From Mr Roger Foord

Sir, There has been much amusing correspondence recently regarding both labels on underwear and upside-down Union Flags.

Some thirty years ago I purchased a pair of Union Flag-designed Y-fronts. I must admit that I possibly wore them back-to-front a couple of times, but never upside down.

Yours faithfully,
ROGER FOORD,
Chorleywood, Hertfordshire. October 20

TURNER AGAIN

From Mr Colin Logue

Sir, Having looked at the state of my desk this morning I think I'm eligible for the Turner Prize (report and leading article, October 20). *Regards,*
C. LOGUE,
Pennine Tools Ltd, Huddersfield, West Yorkshire. October 21

JUST IN CASE

From Mr Trevor Elliott

Sir, On Monday, November 8, you will reach issue no. 66,666.

In order to placate the Devil, ought you not to take a leaf out of the supermarkets' book and number it 66,665.99?

Yours faithfully,
TREVOR ELLIOTT,
Sheffield, South Yorkshire. October 21

From Mr Simon Arter

Sir, I was able to share your celebrations of your 66,666th issue today.

Audrey, my trusty motor vehicle, clocked up 66,666 miles as we passed Andover on the A303 this morning. *Yours etc,*
SIMON ARTER,
North Tidworth, Wiltshire. November 13

WINTER WOOLLY

From Mr Gavin Littaur

Sir, "Nobody knows why" the woolly mammoth became extinct (picture caption, October 19). Perhaps it got bored with frozen wastes and sensibly travelled south to warmer climates, where a woolly covering was otiose and decidedly unfashionable.

Yours faithfully,
GAVIN LITTAUR,
London NW4. October 21

A GIANT STRIDE

From Mr J. J. C. Rylatt

Sir, It is heartening to see that British engineering has conceived as impressive a structure as the London Eye.

Can we now expect our biologists to follow suit by providing a hamster to power it? *Yours faithfully,*
JAMES RYLATT,
Uckfield, Sussex. October 21

HOPES OF A CLERGY WIFE

From Mrs Sally Vigeon

Sir, As the wife of a retired clergyman I read with interest your Diary item about Eileen Carey hoping her archbishop husband would retire sooner rather than later.

I do not think many people appreciate how difficult it is for the wife of a clergyman to sit on the sidelines as she watches her husband giving his all to serving his Lord and humanity; and getting more and more worn-out in the process. Even in retirement, priests are usually helping out somewhere. It is very easy to forget that there is someone at home hoping that there will be some time for them to do things together while they are both able to.

I think we deserve some time when we are not being asked to share our husbands with the world. I do hope Dr Carey will take notice of his wife's feelings and go at "the perfect time" when he turns 65.

Yours etc,
SALLY VIGEON,
Bromsgrove, Worcestershire. October 23

From Mr George Hubbard

Sir, Sally Vigeon is right - we clergy wives deserve a break. I haven't had a decent cheese and onion pie since my wife was ordained. *Yours faithfully,*
GEORGE HUBBARD,
Willingham, Cambridge. October 26

From Mr Cranstoun Gill

Sir, Hard luck, Mr George Hubbard. We eat much better since my wife was ordained. I do the cooking. *Yours faithfully,*
CRANSTOUN GILL,
Hale, Altrincham, Cheshire. October 29

From Mr John Barnes

Sir, Since the Church of England stole my wife for ordination my culinary skills have progressed, with the help of my kitchen bible, from ready-made pizza and coleslaw to full Sunday roast with six different vegetables. May I suggest that my fellow clergy wife, George Hubbard, consult the same volume.

Thank God for Delia! *Yours,*
JOHN BARNES,
Meopham, Kent. October 29

BANKING ON THE FUTURE

From Mr Alan White

Sir, After completing the first transaction with my bank on the Web yesterday I received an acknowledgement stating: "Your Payment will be made on Saturday, 30 Dec 1899."

Do I live in hope, or will the past catch up with me? *Yours faithfully,*
ALAN WHITE,
Bath. October 27

FREEDOM TO CHOOSE WHAT WE EAT

From Dr Roy Cecil

Sir, Agriculture Minister Nick Brown refuses to ban French beef. Instead he suggests that British consumers should decide for themselves whether or not to buy it.

As we seem to be being treated as adults at last, might we perhaps be permitted to eat British beef on the bone if we so choose? *Yours faithfully,*
ROY CECIL,
Datchet, Berkshire. October 28

From Mr Mark H. Levy

Sir, How come the French farmers find the time to go blockading roads and tunnels at the drop of a chapeau? *Yours sincerely,*
MARK H. LEVY,
Knutsford, Cheshire. October 28

From Mr Adrian Williams

Sir, As from midnight tonight I have banned everything French from my household: beans, chalk, cricket, curves, dressing, fries, horns, kisses, knickers, leave, letters, mustard, polish, toast, vermouth and windows.

That'll show 'em!   *Yours faithfully,*
ADRIAN WILLIAMS,
Headington, Oxford. October 28

From Mr John Eden

Sir, This morning's 7am news bulletin on Radio 3, which contained an item on the Franco-British beef war, was followed by three Fauré chansons.

Naturally, I switched off. *Yours faithfully,*
JOHN EDEN,
Sutton Coldfield, West Midlands.
October 29

From Mr Colin McLaughlin

Sir, Can I suggest that we all go straight from the four calling birds to the two turtle doves this Christmas?   *Yours faithfully,*
COLIN McLAUGHLIN,
New Malden, Surrey. December 16

MIXED PROVENANCE

From Professor Ian Craft

Sir, Surely Sotheby's should be able to recognise one nation from another.

Lot 550 in their Amsterdam sale catalogue of furniture for November 17 reads: "An English George III Welsh oak dresser. 18th century."   *Yours faithfully,*
IAN CRAFT
(Director), London Gynaecology and
Fertility Centre Limited,
London W1. November 3

From Mrs Imogen Mollet

Sir, Great Bardfield in Essex is a picturesque village well worth a visit for its intrinsic charm. But, if the November issue of *Essex Countryside* is to be believed, "Bardfield Hall dates from the time of the English Civil War, with Tudor additions".

This must surely be a unique architectural achievement.   *Yours sincerely,*
IMOGEN MOLLET,
Saffron Walden, Essex. November 8

From Mr C. J. Williams

Sir, The Essex house described as dating "from the time of the English Civil War, with Tudor additions" is not a unique architectural achievement.

My father, a clergyman in Shropshire in the 1950s, told me of a house in his parish which had, over an upstairs window, a lintel with a date on it. This was considerably earlier than the one on an inscription over the front door.

The owner suggested that this was because "they built the upstairs first".

Yours faithfully,
CHRISTOPHER J. WILLIAMS,
Marford, Wrexham. November 11

From Mrs Liz Calvert Smith

Sir, My own house is Georgian (George V) with an Elizabethan extension (Elizabeth II).   *Yours faithfully,*
LIZ CALVERT SMITH,
Ruislip, Middlesex. November 11

DOUBLE TROUBLE

From Mr R. J. C. Wait

Sir, Many times every day announcers on television and radio try to tempt us with information about websites, always beginning their recital of the relevant codes with the nine ugly, laborious syllables "double-u, double-u, double-u."

May I suggest that they should instead begin with the three one-syllable words World Wide Web, represented by the code letters www. The announcements would be a good deal less irritating.   *Yours faithfully,*
R. J. C. WAIT,
Weston Park, Bath. November 11

DOWNHILL ALL THE WAY

From Mr Ambrose Killen

Sir, Your Law Report (Palmer and Another *v* Bowman and Another, November 10) records that the court found that drainage from higher ground to lower needed no easement for the natural process to occur.

It is a relief to learn that the Court of Appeal has upheld the Law of Gravity.

I remain, Yours sincerely,
AMBROSE KILLEN,
St Albans, Hertfordshire. November 15

FOOTBALL METAPHORS

From Mr Patrick Phillips, QC

Sir, I have noticed that commentators, writers and others nowadays frequently refer to soccer as "our national game". For many years cricket has been recognised by Englishmen and those overseas as our national game. It was well established as such when soccer was in its infancy. Metaphors from cricket have become embedded in our language. The phrase "It's not cricket" came to represent that sense of fair play for which the Englishman was renowned.

Is soccer now our national game? Are its characteristics thought to reflect the Englishman of today? What metaphors has it contributed? I confess I am stumped.

Yours faithfully,
PATRICK PHILLIPS,
Long Melford, Suffolk. November 17

From Mr Ronald Thwaites, QC

Sir, The suggestion that football, a sport that gives us more drama than the RSC, has not provided metaphors to enrich the English language can only have been made by a man who is not on the ball. For from football, a game of two halves, we have had end-to-end metaphors, long before the final whistle.

I must recommend that Mr Patrick Phillips, QC, gets his eyes tested before he is shown a yellow card.   *Yours faithfully,*
RONALD THWAITES,
London EC4. November 22

From Dr Edward Young

Sir, Football may not be cricket, but clearly someone has moved the goalposts.

Yours sincerely,
EDWARD YOUNG,
Earley, Berkshire. November 22

NEW LABOUR BABY

From Mr Nigel Hammersley

Sir, I am sure the whole country is pleased at the news of the forthcoming addition to the Blair household.

Is it too much to hope that, after the next election, Tony will be able to spend more time with his family?   *Yours faithfully,*
NIGEL HAMMERSLEY,
Desford, Leicester. November 20

From Mr D. O. E. Batten

Sir, To be pregnant at 45 may typify New Woman but will not the confinement be an example of Old Labour?

Yours faithfully,
DAVID BATTEN,
Oakham, Rutland. November 20

From Dr John H. Greensmith

Sir, It will be tough with all those late nights and early day motions, screaming and shouting, tantrums . . . but the new Blair babe will just have to get used to it.

Yours sincerely,
JOHN H. GREENSMITH,
Downend, Bristol. November 20

GUNNING FOR GLORY

From Canon Ivor Ll. Davies

Sir, I and many of my colleagues have, over the years, become well-accustomed to being addressed as artillery pieces, but to find that when defence against the feared Napoleonic invasion was needed (Weekend, November 13) Martello towers were built on which it was possible to "swivel and aim your canon", and strong enough to "carry the weight of a heavy canon on the roof", I have to admit that I had not realised how truly my honoured predecessors were the big guns of their day.   *Yours etc,*
IVOR LL. DAVIES,
Lydney, Gloucestershire. November 20

From Canon Dr Derek Whitehead

Sir, Canon Ivor Davies is quite right to point out the perils which attend the confusion of an ecclesiastical rank with a piece of field artillery. I am sure he will agree with me that it is nothing but unfortunate homophony which has led to a canon being defined as a "smooth bore".

Yours sincerely,
DEREK WHITEHEAD,
Uckfield, East Sussex. November 23

From Mr Raymond Durrant

Sir, A man who is a smooth bore is unlikely to be of the right calibre for an ecclesiastical canon's position.   *Yours faithfully,*
RAYMOND DURRANT,
St Albans, Hertfordshire. November 26

LAST RESORT?

From Mr Keith Chambers

Sir, Prisoners should be charged rent (report, earlier editions, November 17)? Will they be evicted if they get into arrears?

Yours faithfully,
KEITH CHAMBERS,
Oakley, Hampshire. November 22

TUBE PRIORITIES

From Mr Richard Mangnall

Sir, I note (report, November 24) that there are to be facilities for mobile phones on the Tube. Having suffered complete suspensions of the Central Line today and yesterday, I wonder if it would be too much to ask for mobile trains?   *Yours faithfully,*
RICHARD MANGNALL,
London W2. November 26

IRON MAIDEN

From Mr Michael Abbott

Sir, I see that Nick Faldo's ex-girlfriend attacked his Porsche with a seven-iron.

Is there a choice of clubs for damaging cars? Perhaps a driver would have been better.   *Yours sincerely,*
M. P. ABBOTT,
Tankerton, Whitstable, Kent. November 27

From Mr G. D. Neely

Sir, P. G. Wodehouse, in his short story *The*

Salvation of George Mackintosh, decreed the club with which a golfer, or his car, should be attacked. Not a driver, nor a seven-iron. "It was unquestionably a niblick shot."

Yours faithfully,
GUY NEELY,
Chislehurst, Kent. December 2

EARLY SONGBIRDS

From Mr Geoff Watson

Sir, This evening we have been visited by our first carol singers of the season.

Have we had the last of our silent nights, I wonder?   *Yours faithfully,*
GEOFF WATSON,
Downend, Bristol. December 1

POINTS OF VIEW

From Lord Brightman

Sir, Your astronomy correspondent tells us today that "Sunset on the 1st is at 15h 50m", while the Editor of "Hours of Darkness" tells us "Sun sets: 3.55pm". I can only suppose that the former has his desk on the ground floor of your publishing house and the latter on the top floor.

I am, somewhat mystified,

BRIGHTMAN,
House of Lords. December 2

OPEN DOOR POLICY?

From Mr Howard Self

Sir, I have reluctantly come to terms with a "Bob the Builder" Advent calendar, but I can't help feeling that "Action Man" and "Match of the Day" Advent calendars send out a rather confused message.

Yours faithfully,
H. J. SELF,
Manchester. December 3

From Dr Alan Calverd

Sir, Being neither a chocoholic nor a Christian, I took little interest in the subject of Advent calendars until today, when my daughter bought one containing Cadbury's products and carrying the slogan "have a Wicked Christmas".

Is Satan challenging God's 2,000-year dominance of the midwinter marketplace?

Yours sincerely,
ALAN M. CALVERD,
Bishops Stortford, Hertfordshire.
December 8

SPACE RESEARCH

From Mr J. White

Sir, I see the European Space Agency is asking 24 men to spend three months in bed to investigate the effects of weightlessness. Extrapolating from observations of my teenaged children who seem to spend a lot of time supine I predict these effects will include mood swings and spots.

Yours faithfully,
J. WHITE,
Rampton, Cambridge. December 6

NET SUPPORT

From Canon W. D. Jones

Sir, Our congratulations to the Reverend Arthur Kennedy for his Balm (News in brief, December 3), an Internet helpline for vicars being bullied by their congregations.

Now, what about Balm II – for congregations bullied by their vicar? *Yours faithfully*,
W. D. JONES,
Tetbury, Gloucestershire. December 7

AS IN LIFE . . .

From Miss Jaqueline Hope-Wallace

Sir, The Guardian's late music and drama critic, Philip Hope-Wallace, was dogged by misprints when reviewing for *The Grauniad* (Doris Gudonov was long remembered).

He would have been amused if he had known that misprints would follow him even in death. "Madly (instead of badly) missed" in an In Memoriam notice in *The Times* (November 8) strikes a slightly Bacchic note. *Yours faithfully*,
J. HOPE-WALLACE,
London SW1. December 7

"ICON" OF INVENTION

From Commander R. E. Williams, RN

Sir, Far from being "product of the century" (report, "Clip that changed working world", December 7), the paperclip has been known by generations of Supply and Secretariat Officers and Ratings of the Writer Branch of the Royal Navy as the "Court-Martial Clip", for its unfailing ability to pick up important papers accidentally and attach them to less important documents, never to be seen again.

The humble pin has no such proclivity. That said, the pin, too, has its disadvantages, especially if the point is not masked between two sheets of paper and, when handled, buries itself in the finger of your very senior boss. *Yours faithfully*,
BOB WILLIAMS
(Deputy Chief Naval Judge Advocate),
Old Naval Academy, HM Naval Base,
Portsmouth. December 10

From Professor Rhys Williams

Sir, It's now perfectly clear that the Royal Navy has been using paper clips in totally the wrong way for decades. They have obviously been used with the lip on the short arm of the clip pointing outwards. This significantly increases the risk of unintentionally picking up extraneous papers.

The lip, it is perfectly obvious, should face inwards thus strengthening the grip of the clip on the papers it is meant to hold. With the lip in this orientation the likelihood of such a slip is greatly reduced.

Yours faithfully,
RHYS WILLIAMS,
Harrogate, West Yorkshire. December 16

From Mr Kenneth Savidge

Sir, Some years ago in the British High Commission in Karachi, I was amused to see a memorandum instructing staff to ensure that papers for His Excellency's attention were always presented with the point of the pin uppermost.

I never discovered the reasoning behind this instruction.   *Yours etc,*
KENNETH SAVIDGE,
Bristol. December 16

From Mr John Byrne

Sir, Metal paperclips damage paper. As an archivist I spend half my days removing them from sheets which they have worn, punctured or, through oxidisation, stained. Staples, embedding themselves the more deeply, are even worse.

They'll none of them be missed.
Yours faithfully,
JOHN BYRNE,
London W8. December 22

From Mrs Pamela Dooner

Sir, The reason for the High Commissioner's instruction on the placing of pins will be painfully obvious to any left-hander who has been "spiked" regularly by the downward pointing variety.   *Yours faithfully,*
P. DOONER,
Surbiton, Surrey. December 23

From Mr Tom Harman Smith

Sir, Many people fail to realise that the common paper clip is in fact the larval form of the wire coat hanger.

Paper clips, as you have noticed, hide then breed in the corners of table drawers and desks, the coat hanger later hatches out and multiplies in empty cupboards.

The recent introduction of plastic paper clips presumably has resulted in the thin and weak plastic coat hangers appearing.

Full research is needed on this matter and I hope one of our new universities will be able to help soon.   *Yours faithfully,*
TOM HARMAN SMITH,
Whitwell, Isle of Wight. December 29

DRESSING THE PART

From Monsignor Graham Adams

Sir, Mr A. Lindsay asks in his letter "when was the last time anyone saw a clergyman (plus dog-collar) in the pub or at the supermarket?"

I took Holy Communion to five parishioners this morning, shopped at a large supermarket in Banbury and called on my way home at a local pub in Cropredy where I had a cheese omelette and a double tomato juice.

I then visited another sick parishioner before settling down for a few minutes to read *The Times.* I am now wasting time writing this letter.

During all these activities I wore a black suit and a Roman collar.   *Yours sincerely,*
GRAHAM ADAMS,
Daventry, Northamptonshire.
December 11

From Mr Erlend Copeley-Williams

Sir, I recently enjoyed the sight, and, all too briefly the company, of a bishop, clerical collar and purple vest very visible, in a sandwich bar at Holborn, Central London.

I suspect the delights of a prawn salad sandwich were his principal concern, but he was very evident amidst the people.

Yours faithfully,
ERLEND COPELEY-WILLIAMS,
Shaftesbury, Dorset. December 11

GETTING ONE'S GOAT

From Mrs Cynthia Deeson

Sir, Maybe the reason why M&S can sell its pashminas at (only) £99 lies in its spokesman's remark (report, December 8): "We buy our fibre from Mongolian goats . . ." Thus cutting out the middleman?

Yours faithfully,
CYNTHIA DEESON,
Harborne, Birmingham. December 14

From Mrs A. E. Razzack

Sir, Having read the arguments about when a "pashmina" is not a "pashmina", I have come to the conclusion that all this is just splitting hairs.   *Yours faithfully,*
AUDREY E. RAZZACK,
Tottenham, London N15. December 14

PERFECT TIMING

From Mr Martin Turner

Sir, Has consumer labelling gone too far? In Sainsbury's recently I saw Christmas trees labelled "Ideal for Christmas".

Your obedient servant, Sir,
MARTIN TURNER,
Northfleet, Kent. December 15

From Dr John H. Greensmith

Sir, Martin Turner is absolutely right to be concerned about Sainsbury's Christmas trees labelled "Ideal for Christmas".

The case should be referred to the Office of Fir Trading.   *Yours sincerely,*
JOHN H. GREENSMITH,
Downend, Bristol. December 17

From Mr David Himsworth

Sir, Dr John H. Greensmith suggests that the matter of the Sainsbury's Christmas trees labelled "Ideal for Christmas" should be referred to the Office of Fir Trading.

We will be happy to advise on the subject if he writes to our branch office at the address below.   *Yours faithfully,*
DAVID HIMSWORTH
(Director), Fir Trading Ltd,
Malton, North Yorkshire. December 18

LONDON MAYORALTY

From Mrs Elizabeth Baker

Sir, We have had an exhausting amount of media coverage of the race for London's mayor.

Let the Princess Royal be mayor of London. Make it a hereditary role - through the female line - and have done with it.

Yours faithfully,
LIZ BAKER,
Street, Somerset. December 16

From Mr Graham Shipley

Sir, The more one sees of the selection shenanigans for London's mayor, the more one realises how untimely was the death of Screaming Lord Sutch.   *Yours,*
GRAHAM SHIPLEY,
London WC2. December 24

LINES OF SUCCESSION

From the Earl of Limerick

Sir, Your Diary column has it that I was "furious" over the Lord Chancellor's after-dinner assertion that hereditary peers were as ridiculous as hereditary poets (or, by more notorious comparison in debate, hereditary plumbers). Not at all.

But his attempted *reductio ad absurdum* did make me reflect that any hereditary plumber would have shared with an old-style peer the advantage of studying his trade from relatively early age, under the mentorship of an experienced practitioner.

As for poets:
The virtues of genes, I insist,
Should not be too lightly dismissed;
If a poll's on the cards
For hereditary Bards –
My name will be found on the list.

Yours faithfully,
LIMERICK,
London W8. December 16

From Mr Rodney Banks

Sir, The Earl of Limerick says that a hereditary plumber would have the advantage of studying his trade from an early age under the mentorship of an experienced practitioner. It would be more accurate to say he might agree to learn the trade. A hereditary plumber would get the job even if he had no training, ability, or interest in it.

He would be free to work when he pleased, perhaps once in a decade, safe in the knowledge that he could not be sacked and that the customer could not seek help elsewhere.   *Yours etc,*
RODNEY BANKS,
Diss, Norfolk. December 22

"COURTIER CULTURE"

From Mr W. L. Abernethy

Sir, I remember, when I was a senior local government official, telling my political masters that the only advice worth having was unpalatable advice, but that if all they

wanted from me was agreement with them, they did not need me.   *Yours faithfully,*
W. L. ABERNETHY
(Comptroller, Financial Services, Greater London Council, 1964–73), Port Erin, Isle of Man. December 17

CHRISTMAS CANCELLATION

From Mr John P. Stratford

Sir, A commercial aired on independent radio in the London area proclaims that it's Christmas every day at Legoland until January 3, "except December 25".

Yours sincerely,
JOHN P. STRATFORD,
Blue Bridge, Milton Keynes. December 20

OPEN LINE

From Mr John D. Guthrie

Sir, Overheard from a mobile phone conversation last night on South West Trains: "I have been trying to keep all this confidential but somehow it has leaked out."

Yours faithfully,
JOHN D. GUTHRIE,
East Horsley, Surrey. December 20

MARRIAGE LINES

From Mr Robert Vincent

Sir, If couples had been allowed to wed on the London Eye it would not have been a case of "Eye Do" (report and leading article, December 20) but rather "I Wheel". It's the bride's father who says "I do".

Yours faithfully,
ROBERT VINCENT,
Andover, Hampshire. December 21

From Dr David Carvel

Sir, You tell us of the wish many couples have to tie the knot aboard the Millennium Wheel. Should the lady change her mind, would this give a new meaning to "not turning up"?   *Yours faithfully,*
DAVID CARVEL,
Glasgow. December 28

SHRIEVAL CONCERN

From Sheriff Neil Gow, QC

Sir, You reported (December 4) that inmates at Longriggend Remand Institution in Lanarkshire now have their own prison radio station, and that suggestions for the playlist include such songs as *Freedom* by Robbie Williams and *Unchained Melody* by the Righteous Brothers.

As the judge responsible for sending quite a few of the inmates there in the first place, I hope the presenters will exclude Eric Clapton's *I Shot The Sheriff* and other such potentially life-threatening numbers.

Yours judicially,
NEIL GOW,
Sheriff Court House, Ayr. December 22

NATIVITY NAIVETY

From Mr Julian Thomas

Sir, When our four-year-old announced he would be Joseph in his nursery's Nativity, there ensued some discussion on the subject. The concept of Joseph being Mary's husband but not Jesus's father (because that was God) was taken on board quite easily.

Six-year-old sister then remarked that Jesus was in charge of everyone. No, God is in charge of everyone, corrected eight-year-old sister.

No, no, retorted four-year-old, God is in charge of the animals, Father Christmas is in charge of the people.

Happy Christmas and best wishes to parents everywhere.   *Yours faithfully,*
JULIAN THOMAS,
Southsea, Hampshire. December 24

From Mr Roger Betteridge

Sir, My weekly copy of the *Mississippi Woodville Republican* pays much attention to matters of the small town's many churches.

Today, not for the first time, the Woodville United Methodist Church gives details of its live Drive-thru Nativity.   *Yours faithfully,*
ROGER BETTERIDGE,
Shardlow, Derbyshire. December 24

ALL EVENTUALITIES

From Mr Kevin Leigh

Sir, I noticed today two leaflets in my local branch of Barclays Bank, "You and Your New Baby – A helping hand when you need it most – A free service for Barclays customers" and "Divorce and Separation – A helping hand when you need it most – A free service for Barclays customers".

One realises that banks are striving for new business, but perhaps Barclays is trying too hard, especially as both leaflets sat adjacent to one another on the display unit.

Yours faithfully,
KEVIN LEIGH,
London EC4. December 27

MISSING SPACECRAFT

From Mr Jim Poolman

Sir, An earth-stopping tribute to man's progress at this celebratory time would be for Nasa to locate its missing Mars Polar Lander spacecraft (reports, December 3–8).

We would surely be excited to delirium if it were perched on bricks, battery missing, aerial snapped, and scratched down the side.

Yours faithfully,
JIM POOLMAN,
Hook, Hampshire. December 27

LOST FOR WORDS

From Mr David Townley

Sir, One slightly sad consequence of the turn of the century will be that we will no longer be able to use the term "turn of the century" to evoke a much earlier age.

Yours faithfully,
DAVID TOWNLEY,
Banstead, Surrey. December 28

MATURED IN THE JAR

From Mr David Gardner

Sir, My wife has just re-used an old jar and we were intrigued to discover that the "best before" date on it was "End Mars 2062". Neither of us can recall what the jar contained originally and we wonder what might have such an unusually long shelf life.

Is there any significance in the month being in French? The rest of the printing is in English.
Yours sincerely,
DAVID GARDNER
Shipston-on-Stour, Warwickshire.
December 28

OCCUPATIONAL HAZARD

From Ms Ann Rachlin

Sir, I find it alarming to note from your Obituary pages that people are now dying in thematic groups.

Last month a quartet of composers conveniently arranged their final codas so that you could feature them all on one page.

A few months before, three ventriloquists threw their various voices into the great beyond – all chronicled on consecutive *Times* Obit pages.

Please inform me when it is the turn of music educators so that I can take extra care crossing the road.
Yours sincerely,
S. ANN RACHLIN,
London NW8. December 29

TIME WARP?

From Mr Mike Nott

Sir, An advertisement for a recently opened shop in Norfolk boasts "antique pine at factory prices".
Yours faithfully,
MIKE NOTT,
Weybread, Diss, Norfolk. December 29

WHEN TO CELEBRATE A NEW MILLENNIUM

From Mr Jason Streets

Sir, The millennium celebration is nothing to do with a certain number of years since an event, it is all about round numbers: in the same way you recently celebrated your 66,666th edition.

I for one prefer palindromes and will be celebrating two minutes after everyone else when my clock reads: 00:02 1.1.2000.

Yours faithfully,
JASON STREETS,
London N6. December 30

ENDURANCE TESTED

From Mr Peter Burian

Sir, I beg you to offer a remedy for the prevalent and tediously unbearable use of "bear with me" each time another party searches for information while on the telephone.   *Yours faithfully,*
PETER BURIAN,
London NW3. December 30

RICH AND POOR

From Mr Peter Orr

Sir, William Rees-Mogg remarks that Shaun Woodward organised a club "called Sybil after one of Benjamin Disraeli's novels". It is perhaps worth recalling that Disraeli gave an alternative title to that work: *The Two Nations*, between whom there is no intercourse and no sympathy; who are as ignorant of each other's habits, thoughts, and feelings, as if they were dwellers in different zones, or inhabitants of different planets; who are formed by a different breeding, are fed by a different food, are ordered by different manners, and are not governed by the same laws . . . THE RICH AND THE POOR.

Disraeli's novel was published in 1845. What has changed?   *Yours faithfully,*
PETER ORR,
Guisborough, Cleveland. December 31

NAME FOR A DECADE

From Mr Tony Vardy

Sir, We still have not resolved the question of how the new decade will familiarly be known. After the Eighties and the Nineties, the "2000s" seems very clumsy, the "Zeros" and the "Noughts" have little appeal, while some favour "the Naughties" (letter, July 16).

As we increasingly live in the information age, a more radical alternative may be suitable. For millions of computer users, next year has become "Y2K". The decade that follows can then logically be known as "the 2Ks", with 2001 being called 2K1 for short, followed by 2K2, 2K3, etc.   Sincerely,
TONY J.VARDY,
Hadley Wood, Hertfordshire. December 31

OPENING BID

From Mr G. L. Perry

Sir, What words are most likely to be spoken first in the year 2000? Can I optimistically open the bidding with: "Well, the lights haven't gone out."   *Yours faithfully,*
GRAHAM PERRY,
Camberley, Surrey. December 31

2000

SAD DEMISE OF DICK BARTON

From Mr Ken Morgan

Paul Heiney claims to have many reasons to "hate" *The Archers*. I have but one: it replaced *Dick Barton, Special Agent*.
Yours faithfully,
KEN MORGAN,
Aughton, Lancashire. January 1

CHEAP JOKE

From Mr J. G. Wishart

Sir, Your invitation to your readers to ensure their place in history by publishing a message in your edition of January 1, 2000, has its attractions but, as a Scotsman, I would prefer to do it the cheap way.
Yours faithfully,
J. G. WISHART,

Milton of Balgonie, Glenrothes.
January 1

A SMALL STEP FOR E-MAIL

From Dr John H. Greensmith

Sir, Is there an e-mail equivalent of first-footing? I offer "fibbing" (from the acronym Fib, first in box) for the recipient and "fobbing" (Fob, first out box) for the composer. *Yours sincerely,*
JOHN H. GREENSMITH,
Downend, Bristol. January 3

WELL, THEY DID ASK . . .

From Mr Brian Jones

Sir, Driving back from Devon recently, I tried to comply with signs that directed me to "use both lanes". Other drivers indicated loudly that they would prefer me to use only one lane. *Yours faithfully,*
B. E. JONES,
Shedfield, Southampton. January 5

GREAT LIES

From Mr C. M. Burgess

Sir, While I was examining my mobile phone bill, having been assured by my most talkative friends that such telephones are cheaper to run than you think, it occurred to me that this advice may be very close to the last lie of the millennium, along with "only ten a day", "just a glass with my meal", "20 per cent free" and "it will be finished on time". *Yours faithfully,*
CHRISTOPHER BURGESS,
Wateringbury, Kent. January 6

From Mr Tom Brooks

Sir, While I approve of Mr Christopher Burgess's choice of great millennium lies, may I, as a lifelong abstainer from television, add: "I only have it for the wildlife programmes." *Yours,*
TOM BROOKS,
Stockland, East Devon. January 10

From Miss L. M. Forbes

Sir, While contemplating Christopher Bur-gess's comments on great lies of the millennium, I overheard the following: "I'll just have another half and then I really must be going." *Yours faithfully,*
LE FORBES,
Ashington, West Sussex. January 13

From Mr Martin Wyness

Sir, May I offer the untoppable: "Oh, I never read *Hello!*." *Yours sincerely,*
MARTIN WYNESS,
Kendal, Cumbria. January 13

From Mr Neil Kennedy

Sir, My contender is the phrase "with great respect", which invariably implies that the addressee has the IQ of a garden gnome.
Yours truly,
NEIL KENNEDY,
Althorne, Essex. January 18

From Mrs P. J. Harford

Sir, What of the great and original lies?
Of adulthood:
> We must have lunch some time.
> The cheque's in the post.
> It really suits you.

Of childhood:
> Everyone else has got one.
> It was like that when I found it.
> All my friends are going.

Yours faithfully,
P. J. HARFORD,
Chippenham, Wiltshire. January 21

From Miss Winifred Stephenson

Sir, I only drink red wine for the sake of my heart. *Yours faithfully,*
WINIFRED STEPHENSON,
Lincoln. January 21

From Mr Adrian Brodkin

Sir, I can't think of any great lies at the moment but I'll get back to you.
Yours faithfully,
ADRIAN BRODKIN,
London N2. January 21

From Miss S. C. Dex

Sir, Your letters remind me that some weeks ago in the city centre here I witnessed a man saying firmly into his mobile telephone: "I am in Wolverhampton."

> Yours truthfully,
> SHIRLEY DEX,
> Cambridge. January 22

From Mr Adam Birchall

Sir, I once tried the same trick as the man in Cambridge – unfortunately on a train.

Having explained to the person on the other end of the phone that I was unavoidably detained in Bristol, the guard helpfully and clearly informed us over the intercom that we were just departing Dover.

> Yours sincerely,
> ADAM BIRCHALL,
> Truro, Cornwall. January 27

From Mr James Nisbet

Sir, "Completed on time and within budget." Yours faithfully,
> JAMES NISBET,
> Cobham, Surrey. January 27

From Mr W. Gordon McPherson

Sir, I am somewhat handicapped in this contest for the greatest lie, as I have never told a lie in all my life.

> I am, Sir, yours virtuously,
> W. G. McPHERSON,
> Huntly, Aberdeenshire. January 27

READERS WHO WRITE

From Mr Ian Summers

Sir, Why do you always print short, witty and pithy letters in the bottom right-hand corner of the page? When you publish this I expect it to be given due prominence in the top left-hand corner, next to the editorial. I remain, etc,
> IAN SUMMERS,
> Killiney, Co Dublin, Ireland. January 7

From Mr Henry Button

Sir, I am surprised that Mr Ian Summers should have such a low opinion of the b.r.h. corner as a site for letters.

According to one school of thought, this is the place of honour and a letter here, in any tally of letters to the paper, should count double, like away goals in international football matches. Yours faithfully,
> HENRY BUTTON,
> Cambridge. January 12

From Mr Geoff Atkinson

Sir, The obvious reason for the relegation of witty and pithy letters to the bottom right-hand corner is that they are written by sad people desperate to get a letter in The Times, but quite unable to compose the sort of long, deep and meaningful text which would qualify for a more prominent position.

I realise, of course, you will give my letter the prominence it deserves. Sadly yours,
> GEOFF ATKINSON,
> Milton Ernest, Bedford. January 12

From Mr Robert Plumptre

Sir, I was pleased to see that you placed Mr Ian Summers's letter where it clearly deserved to be.

I do not suffer from the same delusions of grandeur since you normally do not see fit to publish mine at all. However, I take comfort that our family motto is Sufficit meruisse (It is enough to have deserved).

Should you by any chance relent, any nook or cranny will do. I remain etc.
> ROBERT PLUMPTRE,
> Abingdon, Oxfordshire. January 12

From Mr J. W. Geddes

Sir, One of my year 2000 resolutions is to have a short, witty and pithy letter printed at the bottom right-hand corner.

I tried (and failed) several times to achieve this in 1999, but I almost succeeded in 1998 (April 29) with a letter on wheelie bins when I was awarded a place at the bottom of the third column. Yours etc,
> J. W. GEDDES,
> Dundonald, Ayrshire. January 12

From Mrs Jackie Graham

Sir, Were I to write you a letter, I would not be so unladylike as to tell you where to put it. Yours faithfully,

JACKIE GRAHAM,
Liverpool, Merseyside. January 18

From Mr Michael Crow

Sir, I rarely get to read *The Times* in print, and make do with the Internet version, which does not show the layout of the page.

Perhaps one of your readers could e-mail me and let me know whether this letter appeared in the bottom right-hand corner, or elsewhere. *I remain, etc,*
MICHAEL CROW,
Hamilton Parish, Bermuda. January 18

From Mr David Lilley

Sir, Aren't letters in the bottom right-hand corner about letters in the bottom right-hand corner taking the pith out of a witty tradition? *Yours faithfully,*
DAVID LILLEY,
Ashby de la Zouch, Leicestershire.
January 24

TABASCO, THE WONDER CURE

From Mr Alfred van Veen

Bless Tabasco's founder, Edmund McIlhenny (Weekend, January 8). I have cured my sinusitis by inhaling it; last week when I had a bad cold, a quick sniff before a concert saved my evening. *Yours faithfully,*
ALFRED VAN VEEN,
The Hague, The Netherlands. January 15

PROOF OF THE PUDDING

From Mr John Burls

Sir, My wife, who makes her Christmas puddings in large batches, discovered what she estimated to be a seven-year-old pudding at the bottom of our freezer.

It was duly, and reverentially, steamed for many hours. At the appointed time on Christmas Day the silver foil was removed before our admiring guests – to expose a large, well-steamed bowl of mushroom soup.

We were fortunately well supplied with mince pies. *Yours truly,*
JOHN BURLS,
Harwich, Essex. January 17

GOOD TIMING

From Mr Michael Purches

Sir, Browsing through my new diary, I notice March 8 has been designated National No Smoking Day. With Easter late this year, that day is also Ash Wednesday.

Yours faithfully,
MICHAEL PURCHES,
Abingdon, Oxfordshire. January 17

REFORM FOR LORDS

From Mr J. E. Hok

Sir, I had thought that I might be able to make a useful contribution as a member of the new House of Lords – man of the people, not aligned to any political party, that sort of thing.

But I have just seen the headline above your first leader: "The eunuchs' house".

I've rather gone off the idea. *Yours etc,*
JONNIE HOK,
Farnham, Surrey. January 22

CRIME FIGURES

From Mr Peter Allen

Sir, The statistics indicate that the five safest areas to live to avoid burglary are all in Wales. This must call into question the opening lines of the derogatory old doggerel: "Taffy was a Welshman, Taffy was a thief . . ." *Yours faithfully,*
PETER ALLEN,
Coleford, Gloucestershire. January 25

From Mr J. F. K. Hinde

Sir, Low incidence of burglary in Wales may not really call into question the derogatory old doggerel about Taffy.

Didn't he cross the border to steal English beef? *Yours faithfully,*
JOHN HINDE,
Esher, Surrey. January 28

MOUNTAINOUS MOLEHILLS

From the Reverend Richard Thomas

Sir, Are molehills getting bigger, or is there a new breed of super-mole in England?

The small piles of soil in the school playing field next to Church House, Oxford, are much larger than I remember them as a child, and yesterday I spotted a cluster of huge molehills at the Christian Conference Centre at High Leigh in Hertfordshire.

Surely molehills don't look bigger as we get older? *Yours faithfully,*
RICHARD THOMAS,
North Hinksey, Oxford. January 29

From Mr David Walker

Sir, The "huge molehills" referred to by the Reverend Richard Thomas are the "fortresses" of the mole, which tend to be at the centre of its territory.

They are distinct from the usual, much smaller, heaps of waste soil produced by tunnelling. Usually about a foot high and three across, they have been known to reach two feet high and eight across.

They consist of a labyrinth of tunnels leading to a nest at about ground level. There may also be a cache of paralysed earthworms.

Fortresses containing winter nests are much larger than those with breeding nests, hence the reason for the wide variation in size. *Yours faithfully,*
DAVID WALKER,
Aldridge, West Midlands. February 5

From Mrs J. Marriott

Sir, No, the molehills are not getting bigger, but the moles are looking a lot younger these days. *Yours faithfully,*
JOYCE MARRIOTT,
Pyrton, Oxfordshire. February 5

From Dr A. P. Davidson

Sir, If molehills are looking bigger to your clerical correspondent than when he was a child, perhaps he should try taking off the bifocals. *Yours etc,*
ALEXANDER DAVIDSON,
Shipston-on-Stour, Warwickshire.
February 5

From Mr David Hancock

Sir, Curious thing age. Molehills may be getting bigger but wine bottles seem to be getting much smaller. *Yours sincerely,*
DAVID HANCOCK,
Horton-cum-Studley, Oxford. February 5

From Mr Allan A. Denham

Sir, Perhaps the answer is global worming.
Yours faithfully,
ALLAN A. DENHAM,
Hets Bank, Lancaster. February 5

From the Reverend H. J. Sutters

Sir, Ever since I was ordained in the diocese of Oxford 60 years ago – and indeed before that – I have heard many people, whom I might otherwise have respected, accused of making mountains out of molehills – not least in matters ecclesiastical.

Now we have it on the highest authority that this has indeed happened, in immediate view of the diocesan office window.

Will Mr Thomas, as the Bishop's official mouthpiece, let us know if mole-engineered mountain-building is agreed diocesan policy for the 21st century? *Yours in trepidation,*
JOHN SUTTERS,
Oxford. February 9

"That mole's getting personal!"

From the Reverend Alan M. Barker

Sir, Might these waste piles be appropriately referred to this year as "molennium domes"?   *Yours faithfully,*
ALAN M. BARKER,
Alford, Lincolnshire. February 15

CRICKET THERAPY

From Mr Neville Denson

Sir, How dare Michael Atherton say that county cricket "serves no purpose whatsoever" (report, Sport, January 26).

It serves the very useful purpose of giving whingeing old gits like me the opportunity to sit in the rain on a virtually empty ground and complain about most things – including county cricket.   *Yours faithfully,*
NEVILLE DENSON,
St Bees, Cumbria. February 1

HISTORIC NAME

From Mrs Charles Mills

Sir, You report, rather tendentiously, that Noel Gallagher "threatened" to call his daughter Fanny.

Nelson married one, Keats had one as a lover and another as a sister, and Trollope had one for a mother. The Gallaghers could have done a lot worse.   *Yours faithfully,*
FANNY MILLS,
Crediton, Devon. February 3

WITCHCRAFT AMONG THE EGGSHELLS

From Mr Michael Butterley

Comments on the shells of boiled eggs have been woefully incomplete (Weekend, January 29). You must invert the empty shell and stave it in with the back of the spoon. This practice, once mandatory among West Country seafaring communities, prevents witches going to sea in the local vessels and putting mariners in danger. Why take risks?   *Yours faithfully,*
MICHAEL BUTTERLEY,
Taunton, Somerset. February 5

From Mrs Ann James

I don't care how mummy takes off the top of my egg, so long as I can have "sol–gers".
Yours faithfully,
ANN JAMES,
Bury St Edmunds, Suffolk. February 5

SEASONAL SIGN

From Mrs M. V. Dover

Sir, The first baby beach-ball landed on our lawn yesterday.

Is this a more reliable sign of spring than the first cuckoo?   *Yours sincerely,*
M. V. DOVER,
Liverpool. February 15

From Mr Jonathan Dover

Sir, The first beach ball of spring may have already landed on my mother's lawn in Liverpool, but this morning the first snowball of the winter was thrown at me from mine.   *Yours faithfully,*
JONATHAN DOVER,
Salford. February 17

VADIM'S WIVES

From Mr Lawrence Brewer

Sir, Reading your obituary of Roger Vadim (February 12) it seemed to me that the list of his glamorous wives amounted to a promotion of heterosexuality. I found myself forming the postscript "He ever married".
Yours faithfully,
LAWRENCE BREWER,
Peopleton, Worcestershire. February 16

HEAVENLY GUIDANCE?

From Mr John Webb

Sir, While singing Psalm 75 at Evensong yesterday I noted a topical warning from the Psalm book: "I said unto the fools, Deal not so madly."

I don't think I'll join the rush to buy the latest dot.com offering after all.
Yours faithfully,
JOHN WEBB,
Alfriston, East Sussex. February 21

COOKERY HINT

From Mrs Josie Tuplin

Sir, I have just found on the back of a packet of sun-dried tomatoes the perfect recipe for the busy working parent at the end of a long day. It reads ". . . then add 100g of rocket and wilt slightly".

Yours faithfully,
JOSIE TUPLIN,
Prenton, Wirral. February 21

BIRD SOUNDS

From Mr Henry Page

Sir, My wife, a keen and knowledgeable birdwatcher with a collection of over thirty bird songs on disc, said that the distant cuckoo I heard today was indeed a record.

Yours faithfully,
HENRY PAGE,
Fakenham, Norfolk. March 4

RHYMES REMEMBERED

From Lord Wright of Richmond

Sir, I am glad that you published an example of Ronald Hope-Jones's inventiveness with limericks in your obituary today.

He was deservedly the winner of a competition, set by Green Label wines in the 1970s, with the following entry:

When last I had dinner with Mabel
I ordered five Deinhard Green Label.
We had two with the meat
and two with the sweet:
The fifth we had under the table.

Yours sincerely,
PATRICK WRIGHT,
House of Lords. March 6

From Mr G. M. Wedd

Sir, The correspondence about the Green Label limerick has reminded one of your older readers of the fashion for rhyming advertisements in the middle of the last century. An advertisement which sticks in the memory for 50 years cannot be bad. Two examples:

Pamela's party was better than mine;

The minx got her drinks from Victoria Wine.

A very good example from a series by the Wool Marketing Board:

"Avast, you scum!" cried Captain Bligh
(Three months adrift) "The shore is nigh!"
He seized his log. "We owe salvation
To pluck – to faultless navigation –
To discipline – to lack of gin -
To wearing wool against the skin;
This last, a most essential rule:
There is no substitute for wool!"

Alas, I have forgotten the ending of the one which began:

When Brummel (Beau), the swell of swells
Electrified the Brighton Belles ...

Yours faithfully,
GEORGE WEDD,
High Littleton, Somerset. March 22

From Viscount Norwich

Sir, My mother used to love to recite the following:

Hark! From Windsor's royal terrace
What glad sound delights the ear?
"Goodness! What a lovely waistcoat!
Where did you get it, Albert dear?
'Tis the very height of fashion,
You must buy a dozen others!"
And the Prince, enraptured, answers:
"'Tis the work of – Baker Brothers!"

I am not absolutely sure – and nor, I think, was she – about the name in the last line. Perhaps someone will confirm or correct; I hope so.   *Yours faithfully,*
JOHN JULIUS NORWICH,
London W9. March 23

From Mrs Robin Otter

Sir, The Wool Marketing Board certainly had some excellent advertisements. One that I recall from the Sputnik 1950s read:

The trouble with a satellite
Is where to put the cat at night.
For if you want your mind at ease
How can you let poor pussy freeze!
The answer reads on your computer –
A woolly overcoat will suit her.

From sheep to bleep all know the rule:
There is no substitute for wool!

Yours sincerely,
ELISABETH OTTER,
Tewksbury, Gloucestershire. March 25

From Mr Peter Rogan

Sir, An advertisement memorised on the way to the office by Tube about fifty years ago went:

King Arthur's Knights sat sullen eyed.
"What ails thee all?" the Monarch cried.
Said one, "It's this round table, sire.
The lads out here can't feel the fire."
Quoth Guinivere, "Poor faithful knights,
I'll knit them all a pair of tights."
Morale was saved, which proves the rule:
There is no substitute for wool!

Yours faithfully,
P. ROGAN,
Rye, East Sussex. March 25

From Dr C. R. McGavin

Sir, May I offer the following from the London Underground in the 1960s?

"Well, shiver my timbers," said Nelson to Emma,
"I'll have to admit it – I'm in a dilemma.
Though Cockburn's a port that's far famed and renowned,
When it comes to pronounce it, my tongue runs aground."
Lady E's smile showed a cute little dimple
As she said, "My dear Nelson, it's really quite simple.
The 'O' is as long as a midsummer's day,
And you turn your blind eye to the 'C' and the 'K'." *Yours faithfully,*
CLIVE McGAVIN,
Yelverton, Devon. March 25

From Mr Douglas Jackson

Sir, I always thought the best wool rhyme was:

An arrow pinned the sheriff's wig
Against the wall; he danced a jig.
"What gives this Robin Hood his nerve,
His vim, his valour and his verve?"
"We do not know," they cried, "unless

It is his all-wool battledress.
"In winter warm, in summer cool,
There is no substitute for wool!"
They don't write them like that any more.

Yours etc,
DOUGLAS JACKSON,
Prestwich, Manchester. March 25

From Mr Malcolm Bruce-Radcliffe

Sir, I learnt the following travelling on the Tube in 1951–52, at the impressionable age of 13.

Before Queen Anne Boleyn was sacked
She'd got her suitcase ready packed,
And labelled it, in letters large,
"The Bloody Tower, per Royal Barge."
Her friends all praised her savoir faire,
Until they missed their underwear.
For Anne, you see, was no one's fool,
There is no substitute for wool!

Yours faithfully,
MALCOLM I. BRUCE-RADCLIFFE,
Lymington, Hampshire. March 27

From Mrs Sue Webb

Sir, Not only wool was advertised in rhyme:

Hey nonny nonny no
Listen to my tale of woe.
All my neighbours; all my friends
Enjoy their Co-op dividends,
But I am such a foolish shopper,
I haven't saved a single copper.

Yours faithfully,
SUE WEBB,
Winchester, Hampshire. March 27

From Mr A. Goldstein, FEng

Sir, The wool verse comes in various attractive versions. Ever topical is one by a senior civil servant:

When Ministers begin to grouse
At awkward questions in the House
When politicians face distress
At odd disclosures in the press
We look for stuff of fitting size
For pulling o'er our master's eyes
We then recall the golden rule:
There is no substitute for wool!

Yours faithfully,

ALFRED GOLDSTEIN,
Edenbridge, Kent. March 27

From Miss H. M. Sands

Sir, In the 1940s I worked in a government office where this adaptation of the final couplet was often quoted:

> Before the interviewing panel
> There is no substitute for flannel.

Yours faithfully,
MARJORIE SANDS,
Orpington, Kent. March 27

From Mr Joseph and Mrs Anna Horovitz

Sir, We are flattered that our Sputnik rhyme,

> The problem in a satellite
> Is where to put the cat at night ...

was remembered, almost correctly, by your correspondent.

The resulting wool advertisement, illustrating the delights of domesticity in space, appeared on London Underground. As a reward we received the poster, which we still have, and a cheque for £5, which we seem to have spent.   *Yours faithfully,*
JOSEPH HOROVITZ,
ANNA HOROVITZ,
London W2. March 29

From Dr R. L. Marshall

Sir, I hope I am not, by exposing it, putting at risk my simple faith in the authenticity of a "rhyming advertisement" for a new edition of the Bible in a Scottish newspaper some time ago:

> Holy Bible, writ divine
> Leather bound at one and nine.
> Satan trembles at the knees
> To think of Bibles priced like these.

Yours faithfully,
R. L. MARSHALL,
Woodhouse Eaves, Leicestershire. March 29

From Mr Michael Brown

Sir, At a time when we were less polarised about Europe, the Wool Marketing Board ran an entertaining advertisement on the Underground along the lines of:

> "What, fly the Channel, oh ho ho,"

> The critics scoffed at Bleriot.
> "You'll freeze, *mon ami*, in that thing
> There's nothing there save wood and
>   string."
> But icing caused him no distress,
> He dressed in wool
> (How did you guess).
> The moral of this story's plain,
> *Rien ne remplace la laine.*

Before "Poems on the Underground", too!
Yours faithfully,
MICHAEL BROWN,
Market Rasen, Lincolnshire. March 29

From the Reverend Kevin M. Pelham

Sir, To refresh George Wedd's memory and relieve the suspense he undoubtedly raised among untold numbers of your readers, the verse whose opening couplet he quoted goes like this:

> When Brummell Beau, the swell of swells
> Electrified the Brighton Belles,
> The Prince would hover in the offing,
> Killing romance with fits of coughing.
> Another cold, Sire? Listen, do:
> To be well dressed, be wool dressed too.
> In elegance it is the rule;
> There is no substitute for wool!

Yours faithfully,
KEVIN M. PELHAM,
Carshalton, Surrey. April 1

From Miss Veronica Hitchcock

Sir, Although I have difficulty recalling the plot of a film I saw last week, I well remember the lines learnt in an Underground train 50 years ago:

> King John in one fell splash (or splosh)
> Lost bag and baggage in The Wash.
> His courtiers wept as all went down –
> The orb, the sceptre and the crown.
> "Mere gems," said John, "a fig for those,
> But what of vest, pants, shirt and hose?
> Without these things I cannot rule;
> There is no substitute for wool!"

Yours faithfully,
VERONICA HITCHCOCK,
London SW1. April 1

From Mr Raymond Berger

Sir, This wool ad was seen on the Tube in the early Fifties, after the great success of the film *Quo Vadis* ("Where are you going?"):

"Quo vadis?" cried the palace guard.
"Upstairs," yelled Nero, running hard.
"My wardrobe must be saved tonight,
before the looters heave in sight.
The blaze is cosy now," said Nero,
"But mercury returns to zero.
And when the nights grow long and cool
There is no substitute for wool!"

Or here is an even earlier ad, seen while riding on the bus to school in the Forties:

At Auntie Sue it's any old brew
At Auntie Meg's the stuffs all dregs,
While dear Aunt Jane pours out pure rain.
But Mother sees – we've Co-op teas.

Yours sincerely,
RAYMOND BERGER,
Exeter, Devon. April 3

From Mr Ian S. Lockhart

Sir, This piece of Cockburniana is from the Underground of the Sixties:

Said King Charles to his court
"I enjoy a good port,
But it must be a wine that's just right."
Said a courtier game
"If I tell you the name
Of the best will you make me a knight?"
The King nodded his head
And the courtier said
"Cockburn's port is the port for a king.
But remember to say it without the CK."
And they all cried
"Long Live Harles the Ing!"

There was also a piece rhyming Cockburn with Holborn and Woburn which involved businessmen and dukes.

It would be good to see a revival.

Yours truly,
IAN S. LOCKHART,
London NW8. April 3

From Mrs Felicity Wood

Sir, Travel by Tube in my student days was also enlivened by the International Wool Secretariat's splendid advertisements, including:

Arriving for her pas-de-deux
The ballerina caused a stir,
For underneath a froth of white
A pair of stockings came in sight.
When challenged to explain her act
She replied: "It is an undoubted fact
These ballet tights are tu-tu cool
There is no substitute for wool!"

Yours sincerely,
FELICITY WOOD,
Newbury, Berkshire. April 5

From Mrs Imogen Thomas

Sir, I remember that after the long, straight, turnpike roads had been built on the East Coast of America, there were found to be a number of road accidents caused by drivers nodding off.

To keep them alert, billboards were placed at intervals with quiz questions, followed sometime later by the answer, or verses, one line at a time.

My favourite on the route from New York to Florida was advertising Burmah Shave:

The shave that made
The gardener's daughter
Plant her tulips
Where she oughter.

Yours faithfully,
IMOGEN THOMAS,
Lyme Regis, Dorset. April 5

From Mr David Peacock

Sir, Whilst crossing London by Tube in 1953 to see my girlfriend (we celebrate our 44th anniversary in July) I memorised –

When William Tell reached for his quiver
He saw his son begin to shiver.
"Art frightened, lad, to face the arrow?",
"No, Dad, just frozen to the marrow."
They fixed him up with scarf and sweater,
And Will took aim again. "That's better
Lad," said he as Whang! he shot.
The apple fell, the boy did not.
Which goes to prove the golden rule;

There is no substitute for wool!
– a verse that has entertained me and, I hope, many captive listeners over the subsequent years.
Yours faithfully,
DAVID PEACOCK
Godalming, Surrey. April 5

From the Dean of Merton College, Oxford
Sir, The wartime Minister of Food, drawing on popularity such as no one in government enjoys today, authorised a memorable poster:

Those who have the will to win
Cook potatoes in their skin,
For the sight of wasted peelings
Deeply hurts Lord Woolton's feelings.

I still do.
Yours faithfully,
THOMAS BRAUN,
Oxford. April 8

From Mr Ivor Davies
Sir, During WW2 I was learning to fly in Arizona and cannot forget the successive (non-rhyming) roadside billboards seen outside Phoenix.

Ain't no cowhand
Ain't no politician
But when crooks pop up
He's in there shootin'
ROACH for Sheriff!

I can't remember if he was elected.
Yours faithfully,
IVOR DAVIES,
Goring-by Sea, West Sussex. April 8

From Mr Colin Pearson
Sir, I suspect the wool marketing campaign was subtly altered to reflect the passage of time. By the mid-1960s there was a verse which ran:

Yon canny Highland crofters keep
A breed of crease-resistant sheep.
They weave wee woollen skirts and slacks,
And sell them to the Sassenachs.
Wool keeps its shape, it's bound to please –
You've nae seen sheep with baggy knees!
At birth bairns learn the Highland rule;
There's still nae substitute for wool!

Yours faithfully,
COLIN PEARSON,
Loughton, Essex. April 8

From Mrs Hilary Brown
Sir, How amazing that so many of us can still summon up these wool verses. Could it be because the punchline is true?

"Our lexicon is finished now,"
Said Dr Johnson, "But I vow
This entry, 'Wool', is not our best;
'The hair of sheep' – how ill expressed!
For wool's the very stuff of life,
It warms our bed, it decks our wife.
Be pleased to add, and under-rule;
There is no substitute for wool!"

Yours sincerely,
HILARY BROWN,
Battle, East Sussex. April 13

From Mr Peter Shorrock
Sir, The latest selection of wool ads reminded me that buried away in the recesses of my memory was this:

When Casanova went to town,
He always took his dressing-gown,
His bed-socks and his knitted gloves –
Which mystified his lady loves.
One gentle temptress asked him, "Why?"
Quoth he, with an experienced sigh,
"Madam, I used to catch all kinds
Of chills through those Venetian blinds,
So learnt this lesson in love's stern school;
There is no substitute for wool!"

Yours faithfully,
PETER SHORROCK,
Aston Abbotts, Aylesbury. April 13

From Mrs Phyllida Gardner
Sir, I am extremely grateful to David Peacock for quoting the William Tell wool rhyme in its entirety. My brother-in-law, the late David Livingstone, wrote it.

I have been asking round the family about it and so far we had only managed to remember part of it. It is a great relief to be put out of our misery.
Yours sincerely,
PHYLLIDA GARDNER,
Shipston-on-Stour, Warwickshire. April 15

From Mr Peter Mottley

Sir, Your correspondent Colin Pearson is correct: the wool marketing campaign was altered to include the word "still" in the last line during the mid-1960s.

As a young advertising copywriter, I was charged with writing the new series to revive the original verses, which had been written by, I believe, Bernard Holloway, the editor of *Punch*.

The new series was intended to combat inroads into the market by man-made fibres. Hence, as well as verses extolling warmth and comfort, the "crease-resistant sheep" – and, a rhymer's nightmare, "machinewashable".   *Yours etc,*
PETER MOTTLEY,
Pangbourne, Berkshire. April 15

From Mr Ivor Davies

Sir, Mr Roach (my letter, April 8) was elected.

My son in San Francisco, who thinks I am slightly in my dotage, sent me the Web address www.mcso.org/hx__sheriffs.htm which includes a picture of Ernest W. "Goldie" Roach, Sheriff of Maricopa County, Arizona, 1945-46.

The power of the Web!   *Yours faithfully,*
IVOR DAVIES,
Goring-by-Sea, West Sussex. April 15

JUST A DOT CON?

From Mrs Sue Pheasey

Sir, I am thinking of setting up an Internet business selling bubbles and cannot choose between tulips.com and groundnut.com.

Yours etc,
SUE PHEASEY,
Solihull, West Midlands. March 17

From Mr Keith Muir

Sir, All of this excitement about the Internet and the dot-com flotations has finally made its mark in our remote northern corner.

Donald, the long-serving barman in the Commercial Hotel in Thurso, is now universally known as Don-Com.

Yours sincerely,
KEITH MUIR,
Thurso, Caithness. March 24

From Mrs Ann Hughes

Sir, Internetspeak is flourishing in the remote South West also, where a group expedition to see the Welsh National Opera in Plymouth last week was, during the arranging, referred to as Turandot-com.

Yours sincerely,
ANN HUGHES,
Par, Cornwall. March 28

NO SENSE OF DIRECTION

From Mr David Simons

Sir, I read that a dentist is alleged to have "grabbed a senior colleague by the genitals and tried to throttle him" (report, earlier editions, March 28).

They obviously don't teach anatomy as well today as they did when I was a dental student.   *Yours faithfully,*
DAVID SIMONS,
Baslow, Derbyshire. March 31

From Mr Alan Hadfield

Sir, Some ten years ago I saw a document describing an active recidivist who, according to the reporting officer, had "one testicle removed, scar in middle of forehead".

Yours sincerely,
ALAN HADFIELD,
Maidstone, Kent. April 4

HOW MANY "OUGHS"?

From Mr Robert Pennant Jones

I claim two more "oughs" than Sir James Hanley in his question for Two Brains (Weekend, March 25). I composed this in the 1960s when a German complained how difficult English was to pronounce: "That rough bough we saw as we passed through Lough Neagh – do you remember, you had hiccoughs – ought to be made

into a trough for kneading dough thoroughly."   *Yours faithfully,*
ROBERT PENNANT JONES,
London SE1. April 1

THAT'S HANDY

From Mrs Janet Whitby

Sir, My husband and I were amused to discover over breakfast this morning that according to your report ("Hand signals for sexual orientation", March 30) we are both lesbians.   *Yours faithfully,*
JANET WHITBY,
Highgate, London N6. April 1

SAINSBURY'S BACON

From Mr David Meredith

Sir, As one of this country's greatest patrons of the arts Sir Robert Sainsbury (obituary, April 4) acquired 13 Francis Bacon paintings. In his autobiography *Never A Normal Man* (HarperCollins, 1997) Daniel Farson wrote delightfully of an evening spent viewing paintings in the Sainsburys' London home:

As we continued up the stairs I turned brightly to their son, David Sainsbury, trying to think of the right thing to say as I recognised a Bacon portrait: "I say, that's an awfully good likeness of your father."

"Yes," agreed David Sainsbury stiffly. "Except it's my mother."   *Yours faithfully,*
DAVID MEREDITH,
Aberystwyth, Dyfed. April 7

CRIMINAL CLASSES

From Mr Tom Pike

Sir, Mark Inglefield's Diary item today, reporting Jonathan Aitken's praise for the room service at Chelsea nick, reflects, perhaps, the respect in which the police there hold the locals.

It reminded me of the occasion when, visiting the Tower, I asked a yeoman warder, at the request of my granddaughter, where the Torture Chamber was.

He replied, rather coldly I thought: "This, Sir, is not that kind of prison. Here we have a better class of criminal."   *Yours faithfully,*
TOM PIKE,
Beckenham, Kent. April 10

From Mr Alfred Finer

Sir, A propos class consciousness in prisons, I recollect, as a prison visitor at Pentonville in the early Sixties, leaving the prison one afternoon with the governor. At the entrance were a group of young women who had been visiting their menfolk. They were attired in miniskirts and flesh-coloured stockings with suspenders visible when they moved.

The governor was somewhat shocked and said: "Now move along ladies, I don't want you giving the place a bad name."

Yours faithfully,
ALFRED FINER,
London N3. April 18

MAN EATING DOG

From Professor Roy Harris

Sir, The much maligned hyphen still has a role to play in communication. I cite your alarming report (April 11) concerning the "hot dog-munching sports fans" who allegedly fill baseball parks in the US. This surely deserves an addendum to Fowler's apoplectic entry on the subject?

Yours faithfully,
ROY HARRIS,
Oxford. April 17

From Mr Peter Mackintosh

Sir, A hyphen inadvertently omitted can have as much effect as one misplaced.

I recall that, some years ago, the secretary of the Standard Chartered Bank's sports club, writing for the bank's UK house magazine, reported that "some twelve hundred odd people" had attended the bank's annual sports day.   *Yours faithfully,*
PETER MACKINTOSH,
Brecon, Powys. April 27

A MODERN TALE

From Mrs Maureen Johnson

Sir, I wonder what Michael Portillo meant by "Beatrix Potter sentimentality"?

Doesn't he know that Peter Rabbit came from a one-parent family? Mr Rabbit was put in a pie by Mr McGregor for trespass and theft from the McGregors' garden, and Peter and his friend, Benjamin Bunny, were set on the same delinquent career.

Nor was Benjamin's father above administering corporal punishment to the two rascals when it seemed fit, even though they were only following parental example.

Seems pretty realistic to me.

Yours faithfully,
MAUREEN JOHNSON,
Ilkley, West Yorkshire. April 19

PROPHETIC WORDS

From Mrs Elizabeth Charles

Sir, I read today that a biscuit from the 1907 South Pole expedition led by Sir Ernest Shackleton fetched £4,935 at auction at Christie's.

Yesterday I happened to read the following extract from the diary of Shackleton's right-hand man, Frank Wild, whilst on the polar trip:

Shackleton privately forced upon me his one breakfast biscuit, and would have given me another tonight had I allowed him. I do not suppose that anyone else in the world can thoroughly realise how much generosity and sympathy was shown by this; I DO by GOD I shall never forget it. Thousands of pounds would not have bought that one biscuit. *Yours faithfully,*
ELIZABETH CHARLES,
Saffron Walden, Essex. April 21

A COOL HEAD

From Mr David Perril

Sir, I was delighted to read that, in France at least, the "sartorially cool" have aban-

doned the baseball cap in favour of the beret. But is it possible to wear a beret back to front? *Yours most sincerely,*
DAVID PERRIL,
Girton, Cambridge. April 25

HELPLINE HELL

From Mr Christopher Towlson

Sir, How many of us get frustrated and angry when trying to contact a helpline, only to hear a recorded message with "six options" or more and then, after listening to every one, find that none deals with our particular requirement?

Solution? Select the option which asks if you are having difficulty paying your bill. It's amazing how quickly a human voice emerges at the other end of the line.

Yours etc,
CHRISTOPHER J. TOWLSON,
London EC2. April 26

From Mr David J. M. Turner

Sir, Mr Christopher Towlson suggests that to get a quick answer when faced with a recorded message one should select the option for those having difficulty paying their bill.

For an even faster response do not select any option. The message system will assume that you are using a pulse phone, thus unable to make a selection, and put you straight through to the next available operator.

Yours faithfully,
D. J. M. TURNER,
Innsworth, Gloucester. April 29

A THEORY ON ECONOMICS

From Mr Bernard Hypher

Sir, In the appointments column of the Court & Social Page (April 19) Manchester University announced that one of its staff had a "change of Professorial title" from Professor of Mathematical Economics to Professor of Economic Theory.

This change at such a senior level has me pondering the implications. Does it mean

that the university has reached the conclusion that economics is not to do with numbers, but with ideas? If so, I am afraid it confirms my fears about the results of the application of economics to the running of countries. *Yours faithfully,*
BERNARD HYPHER,
Poole, Dorset. April 27

From the Reverend Peter Dawson

Sir, Mr Bernard Hypher's letter on the study of economics brought to mind the advice given on my arrival at the LSE as an undergraduate nearly fifty years ago.

The director informed the new intake that economics was unique among university disciplines in one important respect.

In all other subjects, the questions set in final examinations changed every year but, said Sir Alexander Carr-Saunders, "in economics we keep the same questions and change the answers".   *Yours faithfully,*
PETER DAWSON,
Ockbrook, Derby. April 27

KING AMONG HUSBANDS

From Mr Bernard Kaukas

Sir, The emollient sentiments in your leader today, "History's monsters all had their caring side", were never better expressed than by the Oxford historian who greatly admired Henry VIII.

"The latter years of that excellent monarch's reign," he wrote, "were clouded by much domestic unhappiness."   *Yours faithfully,*
BERNARD KAUKAS,
Savage Club, London SW1. April 29

I LOVE YOU BUG

From Mr Oliver Chastney

Sir, I have been checking my e-mails with particular care today, noting that "Within minutes the virus ... sends itself to every e-mail address in employees' electronic address books, infecting the e-mail facilities of subsidiary companies, clients and friends across the world" (report, May 5).

Nothing! Does nobody love me?
Yours faithfully,
OLIVER CHASTNEY,
Cringleford, Norwich, Norfolk. May 6

From Mr Peter Vincent

Sir, A study of social history reveals that the words "I love you" are often followed by a virus.   *Yours etc,*
PETER VINCENT,
Radlett, Hertfordshire. May 12

CLEVER FJORD-BANK GLYPHS

From Mr Ray Ward

In Two Brains (Weekend, May 13): "The quick brown fox jumped over the lazy dog" does not contain the whole alphabet, having no s. It should be: "The quick brown fox jumps over the lazy dog" (35 letters). Raymond Keene's shorter answer, of 32 letters, is: "Pack my box with five dozen liquor jugs". One of 31 letters is: "Jackdaws love my big sphinx of quartz".

The ultimate has only 26 letters but is very contrived, supposedly describing an eccentric's annoyance at finding inscriptions on the side of a steep sea inlet in a rounded valley:"Cwm fjord-bank glyphs vext quiz".
Yours faithfully,
RAY WARD,
London SE16. May 20

VIRTUAL ODYSSEY

From Mr David Webb

Sir, I'm very impressed with Mike Roots (report and photograph, May 19) who is cycling around the world without leaving his front room.

I've taken this virtual approach a stage further by remaining in bed and imagining that I'm in my front room cycling around the world. So far I've reached Derby and hope to reach Birmingham in September.

Yours exhaustedly,
DAVID WEBB,
Beeston, Nottingham. May 20

CARTLAND FUNERAL

From Mr Mike Clark

Sir, I was touched by Barbara Cartland's concern for the environment in being buried in a cardboard coffin under her favourite oak tree. May we spare a silent moment for the many trees sacrificed to feed her writing habit? *Yours faithfully,*
MIKE CLARK,
Weybridge, Surrey. June 1

TRAFFIC CALMING

From Mr Steve Portch

Sir, Our local council recently, and inadvertently, provided a most effective traffic-calming measure on the approach to our village – resurfacing with tar and loose chippings. It would seem that drivers are more concerned with their paintwork than with speed limits. *Yours faithfully,*
STEVE PORTCH,
Kineton, Warwickshire. June 2

DARK DAYS OF WAR RECALLED

From Mr Quentin Matthews

Sir, Reading *The Times* yesterday I was drawn to a report in which a former prisoner of war, Tim Mahoney, spoke of his escape with a friend from German captivity.

That friend is my father, Robert Matthews, who has tried many times over many years to contact Tim Mahoney, even placing an advertisement in a magazine he thought Tim might read.

Yesterday my father spoke on the telephone to his friend "back from the dead" for the first time in decades. They plan to meet up, along with another friend who escaped with them, "Taffy" Morgan.

Thank you for having made some old soldiers very happy. *Yours faithfully,*
QUENTIN MATTHEWS,
Farlington, Portsmouth. June 2

ROAD SIGNS

From Mr Gerald Moggridge

Sir, Spare a thought for the overseas visitor who may not be familiar with all the idioms of the English language and who encounters the three signs I came across recently along a West Country road. In fairly close proximity they announced "farm eggs", "fresh-cut flowers" and "cat's eyes removed". *Yours faithfully,*
GERALD MOGGRIDGE,
Sutton, Surrey. June 5

From Mr Anthony G. Phillips

Sir, Recent letters on the subject of road signs remind me of the time when the idea of English towns being linked with communities on the Continent first became popular.

Not wishing to be outdone, an enterprising farm shop on the Wiltshire/Dorset border proclaimed on its sale board: "Potatoes – twinned with Pommes De Terre."

Yours faithfully,
ANTHONY G. PHILLIPS,
Salisbury, Wiltshire. June 13

From Professor Emeritus Alan Henry

Sir, Some years ago, when driving through Kinross, I came across what has always remained my favourite road sign.

On the post announcing one's arrival in Crook of Devon someone had added "Twinned with the Thief of Baghdad".

Yours sincerely,
ALAN HENRY,
St Andrews, Fife. June 16

From Miss Annie Byfield

Sir, I shall never forget the road sign that I saw while visiting Liverpool about 20 years ago. It read: "Mersey Docks and Harbour Board", beneath which some musical wag had added, "and little lambs eat ivy".

Yours faithfully,
A. R. BYFIELD,
London E5. June 19

From His Honour Judge Teare

Sir, My favourite signpost graffiti adorned the sign towards two Lincolnshire villages: "To Old Bolingbroke and Mavis Enderby",

underneath which had been added "God's gift of a daughter".   *Yours faithfully*,
JONATHAN TEARE,
Lincoln Crown Court, Lincoln. June 19

From Major John FitzGerald (retd)

Sir, I, too, have memories of that fingerpost saying: "To Old Bolingbroke and Mavis Enderby". The photograph that I took in 1973 showed the sign to have been improved with the words "a son". Perhaps the sex change was included in the rearrangements later that year for local government in the county.   *Yours etc*,
JOHN FitzGERALD,
York. June 21

From Mr Trevor Lyttleton

Sir, On the way to Glengariff in Ireland a few years ago I saw the following: "Beware! Extreme Danger! Church Entrance Ahead!"   *Yours faithfully*,
TREVOR LYTTLETON,
London W1. July 21

From Lord Millett

Sir, The shortest ambiguous sentence I have come across is a road sign found everywhere in New York. It consists of three words: "Fine for Parking."

But I would not like to argue the point with a New York traffic cop.
Yours faithfully,
MILLETT,
House of Lords. June 23

From Professor Emeritus Deryke Belshaw

Sir, At the risk of implying that Professori Emeriti are engaged primarily in a search for esoteric road signs, I wish to bring to wider attention the following sign in English and Hindi located beside the road from Kalimpong to Gangtok, Sikkim State in the Himalayan region of India: "If you wish donate blood, kindly do so at Blood Bank, not on National Highway 31A!"

This wordy expression of concern with travellers' welfare was painted on the outside of a 300-degree bend.   *Yours sincerely*,
DERYKE BELSHAW,
Norwich, Norfolk. June 26

From Mr Ernest Spacey

Sir, Travelling near Washington DC about 24 years ago, I saw a large billboard by the roadside. Beautifully painted in letters a foot high, was the legend: "DISREGARD THIS SIGN".   *Really and truly*,
ERNEST SPACEY,
Bradford, West Yorkshire. June 26

From Mrs Anna Lee

Sir, Not all New York road signs are ambiguous. About four years ago I saw one on Fifth Avenue, standing guard over a double yellow line with the uncompromising words: "Don't even think about parking here."   *Yours faithfully*,
ANNA LEE,
Hayfield, High Peak. June 30

From Dr R. A. Dutton

Sir, The oddest road sign I have seen was in Dhahran at the close of the Gulf War – on each major junction was a large sign in three languages stating – "When you see birds falling from the skies, don your gasmask."   *Yours faithfully*,
RICHMOND DUTTON,
Prenton, Wirral. June 30

SOFT VERGERS

From the Reverend Julian Barker
Sir, I came to a small roundabout in France with two exits. One was marked *Toutes directions*, the other *Autres directions*.

Yours faithfully,
JULIAN BARKER,
Repton Vicarage, Derby. June 30

From Dr Henry Hardy
Sir, The one type of road sign not so far mentioned, I believe, in your correspondence is the flatly incomprehensible.

I cannot imagine what drivers in Oxford approaching the Martyrs' Memorial from the north are expected to make of this notice under a sign prohibiting access to motor vehicles:

Except local buses taxis and licensed private hire at any time and except buses " 6pm-10am.

Hello?   *Yours etc,*
HENRY HARDY,
Wolfson College, Oxford. July 3

SEA OF TRANQUILLITY

From Lord Russell-Johnston
Sir, An unadvertised advantage of the Channel Tunnel is that mobile phones do not work during the train's passage under the waves.

And a blessed silence falls.   *Yours sincerely,*
RUSSELL-JOHNSTON,
House of Lords. June 8

ROYAL DIVIDE ON GM

From Mr Pat Fitzgerald
Sir, Is the Royal Family's disagreement over genetically modified food a case for or against selective breeding?   *Yours faithfully,*
P. FITZGERALD,
Belton, Doncaster. June 10

BOUNCING BRIDGE

From Mr Geoffrey Cuttle
Sir, The Millennium Bridge gloriously wobbles into ridicule. I propose that no remedial action be taken but rather that it be permanently closed, magnificently illumi-

nated, and viewing galleries built on St Paul's and Tate Modern so that all can celebrate this monument to the spirit of the age: the triumph of spin over delivery.

Yours faithfully,
GEOFFREY CUTTLE,
Woking, Surrey. June 13

From Mr Peter McGee
Sir, I remember (as one of a group of eight or so Glasgow schoolboys) standing about a third of the way out on the suspension bridge over the River Clyde.

We all jumped up and down hard on the deck at the same time, then timed subsequent jumps until quite a healthy wave became visible, back and forth along the span.

Watching the broadcast of crowds on the Millennium Bridge, did I see some merry side-swayers; rocking the boat, as it were?

Yours faithfully,
PETER J. McGEE,
Banbury, Oxfordshire. June 14

From Mr Robert Sheehan
Sir, An engineer once told me that any fool can build a bridge that won't fall down. The great skill is in building one which only just won't fall down.

I think the designers of the Millennium Bridge are to be congratulated on achieving that aim.   *Yours faithfully,*
ROBERT SHEEHAN,
London SW4. June 15

From Mr Robert Raffety
Sir, Clearly the problem is caused by the wrong type of pedestrian.   *Yours faithfully,*
ROBERT RAFFETY,
London SW18. June 30

RICH DIET

From Mr Michael Nicholas
Sir, A knock on the front door today revealed a crestfallen milkman who presented me with a cheque, left out for him overnight, which had been eaten fully across by a snail.   *Yours faithfully,*
MICHAEL NICHOLAS,

Billingshurst, West Sussex. June 19

A BALANCED EDUCATION?

From Mr B. Plant

Sir, Funding for education is always a contentious issue and often produces anomalies. Some years ago the school for a remote community in Shetland was provided with a seesaw. At the time the school had one pupil.   *Yours faithfully,*
BRIAN PLANT,
Lerwick, Shetland. June 22

WIMBLEDON WIN?

From Mr Vivian Linacre

Sir, A Wimbledon commentator, introduced a match between Miss X and Miss Y yesterday, remarking that: "On paper, Miss X should win easily, but on grass it may be a different story."   Yours superficially,
VIVIAN LINACRE,
Edinburgh. June 29

PUB NAMES

From the Chief Executive of the Brewers and Licensed Retailers Association

Sir, You report that the Culture Secretary has criticised the rebranding of pubs with trendy names such as the Dog and Donut or the Goose and Granite.

In 1710 *The Spectator* called for the appointment of a government official to control the more "absurd" inn signs:

Our streets are filled with blue Boars, black Swans and red Lions: not to mention flying Pigs and Hogs in armour . . .

Yours faithfully,
ROB HAYWARD,
London W1. July 14

From Mr Nigel M. Greenwood

Sir, While I regret the demise of traditional pub names, I nevertheless wonder if all those "Firkin" pubs are to be prosecuted for failing to change their names to the ". . . and 40.914 litres".   *Yours faithfully,*
N. M. GREENWOOD,
Cheltenham, Gloucestershire. July 20

BOUDOIR OF BRASS

From Mr Graham Wallace

Sir, I note that Charles Saatchi has spent £150,000 on Tracey Emin's bed.

Some people will no doubt question how one would justify this value. However, to put it in context, I understand that the average cost of bringing up a child to adulthood is roughly the same and the lasting impression made in a bedroom is almost identical.

If only all young people had Miss Emin's artistic flair then they might be able to sell off their bedrooms to pay for their higher education.   *Yours faithfully,*
GRAHAM WALLACE,
Barnet, Hertfordshire. July 20

From Mr Patrick Waites

Sir, Charles Saatchi might have saved himself a bob or two in 1967 when Alf MacDonald was carried into the Young Contemporaries exhibition in his bed – still fast asleep.

The event was dreamed up between Brian Eno, Alf and myself in Alf's basement flat across the road from Winchester School of Art where he and Brian Eno studied painting.

The inevitable question asked then (the work was rejected) is still pertinent – if it wasn't Art then, is it now?

Of course, I don't recall any underwear – and though Ms Emin is said to have contemplated suicide in her bed, to my mind Alf's was the finer piece; as far as I am aware, he was contemplating absolutely nothing.

Sincerely,
PATRICK WAITES,
Winchester, Hampshire. July 28

GOLF'S LESSONS

From Mr Robert A. Morley

Sir, Whilst P. G. Wodehouse did not subscribe to the same strange views as Simon Barnes on "the footling pastime of golf" (Comment, July 22), he did at least agree that there is more to the game than simply winning or losing:

I attribute the insane arrogance of the later Roman emperors almost entirely to the fact that, never having played golf, they never experienced that strange chastened humility which is brought about by a topped chip shot.

Perhaps Mr Barnes should take up the game. *Yours humbly*,
R. A. MORLEY (Handicap 17),
Southport, Merseyside. July 25

COPING WITH GRAVITY

From Mr Robert C. Swindlehurst

Sir, You report today ("Feminine touch for supersonic fighter") news of the Eurofighter and of a diminutive female who was still able to chat at 9G.

To many a husband this will come as no surprise. My wife is able to chat in a wide variety of extreme conditions and I feel sure that not only would she be able to do so at 9G but she would also be able to complete her shopping list. *Yours faithfully*,
R. C. SWINDLEHURST,
St Anne's-on-Sea, Lancashire. July 25

THE NAMING OF THE NEW WORLD

From Mr Seweryn Chomet

Sir, Speculations about who discovered America are always interesting, especially when viewed against the backdrop of the following entry in Pudd'nhead Wilson's Calendar (as reproduced by Mark Twain): "It was wonderful to find America, but it would have been more wonderful to miss it."

Incidentally, a Russian spin on this has been seen in the form: "It wasn't all that wonderful to find America because it has always been there." *Yours truly*,
SEWERYN CHOMET
(Visiting Research Fellow), King's College London. July 28

FEET ACCOMPLI

From Louise Bailey

I enjoy Nigella Lawson's beauty tips immensely. Regarding feet (The Moment I Wake Up..., July 15), may I suggest a generous amount of petroleum jelly applied before bed and the wearing of bed socks. In the morning, feet are wonderfully soft. As a nurse, this is a tip I often pass on to my patients. *Yours sincerely*,
LOUISE BAILEY,
Penicuik, Midlothian. July 29

PUZZLING POTTER

From Mr John L. Lewis

Sir, I have recently had two 11-year-old grandsons staying with me. I thought I ought to be "with it" so I have been reading the latest Harry Potter book, *Harry Potter and the Goblet of Fire*, a copy of which was brought with them.

I read 210 pages out of the 634 and I have no idea at all what it is about. I have now given up trying.

On page 195, Harry Potter says: "I haven't got a clue what this lot's supposed to mean." This is exactly how I feel. Do other grandparents have the same problem?

Yours sincerely,
JOHN L. LEWIS,
Colwall Green, Malvern. August 7

From Mr Dennis Wilson

Sir, Alas, grandfather John Lewis started with the wrong Harry Potter book. Had he begun reading the first of the saga, *Harry Potter and the Philosopher's Stone*, not only would he have understood it, he might very well have become enthralled by it.

Sincerely,
D. H. WILSON (aged $58^{1}/_{4}$),
Whitchurch, Shropshire. August 8

From Dr and Mrs J. P. Toomey

Sir, We, too, have been reading our grandson's Harry Potter, in our case *Harry Potter and the Philosopher's Stone*.

We found it constantly interesting, we

learnt something of the surrealistic game of Quidditch, and we are now looking out for a matching pair of (not too sporty) broomsticks.   *Yours faithfully*,
J. P. TOOMEY,
E. M. TOOMEY,
Stourport-on-Severn, Worcestershire.
August 15

From Mr Jonathan Collins
Sir, If I read one more reference to Harry Potter in your pages, I shall seriously consider emigrating.   *Yours faithfully*,
JONATHAN COLLINS,
Seaford, East Sussex. August 15

From Ms Leri Price
Sir, Mr Jonathan Collins says he will consider emigrating if he reads another reference to Harry Potter. He can run, but he can't hide. Harry Potter is slowly but surely taking over the world.   *Yours faithfully*,
LERI PRICE,
Rochdale, Lancashire. August 16

SWEET DREAMS

From Mr David Meredith
Sir, I am invariably dreaming when I wake up during the night, whereas I never dream at all when I fall asleep during the day.
Yours faithfully,
DAVID MEREDITH,
Aberystwyth, Dyfedd. August 7

From Mr Ernest W. Ewers
Sir, David Meredith invariably dreams at night, but never if he drops off during the day. The answer is simple. During his daytime nap, he dreams that he is sleeping.
Yours faithfully,
E. W. EWERS,
Aylesbury, Buckinghamshire. August 15

From Mr F. D. A. Mocatta
Sir, Wasn't there the story of the peer who fell asleep and dreamt he was making a speech in the House of Lords, only to wake up and find that he was?   *Yours faithfully*,
F. D. A. MOCATTA,
Berkhamsted, Hertfordshire. August 17

DIGGING FOR VICTORY?

From Mr R. J. Carlyon
Sir, Your Diary notes that Yorkshire Cricket Academy is sending would-be players down t'pit. Will they emerge as seam bowlers?   *Yours faithfully*,
R. J. CARLYON,
Somerton, Somerset. August 10

From Mr Ian Liston
Sir, It is to be hoped that prospective Yorkshire cricketers sent down t'pit don't change their sporting allegiance and emerge as prop forwards instead of seam bowlers.   *Yours faithfully*,
IAN LISTON,
Bolney, West Sussex. August 11

NORMAL SERVICE

From Mr Richard Need
Sir, Yesterday, as my train paused at a station on the Chiltern line, I noticed a rail worker using a blower to clear the opposite platform of fallen leaves. He was blowing them onto the line. Presumably they were the right sort of leaves.   *Yours faithfully*,
RICHARD NEED,
Cheam, Surrey. August 10

PHYSICAL TEST

From Mrs C. M. Fulton
Sir, From the Test match radio commentary on Sunday afternoon: "(The batsman) has two short legs, breathing down his neck." Come again?   *Yours faithfully*,
CYNTHIA FULTON,
Taunton, Somerset. August 11

CHURCH MILITANT

From the Reverend John Williams, Rural Dean of Christchurch
Sir, I have received in the post a question from the Archbishops' Council which, among other requests, asks me for my "martial status". When I was at school I was in the cadet corps and I have an uncle and a brother who served in the Royal Navy. I

wonder whether the Archbishops' Council will regard this as sufficient status to suit their requirements?   *Yours faithfully*,
JOHN WILLIAMS,
Christchurch, Dorset. August 12

From Mr P. M. Hogan

Sir, Your correspondent who referred to a form which, erroneously, asked for his "martial" status, reminds me of an occasion when one of the Goons recounted being asked by a fan for a "singed" photograph. He duly obliged.   Yours correctly,
PAUL M. HOGAN,
King Edward, Banff. August 16

From Mrs Sylvia Jones

Sir, Your correspondence regarding martial (marital) and singed (signed) shouldn't close without mentioning the headline on *The Times* law report (August 11) which read, "Council not liable over fatally locked widows".   *Yours fatefully*,
SYLVIA JONES,
Warminster, Wiltshire. August 19

From Dr K. A. Hillard

Sir, As your correspondence on misprints had clerical origins it is perhaps appropriate to note that a recent issue of *The Church of England Newspaper* repeated that a new refectory at Walsingham was visited by the Archbishop of York, "who unveiled a plague on the building".   *Yours*,
ANTHONY HILLARD,
Worplesdon, Guildford, Surrey. August 28

From Mr David Lane

Sir, A mail order catalogue sent to me this week offers a pair of calvary twill trousers.
Yours etc,
DAVID LANE,
London W1. August 28

UNFINISHED BUSINESS

From Mr N. S. Howard

Sir, Berlin's is not the only wall for which there is pressure for it to be rebuilt.

There is an increasing constituency here which thinks that Hadrian's should be rebuilt also, and substantially higher this time.
Yours faithfully,
NICHOLAS HOWARD,
Penrith, Cumbria. August 18

From His Honour Judge J. P. Wadsworth, QC

Sir, Re Mr N. S. Howard's views on Hadrian's Wall, Beachcomber got there first:

When Hadrian built the Roman Wall to keep the horrid Scots away,

He didn't build it long enough or high enough or strong enough,

And look at us today! (*The Song of the Wall*, i).   *Yours etc,*
JIM WADSWORTH,
Southwark Crown Court, London SE1.
August 21

From Mr Nick Elsley

Sir, No need for rebuilding Berlin's or Hadrian's walls. Just plant a few leylandii.
Yours sincerely,
NICK ELSLEY,
London N20. August 25

THE SEARCH FOR NESSIE

From Mrs Bridget Box

Sir, You report that a special trap may be tried to find the Loch Ness monster. Surely a simpler solution would be to drain the loch to see what is in it.   *Yours sincerely,*
BRIDGET BOX,
Dersingham, King's Lynn. August 19

NATURE AND ART

From Mr Harry Saunders

Sir, I see that a nudity campaigner was arrested naked in London's Exhibition Road. How very appropriate.   *Yours faithfully,*
H. SAUNDERS,
Woodstock, Oxfordshire. August 22

EASTERN FORTE

From Mr Nick R. Thomas

Sir, Your headline "Norwich becomes the new Viagra capital" was followed by "Norfolk is noise capital of regions" in *The Sunday Times*.

Hardly surprising really.   *Yours faithfully,*
NICK R. THOMAS,
Charminster, Bournemouth, Dorset.
August 29

A CORKING IDEA

From Mr Andrew Fleming-Williams

Sir, I was concerned to read in the Wine Society's current annual review that reorganisation of its warehouse had enabled it to deal more efficiently with the Christmas peak by removing bottlenecks.

Yours faithfully,
ANDREW FLEMING-WILLIAMS,
London SW15. August 30

NORTH-SOUTH DIVIDE

From Mr Gareth Price

Sir, From my own frequent observations, I wonder if the North-South divide should be redrawn.

For 25 years I was a resident of Wigan in the poor North and was never once asked for "any spare change". However, since moving to Canterbury in the rich South I am asked this question every day half a dozen times.   *Yours faithfully,*
GARETH PRICE,
Canterbury, Kent. August 31

KNOWING MY PLACE

From Professor Alan Bullock

Sir, Any lingering doubts I might have had about the decline in the status of those involved in full-time education were finally dispelled when my paperboy asked me: "Do you have a high position in your college or are you just a teacher?"

Yours faithfully,
ALAN BULLOCK,
Department of Italian, University of
Leeds. August 31

GOLDEN HELLOS

From Mr J. L. Thorne

Sir, The merchant bank which made an

Oxford Classics graduate such an outstanding job offer in 1982 may have been mindful of the wise words of a Dean of Christ Church many years earlier when he impressed upon his congregation the study of Greek literature "which not only elevates above the vulgar herd, but leads not infrequently to positions of considerable emolument".

What price golf course management and knitwear?   *Yours truly,*
J. L. THORNE,
Hemel Hempstead, Hertfordshire.
September 1

From Sir Robert Sanders

Sir, The most succinct comment I have heard on the relevance of the Classics to a career came from an oil executive to my son's headmaster, when asked why his company continued to recruit Classics graduates.

He replied: "Because they sell more oil."

Yours faithfully,
ROBERT SANDERS,
Crieff, Perthshire. September 2

DEAR MR ESQ

From Mr A. P. Hemming

Sir, For 25 years my chequebooks were printed with my initials, surname and the suffix Esq. The bank then peremptorily substituted the prefix Mr, stating that the term Esq was passe, and I have remained a Mister for 15 years. However, on receiving a cheque, drawn on another bank, in which the drawer's name was printed with Esq, I decided to tease my own bank gently.

My new chequebook has arrived. I am now "ESQ A. P. HEMMING".

Your socially confused servant,
A. P. HEMMING,
Langton Green, Kent. September 1

From Professor J. Brian G. Roberts

Sir, Mr Esq Hemming and I could start a club for social climbers: my telephone company has already bestowed on me the title Mr Prof John B. G. Roberts. I look forward to attaining my Mr Prof Doctorate.

Yours hopefully,
BRIAN ROBERTS,
Malvern, Worcestershire. September 9

From Dr J. R. Crookall

Sir, I read with amusement Mr A. P. Hemming's struggle with his bank to be addressed on cheques with his preferred title.

Some years ago, I was giving my details over the phone to a company and, trying to be clear, I spelt out my name as "J. R. – as in *Dallas* – Crookall". For years after I received various junk mail addressed to J. R. Dallas-Crookall, but at least I knew how my details had been passed on.

I have been called many other things before and since, and such misprints have similarly shown up in the propagation of address lists.

Yours faithfully,
JOHN R. CROOKALL,
Harrold, Bedfordshire. September 12

A LESSON FOR LIFE?

From Mr John Nowell-Smith

Sir, Today's leading article ends with the sentence: "A degree of calm and reflection is now badly needed in higher education."

What qualifications would I need to apply?

Yours faithfully,
JOHN NOWELL-SMITH,
Thame, Oxfordshire. September 2

LOVE 4 E-MAIL

From Mr G. Forbes Abercrombie

Sir, I was interested to read that "lol" stands for "laughing out loud" in Internet communications. At the bridge table it was always "little old lady", not at all the same thing.

Yours faithfully,
G. FORBES ABERCROMBIE,
Rogate, Petersfield. September 6

From Dr Don Taylor

Sir, Oh dear, so "lol" in e-mailspeak means "laughing out loud"?

I frequently use it to mean "lots of love" –

an affectionate but not particularly ardent sentiment.

Perhaps some of my correspondents are "rofl" (rolling on the floor with laughter) at my mistake.

Yours faithfully,
DON TAYLOR,
Southampton. September 8

From Dr Edward Leigh

Sir, While "lol" can mean "laughing out loud" or "little old lady", as a junior doctor I affectionately remember the abbreviation "lolol" to mean "little old lady off legs".

Yours faithfully,
EDWARD D. LEIGH,
The Wellington Health Centre, London NW8. September 8

From Mrs Kathleen B. Cory

Sir, The abbreviation LOL may well have caused confusion among some of your readers, but what about TLC?

This I had always used to mean "tender loving care", but according to my eldest grandson it now means "total load of cr★★"! Not exactly what I had in mind.

Yours faithfully,
KATHLEEN B. CORY,
Edinburgh. September 13

From Mrs J. R. Chilton

Sir, In my youth LOL was the whispered acronym for a living-out-lover. If things went to plan, you moved on to LIL – a living-in-lover.

Naturally, I only learnt of this through hearsay.

Yours faithfully,
MAGGIE CHILTON,
Chipping Norton, Oxfordshire. September 13

From Miss Katerina Bucci

Sir, GAL (get a life), people! If all this Net shorthand is giving you an FB (furrowed brow), BD (big deal). IMHO (in my humble opinion), it's GR8 (great)! RTM (read the manual), and SOL (sooner or later) you will +LY (positively) love it. You'll be BATK (back at the keyboard) in no time.

Yours etc,

KATERINA BUCCI (aged nearly 17), Newport, Isle of Wight. September 13

EASTERN COCKTAILS

From Group Captain H. F. O'Neill, RAF (retd)

Sir, Your obituary of Godfrey Talbot mentioned him drinking a "suffering bastard" at Shepheard's Hotel in Cairo.

This was an effective hangover cure dispensed by Joe, the White Russian barman in the back bar. It was much favoured by those of us in from the desert in 1941 and consisted of gin, brandy, angostura bitters, Rose's lime juice, ginger beer and slices of lemon and orange.

It sent us back to the desert air war in sparkling form.   *Yours faithfully,*
H. F. O'NEILL,
Foston, York. September 11

From Mrs L. A. Smith

Sir, The letter from H. F. O'Neill about the "suffering bastard" cocktail reminded me of a cocktail I drank at the Yak and Yeti Hotel at Kathmandu in 1984.

The drinks menu offered an exotically named selection of cocktails, from which I chose a "Yeti's Smile". I drank one, and the rest of the evening remains a blur.

Thank God I refrained from trying the "Yak's Tail".   *Yours faithfully,*
L. A. SMITH,
Bere Ferrers, Devon. September 21

PETROL PROTEST

From Dr S. R. Gregory

Sir, The present petrol crisis is not all gloom. This morning the road through our village is bereft of traffic, families are walking their children to school, and the local trains to Leeds and Manchester are full of people actually talking to each other.

Have we inadvertently been given a glimpse of a greener and better future?
Yours faithfully,
S. R. GREGORY,
Midgley, Halifax. September 13

From Mr Matthew Wetmore

Sir, Oh boy, don't we love a crisis? Suppliers to our delicatessen urge us to order extra stock, "because we only have enough fuel for the next 24 hours"; customers ask whether supplies will get through; family and friends call to ask about the "situation" in Suffolk. Panic buying of sun-dried tomatoes has started.

Don't mention the war.   *Yours faithfully,*
MATTHEW WETMORE,
Halesworth, Suffolk. September 15

From Dr John McCarthy

Sir, Oil prices, fuel taxes and fuel shortages will bother me little. I return to Kosovo next week where there is a plentiful supply at a very reasonable price.   *Yours sincerely,*
JOHN McCARTHY
(Consultant pathologist),
South Tyneside District Hospital, South Shields. September 15

From Mr Winston Fletcher

Sir, Whichever side you take in the dispute, the petrol blockades surely represent a new triumph in human creativity.

Who would have dreamed countries – indeed continents – could be brought to their knees by a few hundred ill-parked pantechnicons?   *Yours truly,*
WINSTON FLETCHER,
London SW7. September 16

From Mr Anthony Wethered

Sir, I am providing against emergencies.

You are indulging in panic buying.

He is just making things worse for the rest of us.   *Yours faithfully,*
ANTHONY WETHERED,
Marlow, Buckinghamshire. September 22

From Wing Commander David McCann, RAF (retd)

Sir, As a pensioner and – I would like to think – a fine, upstanding citizen, I wonder if the Leader of the Opposition could suggest which installation I should picket in order to improve my lot.   *Yours faithfully,*

DAVID McCANN,
Bracknell, Berkshire. September 22

From Mr David Malaperiman

Sir, I spotted this sign of the times at a Reading petrol station this morning: "Panic buyers now welcome."   *Yours faithfully*,
DAVID MALAPERIMAN,
Grazeley, Berkshire. September 22

DRESS-DOWN FRIDAY

From His Honour Judge J. E. van der Werff
Sir, People who prefer to "dress-down" on Fridays because their suits are uncomfortable are going to the wrong tailors.

Yours faithfully,
J. E. van der WERFF,
London SE1. September 15

ONE CERTAIN THING

From Mr Michael Martin

Sir, Being of a generation for whom grass was for cutting, coke was kept in the coal shed, and someone who was gay was the life and soul of the party, I was relieved to find that, in a certificate of insurance recently received from Lloyds TSB, some things don't change.

Under the heading "Words with special meanings" was the following: "Death means loss of life".   *Yours faithfully*,
MICHAEL MARTIN,
Swindon, Wiltshire. September 16

From Mr Neil A. Parker

Sir, Mr Michael Martin's insurance company is entirely correct to clarify the meaning of death. Some time ago we spent two years in Papua New Guinea, where we learnt that in pidgin died merely meant being seriously ill.

When one finally shuffled off this mortal coil one died finish.   *Yours faithfully*,
NEIL A. PARKER,
Taunton, Somerset. September 18

From Dr Rosemary Harris

Sir, When the insecticide DDT was first coming on to the market we lived in

Northern Ireland and bought some that had been packed locally. The label read "One dose of this and the fly DIES beyond all hope of recovery" (emphasis exactly as in original).

Clearly it was not only in New Guinea that there was some doubt about the meaning of the word.   *Yours faithfully*,
ROSEMARY HARRIS,
Virginia Water, Surrey. September 20

From Dr John E. Downes

Sir, The idea that to "die" does not necessarily mean to progress to final extinction has a Shakespearean precedent. The attendant who brings Cleopatra the asp says: "I would not . . . desire you to touch him, for his biting is immortal; those that do die of it seldom or never recover" (*Antony and Cleopatra*, Act V, scene 2).   *Yours faithfully*,
JOHN DOWNES,
Reading, Berkshire. September 26

From Miss Cheryl Jones

Sir, DDT may well ensure that "the fly DIES beyond all hope of recovery". However, this cannot be said of all insecticides. I have recently bought a preparation to ensure, as I thought, the demise of a small plague of fleas.

Imagine my consternation, therefore, when I read the can, which told me that one application would kill "all adult fleas for up to three months".

I remain, Sir, your obedient servant,
CHERYL JONES,
East Croydon. September 26

From Mr Andrew Hunt

Sir, A recently discarded can of fly killer included the notice that it had not been tested on animals.

No wonder it did not work.

Yours faithfully,
ANDREW HUNT,
Benfleet, Essex. September 27

From Mrs W.Y Jackson

Sir, Mr Andrew Hunt writes of an apparently useless can of fly spray. Perhaps he

should try turning the can around and firmly striking the said fly. I usually find this most effective.   *Yours faithfully,*
W.Y. JACKSON,
Eynsham, Oxfordshire. October 2

From Dr David Crawford

Sir, I have a can of fly spray which "kills bugs dead". I am intrigued as to what other state might result.   *Yours faithfully,*
DAVID CRAWFORD,
Bolton. October 2

From Mr Geoffrey Williams

Sir, I once shot a fly down using a Pledge furniture polish aerosol. He had a perfect finish.   *Yours faithfully,*
GEOFFREY WILLIAMS,
Margate, Kent. October 9

TRANSCENDENTAL WI

From Mr Roger Betteridge

Sir, The splendid Concord (Massachusetts) bookshop has at its centre a long, plain, elegant table to display a changing selection of single items of consequence.

Distinguished writers of the village – Ralph Waldo Emerson, Henry David Thoreau, Amos Bronson Alcott and his daughter Louisa May – jostle for transcendental place.

Last week this honoured position was occupied by the Ladies of Rylstone W.I. Calendar.

New England it seems finds English ladies of a certain age in racy dishabille irresistible.   *Yours faithfully,*
ROGER BETTERIDGE,
Shardlow, Derbyshire. September 16

From Dr Gordon Johnson

Sir, In Rockland, Maine (pop. 6,000), the lobster capital of the world, there is hardly a shop the entire length of Main Street which does not have the Ladies of Rylstone WI Calendar prominently on sale; but then Down-Easterners have a good eye for beauty in full sail.
Yours faithfully,
GORDON JOHNSON

(President), Wolfson College, Cambridge.
September 28

FOOT IN MOUTH

From Mrs J. A. B. Bates

Sir, Today's *Times* contains two choice remarks.

The short obituary of Robert Stainton reports: "On coming down from Oxford he cut his teeth at a prep school at Elstree where he made a deep impression on both staff and pupils." A report about Jean-Marie Messier has the headline: "Messier puts his foot in it."

Thank you for brightening the day.
Yours sincerely,
J. A. B. BATES,
Burton Joyce, Nottingham. September 21

From Mr Robert Greenwood

Sir, Mrs J. A. B. Bates may be amused by two wordplays which caught my attention.

Your report on "Noah's Flood" stated that the wattle and daub village discovered under the Black Sea was the first concrete evidence of submerged habitation.

A few days later BBC News, on the problem of leaves on the line, stated that a liquid spray containing fruit essence was being tried as a solution to the problem.   *Yours sincerely,*
ROBERT GREENWOOD,
Wrenthorpe, Wakefield, West Yorkshire.
September 30

ZERO TOLERANCE

From Mr Robert Brooks

Sir, Today I have received two communications from the Inland Revenue. The first provides details of a refund in the amount of £0.00. A cheque for £0.00 is attached.

The second provides details of the amount I owe – again £0.00. With this the Revenue has kindly provided a Freepost envelope in which I should send it the money.
Yours faithfully,
BOB BROOKS,
Worthing, West Sussex. September 22

From Mr David Le Breton

Sir, For Mr Bob Brooks to bring his communications from the Inland Revenue to their full conclusion, he should send them his cheque for the £0.00 demanded, and request a receipt.   *Yours faithfully,*
DAVID LE BRETON,
Westerham, Kent. September 27

From Mr David Simon

Sir, Mr Brooks was lucky. His demand from the Inland Revenue was for £0.00. My demand was worse – it was for £0.01. But I was told I could pay by instalments.

Yours faithfully,
D. SIMON,
Stokesley, North Yorkshire. October 2

HIGH-HEELED RISKS

From Mrs Vera Roddam Renton

Sir, Las Vegas casino operators want cocktail waitresses to "look their best" by continuing to wear high-heeled shoes (report, September 16).

They would do well to heed my mother's assertion: "Uncomfortable shoes give you lines on your forehead."   *Yours faithfully,*
VERA RODDAM RENTON,
Woodthorpe, Nottingham. September 22

POETRY DEFINED

From Dr Michael Hammet

Sir, Here in Winchester the discussion all evening has been about poetry, following the latest effusion of the BBC's unashamedly intellectual British and World all-comers' welterweight poetry championship (report and leading article, October 5).

Our thoughts turned upon an adequate modern definition of poetry. It clearly had little to do with metre, rhyme, image, mood, or meaning. The consensus was for "Things said in a peculiar voice".   *Yours &c,*
MICHAEL HAMMET,
Winchester, Hampshire. October 7

From Mr Ben Stroude

Sir, Dr Michael Hammet, in defining modern poetry as "things said in a peculiar voice", laments with the rest of us Philistines the lack of structure and meaning in today's works.

You recently ran a highly entertaining series of correspondence recalling the "no substitute for wool" verses of 40 or 50 years ago. Why were they so memorable? Because they scanned, they rhymed and they made sense. There must be a lesson there somewhere.   *Yours sincerely,*
BEN STROUDE,
West Kirby, Wirral. October 10

From Dr John F. James

Sir, Without disagreeing with the definition of poetry proposed by Dr Hammet and friends, the ultimate definition of poetry, ancient or modern, was surely given years ago by Robert Frost: poetry is what is lost in translation.   *Yours faithfully,*
JOHN F. JAMES,
Kilcreggan, Argyll. October 10

From Mr Nigel MacNicol

Sir, Dr Hammet's definition is incomplete. May I propose the addition of this modest verse?

In literature/prose written/with line breaks/inserted at random/intervals.

Yours faithfully,
NIGEL MacNICOL,
Oakham, Rutland. October 10

From Mr Robert Vincent

Sir, A fundamental aspect of modern poetry, apart from not rhyming, is that it should be utterly sad. One's best bet is unrequited love.

Over the years, apart from some paid success with poems of unrelenting cheerfulness, I have always been in with more than a chance when contributing something desperately depressing taking place, say, on a damp, autumnal day. "Her tears fell softly onto golden leaves already drenched with rain, her broken heart, etc, etc . . ."

You really gotta wring the withers to be considered significant.   *Yours faithfully,*

ROBERT VINCENT,
Wildhern, Hampshire. October 14

From Mr W. J. Folkes

Sir, My elder son writes poetry which, I understand, is well regarded. I know that it is good, for I cannot understand a word of it.   *Yours faithfully*,
WILLIAM FOLKES,
Chilworth, Guildford. October 14

From Dr Philip E. Roe

Sir, The best definition of poetry I have encountered was that of the Nobel Prize-winning theoretical physicist Paul Dirac, who hated it.

He learnt that a subordinate wrote poetry in his spare time. He summoned the young man and said: "How can you do both physics and poetry? In physics we try to explain in simple terms something that nobody knew before. In poetry it is the exact opposite."   *Yours faithfully*,
PHILIP ROE,
St Albans, Hertfordshire. October 14

From Commander George S. Pearson, RN (retd)

Sir, Dr Michael Hammet reports from Winchester that the consensus is that a fair definition of poetry is "Things said in a peculiar voice".

If that is to enter the lexicon, how are we to redefine church sermons?   *Yours faithfully*,
GEORGE S. PEARSON,
London SW6. October 14

From Mr Michael Murphy

Sir, A character in one of Trollope's novels defines poetry as stuff that doesn't go right across the page. That, even if hardly modern, should be good enough.

Yours faithfully,
MICHAEL MURPHY,
North Harrow, Middlesex. October 14

From Mrs J. M. R. Baines

Sir,
Is this poetry
Or is this prose?

I really think that no one knows
Any more.   *Yours faithfully*,
JANET BAINES,
Great Addington, Kettering. October 14

From Mr Richard Lines

Sir, I find it sad that a Nobel Prize-winning physicist should have "hated" poetry.

The arts speak to the heart rather than the mind, but in their own way they help to "explain" the world just as much as science does.

Poetry is the most intimate of the arts. To appreciate it one does not need high-tech equipment or expensive opera tickets. It can be enjoyed alone or, better still, read aloud to one's lover.   *Yours faithfully*,
RICHARD LINES,
Upper Norwood, London SE19.
October 19

From Ian Anderson

Sir, William Folkes writes that he cannot understand his son's poems.

I recall that Adrian Plass recounts in one of his books how, feeling very "out-of-things" at his poetry group, he decides to devise a poem as a rather naughty test to see whether he and they really had anything in common.

It was duly received with much serious "Mmmming" and "Yes-ing" which confirmed to him that they didn't, for his "poem" was in fact just a series of clues from one of your paper's crosswords.

Yours faithfully,
IAN ANDERSON,
Cambridge. October 19

From Mr Henry Button

Sir, The poet A. E. Housman, in his great lecture on The Name and Nature of Poetry, said that he had once been asked to define poetry.

'I replied that I could no more define poetry than a terrier can define a rat, but that I thought that we both recognised the object by the symptoms which it provokes in us. One of these symptoms was described

BUT IS IT POETRY?

KRAY'S ELEGY

in connexion with another object by Eliphaz the Temanite:"A spirit passed before my face: the hair of my flesh stood up.'"

(The reference is to Job iv, 15.)

Yours faithfully,
HENRY BUTTON,
Cambridge. October 19

From Mr N. J. Daykin

Sir, *The Radio Times Music Handbook* (1935) says, of the harp:"Unnecessary to describe." This is surely true of poetry also.

Yours faithfully,
NICK DAYKIN,
Norwich, Norfolk. October 19

BOWING OUT

From Mr John C. W. Macnab

Sir, Mr Reginald Kray's funeral (as seen on TV) must have cost someone a few sovs.

Goodbye! magazine, perhaps?

With respect,
JOHN C. W. MACNAB,
Folkestone, Kent. October 12

LEAVES ONLINE

From Mr Stephen Wainde

Sir, As I checked a departure time this morning on the Railtrack timetable website I noticed that it was decorated with autumnal leaves blowing in the wind.

Perhaps Railtrack has more of a sense of humour about seasonal delays than most of the passengers who fall victim to them.

Yours faithfully,
S. M. WAINDE,
Tonbridge, Kent. October 14

UNSETTLED OUTLOOK

From Mr Godfrey J. Curtis

Sir, You report today that BBC staff refer to the ITV's troubled broadcast as "News at When?" I presume this should be preceded by a Whether Forecast. *Yours etc,*
GODFREY J. CURTIS,
Trumpington, Cambridge. October 17

UNCOVERED

From Brigadier B. L. Rigby (retd)

Sir, Why, nowadays, do we appear to "unveil" almost everything? The other day one of our regional TV newsreaders contrived to unveil a new look.

What, one wonders, would Salome have made of it all? *Yours faithfully,*
BERNARD RIGBY,
Saxmundham, Suffolk. October 20

SMELLING OF ROSES

From Mr Andy Bowles

Sir, In an attempt to improve both my knowledge and my garden, I recently bought a "step-by-step" guide to growing and maintaining roses. One of the first things I learnt was that "it's easy to make your own liquid fertiliser by steeping two buckets of sheep manure in a large barrel of water".

I have now decided to remain ignorant.

Yours faithfully,
ANDY BOWLES,
London N19. October 30

From Mr John Jenkin

Sir, I know relatively little about rose growing, but Mr Andy Bowles would notice a distinct and memorable improvement in the taste of his tomatoes over the supermarket product by nourishing them with liquid sheep manure, and at the same time help to benefit our hard-pressed sheep farmers. I speak from several years' experience.   *Yours faithfully,*
JOHN JENKIN,
Eastbourne, East Sussex. November 1

From Mr Ian Linn

Sir, Mr Andy Bowles encapsulates neatly the urban attitudes which bring the country dweller to despair. He clearly loves to smell the roses, but is too delicately nurtured to become involved in the earthy processes by which their beauty is achieved.   *Yours faithfully,*
IAN LINN,
Exminster, Exeter. November 1

From Mr David Malaperiman

Sir, An alternative, but perhaps more accessible, organic liquid feed for the townies' roses and tomatoes is obtained from nettles.

Simply fill an old bucket with nettles and add a little water. Cover, leave for a week or so and add a few drops of the resultant liquid to your watering can. The only drawback is that its noisome smell is worse than that of the sheep manure-based solution.

I've tried both over the last 20 years, but nettle-fertilised roses smell sweeter and the vegetables definitely taste better.

Yours faithfully,
DAVID MALAPERIMAN,
Grazeley, Berkshire. November 4

From Mr John Weber

Sir, Perhaps I may recall a saying I heard more than half a century ago, that although lust is the root of love, the rose is more lovely than its root.   *Yours faithfully,*
JOHN WEBER,
South Cadbury, Yeovil. November 4

From Mr Richard Griffith

Sir, Many years ago we put nettles in our water butt to make liquid organic feed.

The garden thrived until one day we found our neighbours undertaking extensive excavations to locate their sewer in order to investigate an all-pervading odour infiltrating their house and garden.

Yours faithfully,
RICHARD GRIFFITH,
London W4. November 7

From Mr Charles Stringer

Sir, My problem with roses is visual rather than olfactory.

New to rose growing, I sought advice from books and journals on pruning, all of which insist that the cut should always be made above an "outward-pointing bud". I have found great difficulty in identifying such buds; mine invariably point in another direction altogether.

Inquiries in my local pub, the source of so much information in these matters, indicate that other novice rosegrowers are experiencing the same difficulty.

Yours faithfully,
CHARLES STRINGER,
Hertford. November 7

From Mr Neville Denson

Sir, I knew a man who grew the most wonderful dahlias. When I asked him the secret he told me that he fed them on Mackeson Stout. It was some time later that he added that he did this each evening on his return from the village inn, after enjoying the stout.   *Yours faithfully,*
NEVILLE DENSON,
St Bees, Cumbria. November 7

From Mr Paul Rose

Sir, I commend llama manure to your rose-growing correspondents. I have used it with great success.

Affectionately known among llama owners as "llama beans", it is almost odourless and can be applied immediately after its pro-

duction. When dried it can also be used as fuel for fires, giving off a slightly aromatic scent.   *Yours faithfully,*
PAUL ROSE,
Stockleigh Pomeroy, Devon. November 13

LEFT-HAND DRIVE

From Mr David P. Stead

Sir, You report the plan for drivers to use the hard shoulder.

Perhaps, for practice, they could first be encouraged to use the nearside lane?

Yours faithfully,
DAVID P. STEAD,
Balscote, nr Banbury. October 27

RAILWAY MISERY

From Mr Mark Solon

Sir, A colleague tells me his local station-master made the following announcement yesterday: "We are sorry for the substantial delay. This is due to leaves on the lines, and further due to those leaves still being attached to the trees."   *Yours faithfully,*
MARK SOLON,
London EC1. November 3

A HIGHER CALLING

From Mr Graham Breeze

Sir, In circumstances where lesser mortals reach for the expression "it does not take a rocket scientist", to whom do rocket scientists defer?   *Yours faithfully,*
GRAHAM BREEZE,
Hawksworth, Leeds. November 7

From Mr David Green

Sir, Graham Breeze asks to whom rocket scientists defer. Presumably the answer is the Prince of Wales (report, same day).

Yours faithfully,
DAVID GREEN,
Haverfordwest, Pembrokeshire. November 8

From Mr John Faichney

Sir, Rocket scientists are clever, but they perforce defer to rocket engineers if they wish to realise their ideas.   *Yours faithfully,*

JOHN FAICHNEY,
Barnard Castle, Co Durham. November 8

From Mr Trefor Edwards

Sir, We humble rocket scientists find this adulation hard to cope with – even Shania Twain sings our praise. We, in turn, should look to our intellectual heroes for inspiration but, if truth be known, we actually defer to our wives.   *Yours faithfully,*
TREFOR EDWARDS,
Rutherford Appleton Laboratory, Chilton, Didcot. November 11

From Mr Niall Crosby

Sir, As a medical student I am frequently reminded by neurosurgeons that I am "not studying rocket science". A friend who is studying astrophysics is often told during lectures on rocket science that he is "not studying brain surgery".   *Yours faithfully,*
NIALL CROSBY,
Selly Oak, Birmingham. November 11

From Dr Cris Whetton

Sir, As a former rocket engineer, I defer to the cleaners, they being the only persons in any organisation who know what is really happening.   *Yours faithfully,*
CRIS WHETTON (Technical Director),
ility Engineering, Tampere, Finland.
November 11

From Mr Tony Scarisbrick

Sir, It does not take the brains of an archbishop nor a size ten in hats to work out to whom rocket scientists should defer.

Yours faithfully,
TONY SCARISBRICK,
Berwick upon Tweed, Northumberland.
November 11

From Mr Robert Yeoman

Sir, I find that teenagers know everything.
Yours faithfully,
ROBERT YEOMAN,
Malvern, Worcestershire. November 11

From Miss Leah Tardivel

Sir, Trefor Edwards wrote, with reference

to rocket scientists: "If truth be known we actually defer to our wives." Are all rocket scientists married? More to the point, are all rocket scientists male?   *Yours faithfully,*
LEAH TARDIVEL,
Canterbury, Kent. November 15

From Professor David Thomas
Sir, I find I get more common sense from watching 30 minutes of Ricky Tomlinson and *The Royle Family* than I hear in a whole evening with my neurosurgeon and astrophysicist friends.

What's more, I am sure they would agree with me.   *Yours faithfully,*
DAVID THOMAS,
Tettenhall, Wolverhampton. November 18

From Mr Paul Jones
Sir, To whom does a rocket scientist defer? If the rocket scientist happens to be Wernher von Braun then he defers to whichever political system happens to be paying him.   *Yours,*
PAUL JONES,
West Bridgford, Nottinghamshire.
November 18

From the Reverend Roger Holmes
Sir, I vividly remember, circa 1975, the renowned Professor Tom Torrance of Edinburgh University saying in a lecture: "Now take something simple, like astrophysics." But then he was professor of that queen of sciences, Divinity.   *Yours sincerely,*
ROGER HOLMES,
York. November 18

CHRISTENING GIFT?

From Mr Martin Wall
Sir, The naming of children can indeed be tricky (report and leading article, November 4). When faced with this task for our first son, we quickly rejected Walter, as a career in carpet fitting seemed to be suggested. We settled for a seemingly safe Matthew.

Our son is now known to one and all as Matt Wall; something we might wish to gloss over.   *Yours faithfully,*

MARTIN (aka MAX) WALL,
Worcester. November 9

From Mr J. M. C. Clark-Maxwell
Sir, According to family tradition, my grandfather, a slightly deaf parson of forbidding appearance, once christened a girl John.

When he said: "Name this child", a timorous godmother seemed to say "Lucifer", even though asked twice. Refusing to accept such a name he continued sternly: "I baptise thee John in the name of the Father, the Son and the Holy Ghost."

Afterwards it was explained to him that the godmother had said: "Lucy, sir."
Yours faithfully,
JOHN CLARK-MAXWELL,
Swallowfield, Berkshire. November 14

From Sir William Whitfield
Sir, When in the 18th century, the Whitfield family through misfortune lost Whitfield Hall in Northumberland, their ancestral home since the 12th century, a distraught daughter, having married a gentleman of the name Hall, christened her newly born son Whitfield, that there should remain in the family a Whitfield Hall.

The Hall survives, the child does not.
Yours faithfully,
WILLIAM WHITFIELD,
St Helen Auckland, Durham. November 14

UNDERCOVER THEORY

From Professor David Thomas
Sir, For the last three years running, but on average seven days later in the year than in each previous year, I have woken up feeling cold, to discover that the whole duvet has somehow moved to my wife's side of the bed during the night.

Is this delayed phenomenon further evidence that global warming is occurring?
Yours faithfully,
DAVID THOMAS,
Tettenhall, Wolverhampton. November 13

From Mr David Beech

Sir, Professor Thomas needs my help. Whatever the global weather pattern, if the duvet ends up with me my wife explains that I have unconsciously pulled it; if it is found entirely with my wife I am told that I have inadvertently pushed it.

This is irrefutable evidence of marital harmony - nothing more.   *Yours faithfully,*
DAVID BEECH,
Retford, Nottinghamshire. November 16

From Mrs Catherine Bradshaw

Sir, While Professor Thomas's chilly awakenings may be a sign of global warming, I feel they are more probably the proof of that old adage: "One good turn gets most of the duvet."   *Yours faithfully,*
CATHERINE BRADSHAW,
Harrow. November 16

From Mr David E. Perril

Sir, The phenomenon described by Professor David Thomas is known as Quilt Drift, possibly related to Continental Drift.

Anecdotal evidence suggests an alarming increase since the beginning of the month, and those at risk should take the precaution of placing sandbags along the edge of the quilt on their side of the bed.

Yours faithfully,
DAVID PERRIL,
Girton, Cambridge. November 16

From Mrs Joan Atkins

Sir, There is an easy solution to Quilt Drift, adopted many years ago in this house. One bed, two duvets, no problem.

Yours faithfully,
JOAN ATKINS,
Little Shelford, Cambridge. November 20

From Dr Chris Pond

Sir, It is no surprise that the inexorable increase in duvet sales in the 1970s and 1980s almost exactly matched that of the divorce rate. Eschew this uncivilised alien invention altogether, return to sheets and blankets, and all will be well.   *Yours faithfully,*
CHRIS POND,
Loughton, Essex. November 20

From Mr David Kirwan

Sir, In this household we have implemented a method of combating Quilt Drift that does not require sandbags.

The use of two or three 7kg Yorkshire ter-

Quilt drift

riers, one at least of which is guaranteed to growl threateningly when asked to move, will effectively secure the quilt against all movement, whether involuntary drift, or determined tug.

There is the added advantage that neither human occupant can roll out of bed, nor indeed move at all, during the hours of slumber.   *Yours faithfully,*
DAVID KIRWAN,
Oakfield, Sale, Cheshire. November 21

From Mrs M. Button
Sir, Pleasant dreams and sweet repose, half the bed and all the clothes.   *Yours sincerely,*
M. BUTTON,
Great Ayton, North Yorkshire. November 21

From Mr Brian Rhodes
Sir, Why is it that a duvet moving in my direction is being pulled but moving in my wife's direction is being pushed?
Yours faithfully,
BRIAN RHODES,
London W4. November 27

From Mr Edwin Smith
Sir, To those not fortunate enough to own a string of Yorkshire terriers might I suggest that a strip of Velcro could well stop the Drift.   *Yours sincerely,*
EDWIN SMITH,
Kilburn, York. November 27

From Mr L. I. Elias
Sir, Gentlemen who find they are not getting a fair share of the domestic duvet need to spend more time in the arms of their wives.   *Yours faithfully,*
LYNDON ELIAS,
Didcot, Oxfordshire. November 27

From Mr Leslie Baker
Sir, Have you ever tried to pull back your share of the duvet from the wife at four in the morning? Yet this is the same woman who a few hours earlier could not get the top off the pickle jar.   *Yours faithfully,*
LESLIE BAKER,
Solihull, West Midlands. December 2

WRONG-FOOTED
From Mr Anthony Williams
Sir, I see that Jean Marsh suggests that "wearing more than one article of leather is ill-advised for any man over 49" (Times2, November 17). Call me out of touch, but I think I look sillier hopping on one foot than wearing both shoes.   *Yours faithfully,*
ANTHONY WILLIAMS,
Exton, Devon. November 20

GRACE BUT NO FAVOUR
From Mr Keith Chambers
Sir, Perhaps ITV's alleged dirty tricks (report, "BBC fury as Tarrant buries Meldrew", November 21) were in revenge for the BBC killing off Grace Archer on ITV's opening night 45 years ago.   *Yours faithfully,*
KEITH CHAMBERS,
Basingstoke, Hampshire. November 22

DESIRABLE ADDRESS
From Mrs Sue Vernon
Sir, In the early days I created my silly personal e-mail address, not realising it would later become a source of professional embarrassment.

Seeing your headline, "Rush likely for 'dotty' new Web addresses", I think I'll keep it after all.   *Yours faithfully,*
SUE VERNON,
Wallington, Surrey
svdotty@aol.com. November 22

SING SING?
From Mr Brian M. Poag
Sir, In your list of church services (Sunday Worship, November 18) I was delighted to read that the Choir of St Bride's was doing Byrd for the 6.30pm Prison Service. How very apt.   *Yours faithfully,*
B. M. POAG,
Beckenham, Kent. November 24

WOT, NO PRESIDENT?
From Dr Martin Toal
Sir, I recently observed on the Internet that

St Chad, the English bishop of the 7th century, does not appear to be a patron saint for any particular cause.

This seems such a shame when there is now clearly a vacancy for a patron saint for presidential elections.   *Yours sincerely*,
MARTIN TOAL,
Stoke Poges, Buckinghamshire.
November 25

From Mrs S. E. Chown

Sir, I don't know – there is a lot to be said for making a simple cross on a piece of paper with a pencil attached to a bit of string.
Yours faithfully,
S. E. CHOWN,
Dorchester, Dorset. November 25

MOBILE PHONES

From Dr John Burscough

Sir, The ban on mobile phones in British hospitals must remain. Otherwise the corridors will echo with cries of: "I'm on the trolley".   *Yours faithfully*,
JOHN BURSCOUGH,
Wrawby, Brigg, North Lincolnshire.
November 25

ORDEAL BY WATER

From Mr Rodney Legg

Sir, There is talk from time to time about substituting for England's imported national saint a native-born candidate. Now we have experienced the wettest autumn on record, consideration should be given to St Swithin, Bishop of Winchester between 852 and 862.

Having a Bank Holiday on or near his day, July 15, would provide an opportunity to start filling sandbags.   *Yours sincerely*,
RODNEY LEGG,
Wincanton, Somerset. November 28

SEX AND SHOPPING

From Mr R. Wilson

Sir, Assuming that half the population are men and half are women, then if, according to Dr Thomas Stuttaford's article on shopping sprees, one in five of women are shopaholics, and one in ten of the population are shopaholics, no men at all can be included among the shopaholics. Or have I missed something?   *Yours faithfully*,
RICHARD WILSON,
Stafford. December 1

AGE OF CHANGE

From Mr Henry Guly

Sir, Edward George did not need to be knighted to change his name, as reverting to the name on one's birth certificate appears to be a normal development in middle age for middle-class males.

My address book is full of Michaels (previously Mike), Anthonys (formerly Tony) and at least two Daves who have metamorphosed into Davids.

How should I respond? Should I rejoice in a sign that, perhaps, student excesses have now been left behind or regret it as evidence of the onset of pomposity? I have the advantage of a name that has never been shortened.   *Yours faithfully*,
HENRY GULY,
Horrabridge, Devon. December 11

From Dr Timothy Chambers

Sir, One of the minor compensations for possessing a forename that is commonly abbreviated is that when one is addressed by one's full name by a family member one knows one is in trouble.

Happily most of the time one remains your obedient and untitled servant.

TIM CHAMBERS,
The Athenaeum, London SW1. December 11

From Mr H. J. Lane

Sir, I, like Mr Guly, am a Henry, but it is only my wife who addresses me thus. All my friends call me Harry, my sisters call me Hal and to my other relatives, in London, I am Aitch.   *Yours faithfully*,
H. J. LANE,
Hatfield Peverel, Essex. December 18

From Mrs Hilary Cotter

Sir, It can be important to remember what you were called at certain periods of your life, particularly when it comes to signing Christmas cards.

At school I was Hil, to certain old friends I am Dilly, and to a former employer and his family I am Hilly. Although no one now calls me Hilly Bags, I was happy to be called it by its originator, the cricket commentator Rex Alston, and presumably Brian Johnston's genius in inventing names rubbed off on to him. I was happy when he used it, but anyone else would have had short shrift.

Yours, etc.,
HILARY COTTER,
Rudgwick, West Sussex. December 18

From Mr Ian Davies-Llewellyn

Sir, My mother christened me Ian with the specific aim that it could not be shortened. My father has spent the last 35 years testing her patience by calling me E.

Yours faithfully,
I. M. DAVIES-LLEWELLYN,
Whitchurch, Cardiff. December 27

From Dr Tony Collings

Sir, Like most Anthonys, I'm Tony to everyone except my mother.   *Yours faithfully,*
TONY COLLINGS,
Westcliff on Sea, Southend. December 27

From Mr Len Cacutt

Sir, "Moff" ("My old fat friend") is the gentle pet name given me by my son Ian. He addresses letters to me with "Moff" and I reply in kind, as "Yoff".   *Yours faithfully,*
LEN CACUTT,
Carshalton Beeches, Surrey. December 28

From Mr Richard Candy

Sir, I have long suspected that my parents christened my elder brother Thomas and my younger sister Harriet so that any old Tom, Dick or Harry would know our pet names.   *Yours faithfully,*
RICHARD CANDY,
Buckhurst Hill, Essex. January 1

ONE GOLD RING

From Mr David Norbury

Sir, How is it that, on seeing her favourite jewellers to be open, and perhaps influenced by the season, my wife can declare her wedding ring to be worn out and in need of immediate replacement, when mine of obviously similar vintage is fine?

Perhaps I should be grateful she did not ask for five.   *Yours faithfully,*
DAVID NORBURY,
Guilden Sutton, Cheshire. December 13

From Mrs Frances Manson

Sir, In today's Letters to the Editor only one came from a woman.

Mr David Norbury, in his letter, wonders why his wife needs a new wedding ring when his is still fine. Could it be that while one of them is scrubbing the bath with abrasive cleaning products or working in the garden with her hands covered in gritty soil, the other is sitting in an armchair reading *The Times*?   *Yours faithfully,*
FRANCES MANSON,
Robertsbridge, East Sussex. December 18

From Mr A. C. Waddelove

Sir, Should not your correspondent be grateful for the fact that it was only the wedding ring which his wife wished to replace?   *Yours,*
ADRIAN WADDELOVE,
Malpas, Cheshire. December 18

RELATIVE VALUES

From Mr Grahame Jelbart

Sir, Prolonged convalescence has led me to watch quiz shows on television. I was intrigued that today the same question (the alter ego of the writer Ruth Rendell) was valued at no more than £2,000 on *The Weakest Link* but £32,000 on *Who Wants to be a Millionaire?* And the latter gave a choice of answers.   *Yours faithfully,*
GRAHAME R. JELBART,
London SE21. December 15

RETAIL EYE THERAPY

From Mr Richard Crisp

Sir, Boots is offering a laser eyesight cure at their Regent Street store.

At a quoted price of £1,250 per eye, I think I'll wait until they have a "three for the price of two" promotion.

Yours faithfully,
RICHARD CRISP,
Weybridge, Surrey. December 16

From Mr John Turner

Sir, My local branch of Boots can't even organise its sandwiches into logical categories, so I am certainly not letting them anywhere near my eyes with a laser.

Does the 20 minutes include the time queueing to pay? *Yours faithfully,*
JOHN TURNER,
St Albans, Hertfordshire. December 16

VEGETABLE MATTER

From Mrs Stella Noble

Sir, Working on the principle that when mixing a dry Martini it is sufficient to have a bottle of vermouth on the sideboard, I shall be adopting a similar strategy when considering the traditional festive vegetable: it is sufficient when serving sprouts to prepare them and leave them in the kitchen. *Yours faithfully,*
STELLA NOBLE,
Handforth, Cheshire. December 22

PAWS FOR THOUGHT

From Commander D. Morgan, RN

Sir, Do all cats find computers irresistible? No sooner do my wife or I switch on our PC to type a letter such as this than our cat will appear from wherever she has been hiding, and insist on adding her contribuqtzxion. *Yours sincerely,*
DAI MORGAN,
Bassett, Southampton. December 26

From Mrs Sue Darge

Sir, Our cat is happy to sit on a lap when we use the computer. In the evening, so familiar is she with the sequence of shutting down noises that she now takes off at speed to hide, knowing that our next move will be to put her out for the night. *Yours faithfully,*
SUE DARGE,
Worcester. December 30

From Mr Peter Hutchinson

Sir, There are historical precedents for the ambulatory habits of Commander Morgan's cat: in the early 18th century Domenico Scarlatti's cat was pacing up and down his keyboard, supposedly creating the theme for the piece now known as the Cat's Fugue.

It says much for the adaptability of the species that our feline friend has become computer-literate without the need for any government-sponsored training course.

Yours sincerely,
PETER HUTCHINSON,
Haywards Heath, West Sussex. December 30

From Mrs Rachel Pearson

Sir, Commander Morgan should perhaps refrain from using his mouse.

Yours faithfully,
RACHEL PEARSON,
Bury St Edmunds, Suffolk. December 30

QUEEN'S ENGLISH

From Mrs Marilyn Cuthbert

Sir, Her Majesty's voice may be 'eading dahn Sarf (leader, December 21), but she will not be a real Estuary user until her spelling follows suit. One of my cherished moments as a teacher came when an Essex pupil, wanting to put my name on her exercise book, asked: "Do you spell your name with one F or two?" *Yours faithfully,*
MARILYN CUTHBERT,
Edinburgh. December 26

LOST IN TRANSLATION

From Dr Anthony Clayton

Sir, The following notice was placed on the wall of the corridor outside my room in a Paris hotel at which I was staying recently:
ATTENTION

PEINTURE FRAICHE.
FRENCH PAINT. *Yours faithfully,*
ANTHONY CLAYTON,
Lower Bourne, Farnham. December 26

A TEST OF FAITH

From Mr Daniel Neal

Sir, It seems quite bizarre how the name of the subject my mother teaches has undergone so many changes.

It was called Divinity, then Scripture, followed by Religious Instruction, Religious Knowledge, Religious Education and now Religious Studies.

Perhaps an expert in chaos theory could hazard a guess as to the next title. *Yours sincerely,*
DANIEL NEAL,
Deal, Kent. December 28

From Mrs M. M. Robinson

Sir, Divinity is not the only school subject to have undergone a series of name changes over the years.

Cookery became domestic science, then home economics, then food technology. Where will it all end – nutritional pharmacology? *Yours faithfully,*
J. A. ROBINSON,
Ightham, Kent. January 4

From Dom John Wisdom

Sir, As a boy I had RE, RI, RK, and RD (doctrine) classes, and now teach Catholic instruction at a prep school.

Not much really changes though – the lessons are still based on the Penny Catechism, and the children (and the school's website) still have trouble spelling "religious".

Yours in Christ,
JOHN WISDOM,
Cranham, Gloucestershire. January 4

From Mrs Stella M. Fookes

Sir, When I was at school in the North of Scotland in the 1920s, we just called it Bible (and it was, too – we had to learn chunks of it by heart). *Yours faithfully,*
STELLA M. FOOKES,
Reading, Berkshire. January 4

From Mr Ivor Davies

Sir, Concerning the many names for what will always be, for me, divinity lessons, I suggest that it should now be called "lip service". *Yours faithfully,*
IVOR DAVIES,
Goring-by Sea, Worthing, West Sussex.
January 4

ANOTHER YEAR WISER

From Mr Michael J. Blyth

Sir, We are now well into the last month of the last year of the 20th century and, indeed, of the millennium. However, little appears to have been said about plans to mark this momentous occasion. Has it, by any chance, been overlooked?

Yours faithfully,
MICHAEL J. BLYTH,
Haywards Heath, West Sussex. December 28

HEALTH AND HARMONY

From Mr Stephen Bayley

Sir, The other day the Muzak system in the local medical centre waiting-room was playing Bob Dylan's *Knocking on Heaven's Door.*

It really added to a feeling of inner peace and harmony whilst preparing for an interview with the doctor. *Yours faithfully,*
STEPHEN BAYLEY,
Bridport, Dorset. December 29

A DODGY NEW YEAR

From Mr Ernest Todd

Sir, Perusing my new diary, I observe that the first day of what many believe is truly the new millennium may be written, for once, in exactly the same manner in both Great Britain and the United States without causing ambiguity (01/01/01).

I also notice with unease that this has a somewhat binary look about it, and trust my computer understands this date for what it is. *Yours etc,*
ERNIE TODD,
Long Hanborough, Oxfordshire.
December 29

2001

LOOKING BACK IN ANGER

From Mr Dennis Rolfe

Sir, Many years ago I saw Kubrick's film *2001*. That date is now upon us and no manned mission to Jupiter seems imminent. Orwell's *Nineteen Eighty-Four* has been and gone and no *Big Brother* arose. The Eagle's *Dan Dare*, "pilot of the future", was set in 1997, yet no Martian Treens or Mekon have appeared. I now have no more fictional milestones to look forward to.

Is it the future that's not what it used to be, or will it be the past that's not up to my expectations? *Yours faithfully,*
DENNIS ROLFE,
London NW3. January 2

GREATLY EXAGGERATED

From Lord Stokes

Sir, With reference to your interesting report today regarding a 1969 report by the "late Lord Stokes", I hasten to assure you that although I may be sometimes late, I am still very much alive.

A very happy new year to you.

Faithfully,
STOKES,
House of Lords. January 4

WEATHERSPEAK

From Mrs E. J. Sharland

Sir, Not only does our weather appear to be changing, but also the language in which it is described. "Mistiness", although no doubt technically correct, caused a certain amount of alarm, but "sleatiness" is, surely, both invented and unnecessary.

Yours faithfully,
SUSAN SHARLAND,
Lenham, Kent. January 5

From Mr Dave Hepworth

Sir, Isn't "sleatiness" simply a bad spell of weather? *Yours faithfully,*
DAVE HEPWORTH,
Bakewell, Derbyshire. January 6

From Mr Peter Stamford

Sir, When forecasting rain or snow, our weather forecast readers in Ontario will often say: "You will experience active clouds today." The clouds have been very active this winter. *Yours sincerely,*
PETER STAMFORD,
Port Elgin, Ontario, Canada. January 6

BEST OF TIMES?

From Mr David Prockter

Sir, Of the three columns on today's Comment page, Philip Howard's refers to "the best of times and the worst of times", Mary Ann Sieghart's states that "the country can easily find itself in a Micawberish mess" and Richard Morrison's opens with a quotation from Thomas Gradgrind.

What the Dickens is going on?

Yours faithfully,
DAVID PROCKTER,
Marlborough, Wiltshire. January 6

ACCIDENTALLY CREATIVE

From Mr Alan Millard

Sir, I read about creative people being prone to accidents with a mixture of joy and sadness.

As someone who has, among other things, amputated his tie cutting the hedge, melted his polyester trousers lighting a bonfire, watched his glasses being eaten by a cow whilst relaxing in a meadow, ignited his jacket after putting a pipe in the pocket and speared his toe with the prong of a gardening fork, I was pleased to discover that research suggests I might be imaginative and open-minded, but sorry to learn that I am unlikely to succeed as a train driver or air traffic controller.

It seems a shame that creative people like me are likely to be debarred from giving others the ride of a lifetime.   *Yours sincerely,*
ALAN MILLARD,
Lee-on-the-Solent, Hampshire. January 9

LANGUAGE LEARNING

From Mr Ian P. S. Proud

Sir, My late father spoke many languages, Hebrew, Arabic, French, German, two West African dialects and usable Greek and Spanish.

No matter what the language, his advice was that there were only two phrases one needed anywhere in the world: "How much?" and "My friend will pay."

It works, and is a great ice-breaker.
Yours faithfully,
IAN P. S. PROUD,
Ealing, London W5. January 10

MONKEY BUSINESS

From Dr Don Rolt

Sir, Monkey with jellyfish genes (report, January 12)? There must be a sting in the tail.   *Yours etc,*
DON ROLT,
Surbiton, Surrey. January 13

IT'S A WEIGHTY PROBLEM

From Mr Paul D. Mudd

The correct way to calculate your body mass index (Weekend, January 6) is from the subject's mass in kilograms divided by the square of the height in metres.
Yours faithfully,
PAUL D. MUDD,
Wednesfield, West Midlands.January 13

BADGER SOLUTION

From Mr John Rotheroe

Sir, The problem of badgers on farmland (reports, January 10 and 11) is easily solved. Merely extend set-aside to include sett-aside. Subsidies always adjust agricultural attitudes.   *Yours faithfully,*
JOHN ROTHEROE,
Tring, Hertfordshire. January 17

SINGULAR SOLUTION

From Mr Mark Smith

Sir, It's obvious what's wrong with hunting. It's unfair. There should only be one dog.
Yours faithfully,
M. SMITH,
Ely, Cambridgeshire. January 20

SAVING BACON

From Mr Richard Crisp

Sir, I am eating a sandwich labelled "reformed ham". Whatever the ham had done wrong, one presumes it is now cured.
Yours faithfully,
RICHARD CRISP,
Weybridge, Surrey. January 23

From the Reverend John Cosgrave

Sir, Your correspondent Richard Crisp is obviously unaware of the recent declaration by an Italian Roman Catholic theologian that fast food is essentially Protestant in ethos (report, November 10, 2000).

Perhaps the "reformed ham" in his sandwich had not committed an offence, as he had assumed, but was simply derived from a pious, law-abiding Protestant piglet.
Yours etc,
JOHN COSGRAVE,
London SW3. January 30

IN MOODY MODE

From Squadron Leader Jack Arkinstall, RAF (retd)

Sir, The more time I spend on my computer the more I am convinced that, like humans, they have good days and bad days.

For example, I will shut down the computer at night, having had a good day, expecting the same the following day. But my expectations are often too optimistic. Like a rebellious child it disobeys my instructions and produces inscriptions such as:"This programme has performed an illegal operation", but really meaning you.

You press on hoping that the mood will change, but often if you press too hard the screen will freeze and you are powerless to do anything except simulate a power cut, allow things to cool down, then start up again.

Sometimes this is enough to change the mood but not always. *Yours faithfully*,
JACK ARKINSTALL,
Chichester, West Sussex. January 25

From Lieutenant-Commander Alec Tilley
Sir, Like Squadron Leader Arkinstall, I often have to shut down my frozen computer by simulating a power cut, but when I start it up again it reproves me insolently for what I have done, and warns me never to do it again.

Typing in extracts from the Naval Discipline Act about behaving with contempt towards its superior officer has very little effect. *Yours faithfully*,
ALEC TILLEY,
Hambledon, Hampshire. January 30

From Mr David Berry
Sir, Having been associated with aeroplanes, has Squadron Leader Arkinstall forgotten about gremlins? They used to cause havoc in our flying machines but have now obviously moved on to pastures new.

Mind you, some of those old "difficulties" were often attributed to the operator, one Pilot Officer Prune. But it is not for me to cast aspersions – I have the same computer difficulties myself.

Another Squadron Leader (retired), I am, Sir,
Yours faithfully,
DAVID BERRY,
Chippenham, Wiltshire. January 30

From Mr James Blythe
Sir, Not only do computers have moods (I have found a definite link with certain meteorological conditions), but they also appear to have distinct personalities.

I do not regard myself as being superstitious, and I am sceptical of the emotional complexity of most inanimate objects, but I do confess that I try to be sensitive to the feelings of any PC I use, lest it feel undervalued and become difficult to work with.
Yours faithfully,
JAMES BLYTHE,
Fulwood, Preston. January 30

From Mrs Peter Halliwell
Sir, My computer's attitude (ranges from judgmental ("long sentences are difficult to understand") to downright malign. It autocorrected the word "co-operative", from which I had missed the hyphen, to "copulative" in an accountancy report on an elderly client, as in "Mr Smith was very . . ." *Yours faithfully*,
ROMY HALLIWELL,
North Baddesley, Hampshire. February 3

From Captain John Speller, RN
Sir, Last weekend my computer suffered the attention of my two-year-old grandson who, whilst I was away for only a few moments, managed to wipe at least six months' worth of recently acquired computer programming skill from my machine and left me with, worst of all, no calendar.

However, he is a dab hand at programming and operating the video machine, so it is not all negative. *Yours faithfully*,
JOHN SPELLER,
Pitch Green, Buckinghamshire. February 3

From Mr Richard Marques
Sir, I disagree that computers have moods. They are simply powerful toys; thus, like men, they are incapable of having true emotions. *Yours sincerely*,
RICHARD MARQUES,
Balham, London SW12. February 3

From Mr Steve Turner
Sir, The cause of the problem in 97.3 per cent of cases is a simple fault with the nut

attached to the keyboard. I trust you find this useful.   *Yours etc,*
STEVE TURNER,
Enfield, Middlesex. February 3

From Mrs Judith A. White

Sir, My computer never reprimands me for something I have done but always takes the blame on himself, sending me messages as: "This computer has performed an illegal operation and will now shut down."

This reinforces my belief that my computer is male because a) he can only do one thing at a time, and b) he doesn't always understand my perfect instructions.

Yours sincerely,
JUDITH A. WHITE,
Ely, Cambridgeshire. February 3

From Mr David P. Lintott

Sir, I always refer to any machine I work on as "Annie". This was the name of my first girlfriend. She was equally ungiving and unforgiving.   *Yours etc,*
DAVID P. LINTOTT,
Chislehurst, Kent. February 3

From Mr Colin Pountney

Sir, Lieutenant-Commander Tilley should realise that his computer, in this case, is his superior officer.   *Yours faithfully,*
COLIN POUNTNEY,
Broughton, Northamptonshire. February 3

From Squadron Leader Martin A. Locke, RAF (retd)

Sir, Leave the wretched thing switched on. (Oops, sorry.)   *Yours etc,*
MARTIN LOCKE,
Astley, Shrewsbury SY4. February 3

From Mr Clive Standbridge

Sir, The people offering deferential words or gestures to placate their computers are amateurs. The professional response is foul verbal abuse.

Intractable cases warrant physical measures.
Yours faithfully,
CLIVE STANDBRIDGE,
Tylers Green, High Wycombe. February 9

From Mr John Hughes

Sir, After many years' service to the Scotch whisky industry, I was honoured to be appointed a "Keeper of the Quaich".

When I was drafting a piece on my career for inclusion in a forthcoming book about whisky, my computer challenged quaich, preferring quiche.   *Yours sincerely,*
JOHN HUGHES,
Inchbrakie, Perthshire. February 9

A SUITABLE CASE

From Mr John Mellin

Sir, Four suitcases for Posh Spice?

In the 1950s I knew an elderly farmer who embarked on the only holiday of his long lifetime – a trip to the Isle of Man. He stood, in best suit and polished boots, waiting for my father to drive him to the railway station.

"Where is your suitcase?" asked my father. The old man produced a spare shirt collar from his pocket. "Nay, lad," he said, "I'm only going for the week."   *Yours faithfully,*
J. A. MELLIN,
Utley, Keighley, West Yorkshire. January 30

PERFECT PORRIDGE

From Dr Anthony Parsons

Sir, Like Bruce Miller (Weekend, January 13) my family has a porridge recipe: boil 1 jug (1.14l) water, add 1 mug (227g) oatmeal and 1 teaspoon (5ml) sea salt, return to boil, stir, cover, leave for 1 hour. Transfer to casserole; heat in oven for 4 hours.

Yours faithfully,
ANTHONY PARSONS,
St Neots, Cambridgeshire. January 20

From Mr W. Gordon McPherson

Sir, Two recipes have appeared in your columns recently for the making of porridge. What the end product of these can be like I do not know, but it is certainly not Scottish porridge.

This is how you make the real thing, as

used over the years – in my own case nearly a century.

First, throw away your measures, cups and litres and what not. Porridge-making is an art, not a science. All you need is boiling water, a bowl of oatmeal, a little salt and your own common sense, plus a little experience.

Take a handful of meal and trickle it slowly into the pot, stirring with the spurkle all the time, to prevent knotting. After a few minutes, the meal all in and the porridge beginning to thicken, stir in a little salt and set aside to simmer for five to ten minutes, giving a stir now and again. Pour into the plates.

There is a sensuous pleasure in the making of porridge – the delightful aroma from the pot as the boiling water begins to take hold of the meal, the pouring into the plates, which fills the room with scent of warm meal.

The proper way to sup porridge is to have alongside the plate a bowl of top of the milk or cream – a spoonful of porridge, then a dip in the bowl.　　　　*I am, Sir, yours,*
W. G. McPHERSON,
Huntly, Aberdeenshire. January 31

From Professor Calum Carmichael

Sir, When I was a youngster in Port Ellen, Islay, my piping teacher, Alastair Logan, would stir his porridge atop his peat-fired oven, all the time listening intently to whatever piobaireachd I was practising. After the porridge was made he put it in the oven and added some more peat to keep it warm till morning.

Also put into the oven were his large woollen socks, which, so far as I could make out, were never washed. He worked at the Lagavulin distillery and the socks gave off a pleasant odour which I attributed to a combination of heather and Islay malt.

Sincerely,
CALUM CARMICHAEL,
Department of Comparative Literature,
Cornell University, New York. February 2

From Mr Colin MacNeill

Sir, Always eager to improve my own porridge technique (oatmeal, water, salt, leave overnight then boil while stirring), I note that Dr Anthony Parsons recommends one hour standing time followed by four hours in the oven.

Does this mean that a) Dr Parsons eats his porridge at lunchtime, b) he has staff to rise in the middle of the night to prepare it for him, or c) he uses the traditional technique of making the porridge in bulk and pouring it into a drawer, from which portions can be cut and reheated as and when needed?　　　　*Yours faithfully,*
COLIN MacNEILL,
Edinburgh. February 2

From Sir David Serpell

Sir, Prepare porridge how one may, it can still be enhanced, as a family dish, by a treacle well. For this, each breakfaster, while remaining seated, should raise a fully charged spoonful of golden syrup as high as possible above his or her plate, and try to ensure that the descending globule of syrup penetrates the exact centre of the porridge. This can be surprisingly difficult, and a poor aim may be penalised.

Over-enthusiastic parents have been known to show off by standing on their chairs, but this should be discouraged.

Yours faithfully,
DAVID SERPELL,
Dartmouth, Devon. February 2

From Sir Robert Sanders

Sir, My wife, who is English, makes excellent porridge from a recipe culled from *The Scotsman* some 40 years ago.

The whole principle of porridge-making is to continue to add pinches of fresh meal as the porridge boils, so that when the dish is ready you will have a complete gamut of textures from fully boiled to almost raw meal. The moment when the salt is added is also important, for the first and bulkiest portion of the meal should have swelled and burst before this happens.

Tradition prescribes a birchwood bowl with a horn spoon, and that they (porridge to me is always a plural noun) should be eaten standing up.

I submit this letter with some diffidence, first because I make porridge in the microwave with porridge oats, and second because my wife says I might as well save my breath to cool my porridge.   *Yours faithfully,*
ROBERT SANDERS,
Crieff, Perthshire. February 6

From Mr John Farman

Sir, The recent correspondence on the making of perfect porridge has been a revelation for this Sassenach. For me, however, perfection lies in equal measures of porridge oats, milk and water, sweetened to taste and microwaved in a Pyrex basin until boiling causes the mixture to rise. At this stage the lily can be gilded by the addition of slices of peach.

Eat from the basin (and drink from the measure, a standard cup is ideal) for economy of washing up. At least this part should appeal to the Scot.   *Yours sincerely,*
JOHN FARMAN,
Hitchin, Hertfordshire. February 6

From Mrs Maureen Hawkins

Sir, For those without benefit of peat fires, piobaireachd or, God help us, a porridge drawer, may I commend my recipe: two dessert spoons full of porridge oats; mix with approx four fluid ounces of milk; microwave for $5^{1}/_{4}$ minutes on high; add a spoonful of honey to sweeten.

The result is a sort of porridge soup, one of the few things I am able to eat and enjoy on the actual morning of preparation.
Yours faithfully,
MAUREEN HAWKINS,
c/o St Elizabeth Hospice, Ipswich.
February 8

From Dr Anthony Parsons

Sir, Contrary to Mr Colin MacNeill's suggestions, the secret of giving my breakfast porridge four hours in the oven is not rising in the middle of the night but "setting the timer to turn the oven on four hours before breakfast", a useful phrase that was cut from my original letter (Weekend letters, January 20).   *Yours faithfully,*
A. M. PARSONS,
St Neots, Cambridgeshire. February 8

From Mr Jim Christie

Sir, As every woman married to a Scotsman knows, the only person who made perfect porridge was that Scotsman's mother.
Yours sincerely,
JIM CHRISTIE,
Abingdon, Oxfordshire. February 9

From Mr Huw James

Sir, It does not much matter how you prepare your porridge the night before. The important thing is that in the morning you should, before anybody eats it, throw it out.
Yours faithfully,
HUW JAMES,
Llanishen, Cardiff. February 9

A CALL FOR PHONE BOXES

From Mr Paul Motte-Harrison

Sir, Even in this age of mobile phones the telephone box will continue to be of use. Recently I saw an individual enter a box and, either for privacy or to lessen the traffic noise, proceed to make a call on his mobile.   *Yours faithfully,*
P. MOTTE-HARRISON,
Shoreham-by-Sea, West Sussex. January 31

SLEEP DEPRIVATION

From Mr John de Bono

Sir, Ellen MacArthur's success rested on an ability to cat-nap (report, February 13). How do I enter my four-month-old son for the next round-the-world race? He has four hours' sleep a night, with no stretch longer than 20 minutes, and is positively thriving. I am not.   *Yours faithfully,*
JOHN de BONO,
West Kirby, Wirral. February 15

FIRST CUCKOO JOURNALIST?

From Dr David Viner

Sir, Yesterday the first journalist of this year called us here at the Climatic Research Unit at the University of East Anglia to ask: "Is spring getting earlier?"

This beats the previous earliest recording of this annual question (1999 – coincidentally the warmest year of the last millennium in the British Isles) by four days.

Is this a record?   *Yours faithfully*,
DAVID VINER,
University of East Anglia, Norwich.
February 22

E-MAIL'S UPS AND DOWNS

From Mr David Shamash

Sir, Why are e-mail addresses always shown in lower case?

The Internet cares not a jot if the addresses are in upper, lower, or a mixture of cases and it's actually quite difficult to write one out by hand in lower case clearly enough to be unambiguous without using a four-year-old's style of handwriting.   *Yours faithfully*,
DAVID SHAMASH,
Wantage, Oxfordshire. February 28

from professor humphrey hodgson

sir, i agree with mr david shamash (letter, march 1) that the convention for the use of lower case in e-mail is illogical. myself, i blame E. E. CUMMINGS.   *yours faithfully*,
humphrey hodgson,
london n10. march 7

From Mr James Whitehead

Sir, Don't blame e. e. cummings for the exclusive use in e-mail of lower case; none of my computer-literate friends has heard of him.

However, they all know k. d. lang.
Yours faithfully,
JAMES WHITEHEAD,
Great Gransden, Cambridgeshire. March 13

From the Reverend Henry Gordon

Sir, On the subject of upper and lower case

and e-mails. Obviously, with so many free servers the whole industry is under capitalised.   *Yours faithfully*,
HENRY GORDON,
Rhyl, Denbighshire. March 12

From Mr Kevin Lowe

Sir, I am sure that all Internet keyboard-using amateurs will agree that lower case addresses are fine. The problem is with using the shift key to find "@".

I attach the first signature to the petition to substitute ; or ' or No.   *Yours faithfully*,
KEVIN LOWE,
Portadown, Co Armagh. March 14

MURPHY'S LAW, QED

From Mr L. S. Cockerham

Sir, I heard on the radio this morning that 150,000 secondary-school children are going to drop pieces of buttered toast next week in an attempt to verify (or otherwise) Murphy's Law – ie, that if something can go wrong, it will.

They're wasting their time. Under Murphy's Law, a dropped piece of buttered toast will always fall butter side downwards – unless it is being dropped as a demonstration of Murphy's Law.

By the way, what happens to the toast afterwards?   *Yours faithfully*,
L. S. COCKERHAM,
Harrogate, North Yorkshire. March 6

From Mr Howard Toon

Sir, It has long been a matter of fact that buttered toast always falls to the ground sticky side down.

Conformists will be pleased to note that the same is also true of the newly released self-adhesive postage stamps.   *Yours faithfully*,
HOWARD TOON,
Loughborough, Leicestershire. March 6

From Mr Stuart Kind

Sir, Murphy's Law is not tested by the dropping of buttered toast. Murphy's Law, better known as the Law of Unconsidered Outcomes, deals with such matters as the headmaster slipping on the toast and breaking his leg.

One of the chapters in my book *The Sceptical Witness* (Hodology, 1999) considers the matter at length.   *Yours faithfully,*
STUART KIND,
Harrogate, West Riding of Yorkshire.
March 9

From Mr David J. O. Llewellyn

Sir, While Murphy's Law applies when toast falls buttered side down, the same is also true should the piece fall buttered side up. It merely means that Murphy's Law applied at an earlier stage of the process, that is to say, the wrong side of the toast was buttered.   *Yours faithfully,*
DAVID J. O. LLEWELLYN,
Hawkhurst, Kent. March 9

From Mr Julian Dolman

Sir, Never butter the toast until after you have dropped it.   *Yours etc,*
JULIAN DOLMAN,
Shelsley Beauchamp, Worcestershire.
March 9

From Mr Steve Palmer

Sir, It is Sod's Law that decrees that toast will land buttered side down, not Murphy's Law.

Murphy's Law states that if something can go wrong, it will. Sod's Law is that if there are two possible outcomes to a situation, the less favourable will occur.   *Yours faithfully,*
STEVE PALMER,
Penwortham, Preston. March 10

From Mr Terry Cottrell

Sir, For some while now, Murphy's Law has been undermined by open telephone kiosks. Murphy's Law stated that regardless of the direction from which you approached a telephone box, the door was always on the other side.

If this sort of thing is allowed to continue, who knows where it may lead.

Yours faithfully,
TERRY COTTRELL,
Winterbourne Down, Bristol. March 10

From Mr Mike Tait

Sir, I have always understood that Murphy's Law reads in part: ". . . if a number of people simultaneously drop their buttered toast, yours is the only piece to land butter side down".   *Yours faithfully,*
MIKE TAIT,
Malvern, Worcestershire. March 10

From Mr Michael Forrest

Sir, Mr Terry Cottrell mourns the loss of the enclosed telephone box as a public exemplar of Murphy's Law because its door was always on the "wrong" side.

But the new open ones serve equally well. Whichever way the box faces, the wind will always be blowing from that direction.

Yours faithfully,
MICHAEL FORREST,
Sonning, Reading, Berkshire. March 14

From Mr Julian Corlett

Sir, Mr Terry Cottrell wonders where the escalation of Murphy's Law may lead.

This morning my partner broke the yolk of one of two fried eggs being prepared for our breakfast and, citing Murphy's Law, made the unilateral decision that the broken egg was mine.   *Sincerely,*
JULIAN CORLETT,
Scunthorpe, North Lincolnshire. March 14

From Father Bryan Storey

Sir, It is not quite fair to say that Murphy's Law states that if something can go wrong, it will. For that Law is emphatic that when this occurs, it is at the worst possible time.

Yours truly,
BRYAN STOREY,
Tintagel Catholic Church, Cornwall.
March 17

From Mrs Amanda Sloan

Sir, Some time ago there was a televised trial where slices of buttered bread were launched from a "trebuchet". On grass the ratio of butter up to butter down was 50:50, but as soon as a carpet was laid on the landing area the ratio tipped dramatically in favour of butter down.

> *Yours sincerely,*
> AMANDA SLOAN,
> London SW11. March 17

From Dr D. H. Frean

Sir, The proof of Murphy's Law is surely that things sometimes unexpectedly go right. *Yours truly,*
> DAVID FREAN,
> Lichfield, Staffordshire. March 17

From Professor Ian Fells, FREng

Sir, In 1991 I made a TV programme, with Bob Bootle of the BBC, exploring the validity of Murphy's Law.

The programme was scheduled to be broadcast on BBC1 on what turned out to be the first day of the Gulf War, not auspicious timing. For once, however, things went well and, to our surprise, eight and a half million people watched the show.

But the making of the programme itself was dogged throughout by Murphy's Law. Captain Ed Murphy, after whom the law was named by his exasperated commanding officer (Philip Howard's Comment, March 9), was discovered alive and well in the US, but when we went to interview him we found he had Alzheimer's disease and could remember nothing.

When we came to put the voiceover on to the programme the recording apparatus wouldn't work properly, until we discovered that someone had fixed the microphone insert the wrong way round. These kinds of frustrations went on for six tortured weeks.

We finally concluded that it is not Murphy's Law, with its insistence that if a thing can go wrong it will, but O'Reilly's Law we should heed. O'Reilly's Law states that Murphy's Law is wildly optimistic.

> *Yours faithfully,*
> IAN FELLS,
> Newcastle upon Tyne. March 20

From Mr David Wright

Sir, Some weeks ago I was about to comment on Murphy's and Sod's Laws, but I didn't think there would be any interest.

Since then, you've printed many letters (March 6, 9, 10, 14, 17, 20). *Yours faithfully,*
> DAVID WRIGHT,
> Derby. March 22

From Mr Peter Bennett

Sir, In Mr David Wright's letter on Sod's Law, you refer to previous letters published on March 6, 9, 10, 14, 17 and 20. Are these this week's winning lottery numbers?

If I don't buy a ticket, the numbers will come up. *Yours faithfully,*
> PETER BENNETT,
> Harold Wood, Essex. March 23

WELSH WHINGEING

From Mr K. J. Marks

Sir, Following Anne Robinson's gratuitous insult to the Welsh people on the BBC's *Room 101* programme, the Council of Bards should impose a Taffwah. *Yours etc,*
> K. J. MARKS (Welshman in exile),
> Wothorpe, Lincolnshire. March 8

From Mr Michael Bissmire

Sir, It was recently, and controversially, asked: "What are the Welsh for?".

I was brought up to believe that our purpose in God's scheme of things was to keep the Irish and the English apart.

> *Yours faithfully,*
> M. J. BISSMIRE,
> Bissmire Fudge & Co (solicitors),
> Haverfordwest, Pembrokeshire. March 22

EXPENSIVE BABIES

From Mr Ed Thompson

Sir, Having a baby costs £20,000 over the first five years.

Since our son Benedict was born eight weeks ago our social life has collapsed and we have rarely left the house. If we keep this up for the next five years we should see a healthy profit. *Yours etc,*
> ED THOMPSON,
> Southampton. March 8

BROTHERLY LUVVIE

From Mr Philip Havers, QC

Sir, My brother is a famous actor. Or so I thought. According to your Law report to-day he is now also a QC.

It was bad enough being asked: "Are you the actor or the other one?" Now I am not even the other one.   *Yours faithfully,*
PHILIP HAVERS,
London EC4. March 8

From Mr Terry Walsh

Sir, The confusion encountered by Mr Philip Havers, QC, reminds me of the headmaster who at a reunion of his old boys asked one of them: "Was it you or your brother who was killed in the war?"
Yours faithfully,
TERRY WALSH
(Secretary, Alleyn Club), Dulwich College,
London SE21. March 12

EDUCATION GAP

From Mr Tony Hodges

Sir, At 7 o'clock this morning I received an urgent mobile text message from my 18-year-old daughter on a gap year in Sydney. "Hi Dad, how long do you boil potatoes for? We are cooking sausage and mash."

This from a girl who has received the finest education an overdraft can buy. Has the system or the family failed her?
Yours faithfully,
TONY HODGES,
Nottingham. March 12

From Mr James Taylor

Sir, Upon leaving my cavalry regiment in 1982 and taking up residence in London, I certainly did not know how long it took to boil a potato, or even an egg for that matter.

Realising my difficulty, my mother kindly sent me a book entitled *Cooking for Bachelors – A Simple Guide.* Turning to the chapter on cauliflower cheese, it began: "Make a white sauce in the usual way." I am afraid I threw the book away.   *Yours faithfully,*

JAMES TAYLOR,
London SW5. March 15

From Mr Guy Abel

Sir, We get mobile-phone calls from up-stairs – inquiring whether there might be a cup of tea on the go.   *Yours faithfully,*
GUY ABEL,
West Stow, Suffolk. March 15

From Mr David Fillery

Sir, Mr Tony Hodges should not be alarmed that his daughter should ask the cooking time for potatoes. It is not he who has failed her but the system. Obviously the local supermarket had run out of ready-cooked meals.   *Yours faithfully,*
DAVID FILLERY,
West Malling, Kent. March 19

From Mrs Caroline Harwood

Sir, One evening at 9.15 I received a tel-ephone call from my son at Edinburgh University asking me how to cook pheas-ant. Details of making bread sauce, fried breadcrumbs, gravy and other accompani-ments were also sought. After some further exchange of news, he said: "Well, better start cooking, we've got ten coming for dinner in half an hour."   *Yours faithfully,*
CAROLINE HARWOOD,
Pednor, Buckinghamshire. March 19

From Mr John Fidler

Sir, Some few weeks after the marriage of our eldest daughter, she telephoned late on a Sunday morning, and asked: "Is that the Custard Advisory Council?" It was.
Yours &c,
JOHN FIDLER,
Lancaster Royal Grammar School. March 21

TALEBAN'S INTOLERANCE

From Mr Ian McDonald

Sir, Much as we may abhor the destruction of the great statues by Taleban, we should consider the act as a reminder of the Bud-dha's teaching on impermanence.

It may help if we remember that, with an

absolute certainty, there will come a time when nobody will remember Taleban.

Yours faithfully,
IAN McDONALD,
Ness, South Wirral. March 26

WET BLANKET

From Mr Gavin Littaur

Sir, It was a shock to read that the last 12 months were the wettest since records began in 1766. It only rains here twice a week; once for three days and once for four days.
Yours faithfully,
GAVIN LITTAUR,
London NW4. March 27

From the Reverend Nick Percival

Sir, Prior to moving to the North East I was informed that I would encounter wet and windy conditions for three months of the year and that the other nine months are winter.
Yours sincerely,
NICK PERCIVAL,
South Shields, Tyne and Wear. March 30

From Mr John Cosslett

Sir, The Reverend Nick Percival bemoans the absence of summer in the North East. As we walked through the grounds of the Peterhof Palace outside St Petersburg on a beautiful day last August, I realised how lucky I was when my guide told me that it was the first really fine day for five weeks.

"Here," she said, "summer is nine months of anticipation and three months of disappointment."
Yours sincerely,
JOHN COSSLETT,
Cardiff. April 3

From Sir George Engle, QC

Sir, Byron knew what he had left behind: "The English Winter – ending in July, To recommence in August" (*Don Juan*, Canto xiii, stanza 42).
Yours faithfully,
GEORGE ENGLE,
London N6. April 6

From Mr Richard Barber

Sir, Mr John Cosslett's letter on the weather

in St Petersburg recalls some important horticultural advice I heard one April morning, when I was living in the West of Scotland. It was given by the local radio's gardening expert, who said: "At this time of year, you must never forget how, in Scotland, spring can fade imperceptibly into autumn."
Yours sincerely,
RICHARD BARBER,
Kingston upon Thames, Surrey. April 10

GUARANTEED TO LAST

From Mrs Susan Harley

Sir, On my new umbrella there is a notice – "Limited Lifetime Guarantee". How long may I expect it to last?
Yours faithfully,
SUSAN HARLEY,
London W9. March 27

From Mr David Fraser

Sir, I suspect that the life expectancy of Susan Harley's umbrella will revolve around when she takes it on a train, subsequent to which it will join mine in happy retirement at the lost property office.
Yours faithfully,
DAVID G. FRASER,
Littlehampton, West Sussex. March 28

A GAME OF CHANCE

From Mr David Ponte

Sir, Recently I contacted the City of Westminster to request information on gaming for a new project. Two days later I received a package full of useful pointers for those interested in retailing pheasant, duck and guinea fowl.

This is not going to be easy.
Yours faithfully,
DAVID PONTE
(Co-owner) Momo Restaurant, London W1. April 16

BANK HOLIDAY BLUES

From Mr Colin Baser

Sir, Today my wife and I drove from Bristol to our friends in Devon. Most of the journey was in heavy traffic and on several occasions we came to a halt.

While applauding the success of Mr Blair's appeal to us to visit the countryside, I don't think he intended us all to go on the same day.   *Yours faithfully,*
COLIN BASER,
Portishead, Bristol. April 17

From Mr Peter J. K. Tither

Sir, Please, no more bank holidays. We have enough cold, damp, miserable days in this country as it is.   *Yours faithfully,*
PETER J. K. TITHER,
Cydweli, Carmarthenshire. April 17

From Mr Gerald Moggridge

Sir, An extra public holiday to mark Nelson's victory at Trafalgar? What a splendid idea! Will it be backdated?   *Yours faithfully,*
GERALD MOGGRIDGE,
Sutton, Surrey. April 20

PASSING THE BUCK?

From the Reverend J. D. Wright

Sir, It seems quite unjust to blame a safari park antelope for the BSE crisis (headline, April 19). I am sure that it would rather not have been used to make animal feed.
Yours sincerely,
J. D. WRIGHT,
Brighton, East Sussex. April 21

WISDOM OF YOUTH

From Mrs Isabelle Laurent

Sir, Walking with my daughters to school, we passed the third roadworks to spring up at the end of our road in as many months, prompting my five-year-old to say: "Oh look, they're building a new traffic jam!"
Yours faithfully,
ISABELLE LAURENT,
London NW3. April 23

From Mr David Mowat

Sir, Mrs Isabelle Laurent's daughter who saw workmen "building a new traffic jam" is on a par with the roadworks sign in County Wicklow, "Pot holing in progress".

Yours faithfully,
DAVID MOWAT,
Formby, Liverpool. April 26

TEACHERS' 35-HOUR WEEK

From Professor J. N. Fawcett

Sir, My late schoolmaster father, when confronted with complaints from other workers about his long holidays, always replied to the effect that, although he had more days of holiday, he was on holiday only from 9am to 3.30pm whereas their holidays were from 7.30am to 5.30pm.

Yours faithfully,
J. NEVILLE FAWCETT,
Embleton, Northumberland. April 24

CARRY ON CADDY

From Mr Robert Maxtone Graham

Sir, Some eighty years ago my father asked a new girlfriend whether she shared his passion for golf. Shaking her head, the beauty murmured that she did not "even know how to hold the caddy" (report, April 23).

He did not ask for her hand in marriage.
Yours faithfully,
ROBERT MAXTONE GRAHAM,
Sandwich, Kent. April 26

DEMANDS ON NHS

From Dr Peter Hegarty Johnson

Sir, I would like to write a letter about GPs' workload but I really don't have time. Next!   *Yours,*
P. H. JOHNSON,
Wallasey, Wirral. April 28

BASEMENT BARGAIN

From Dr Paul Davison

Sir, Whether by accident or design, today in their Aberdeen branch, Woolworth displayed a sign offering "buy one, get one" for their own-brand batteries.

A canny marketing strategy, but would it work outside Aberdeen?   *Yours faithfully,*
PAUL DAVISON,
Kintore, Aberdeenshire. April 30

TENSION IN THE TORY PARTY

From Mr Tim Evans

Sir, I was amused to spot on your front page today: "Mr Townend, who has insisted that he will not be silenced, refused to comment." *Yours faithfully,*
TIM EVANS,
Leeds, West Yorkshire. May 1

MENTAL PICTURES

From Dr F. B. Rutterford

Sir, You say that Albert Camus described an intellectual as "someone whose mind watches itself". I once heard an intellectual described as someone who can listen to the William Tell Overture without thinking of *The Lone Ranger.* *Yours sincerely,*
F. B. RUTTERFORD,
Dover, Kent. May 7

From Mr John R. Waters

Sir, Many years ago, in the customary arrogance of youth, I rather fancied myself as an intellectual, but then I came across W. H. Auden's poem:

To the man in the street, who,
I'm sorry to say,
Is a keen observer of Life,
The word Intellectual suggests straightaway
A man who's untrue to his wife.

It cured me. *Yours faithfully,*
J. R. WATERS,
Faringdon, Oxfordshire. May 12

From Mr Tim M. Hicks

Sir, I have always subscribed to the theory that a true intellectual is someone who, left in a room alone with a tea cosy, will not attempt to try it on. *Yours sincerely,*
TIM M. HICKS,
Awsworth, Nottinghamshire. May 12

FLEXIBLE FRIEND

From Mrs Pippa Lewis

Sir, My two-year-old granddaughter, passing a fountain, was fascinated by the coins in it. Holding out her palm she said:

"Money please." I searched my purse and pockets but had no small change.

Undaunted, the little hand came out again: "Card please." *Yours faithfully,*
PIPPA LEWIS,
Lydiard Millicent, Swindon. May 8

CANADIANS DEBATE ROLE OF THE QUEEN

From Mr D. J. Doyle

Sir, To change our form of government to a republic (report, May 19) would require the approval of all ten provinces. To get two provinces to agree on the time of day would be a major victory. So the Queen is safe in Canada for a long time.

Yours faithfully,
D. J. DOYLE,
Winnipeg, Manitoba, Canada. May 24

From Mr Paul Woodman

Sir, If Canadians did agree on the time of day there could be some pretty dark mornings in Vancouver. *Yours faithfully,*
P. J. WOODMAN,
Grantham, Lincolnshire. May 25

SUMMER'S LEASE

From Mrs Julie Goddard

Sir, Seeing the fruit tree blossom being blown like confetti across the lawn, I remember the line "Rough winds do shake the darling buds of May" and wonder if the climate has really changed over the 400 years since it was written. *Yours faithfully,*
JULIE GODDARD,
Newbury, Berkshire. May 29

NOT QUITE ETERNAL

From Mr Peter D. Spencer

Sir, If the French think the "eternal flame", which a man tried to extinguish by sitting on it, has been burning since 1921, I could tell them differently.

A couple of years ago my wife and I were at the Arc de Triomphe early one morning. Along came two cleaners to wash and mop the memorial. Unfortunately the water put out the flame, but a cigarette lighter was brought out and normality resumed.

Yours truly,
PETER D. SPENCER,
Leicester. June 4

PLAY ON WORDS

From Mr Anthony Baker

Sir, Your obituary of Jack Watling (May 24) contains a notable mondegreen (mondegreen: non-dictionary word for a mishearing, as in "They ha' slain the Earl o' Moray, And Lady Mondegreen" – instead of "and laid him on the green").

The title of Rattigan's play (which presumably underwent oral transmission at some stage) is not *Wild Sunshine*, but *While the Sun Shines*.   *Yours faithfully*,
ANTHONY BAKER,
Winscombe, Somerset. June 5

From Dr David Gardner

Sir, I am grateful to Mr Anthony Baker for his enlightenment on the nature of a mondegreen. I had laboured for many years under the illusion that the correct term was a gladly.

This derived from my childhood memory of singing in Sunday School a hymn with the line "Gladly, my cross-eyed bear".

Yours sincerely,
DAVID GARDNER,
St Albans, Hertfordshire. June 13

From Mrs P. M. Hickley

Sir, When I was a child my father was watching me and my friends learning a folk dance to the tune *A Merry Conceit*. On asking the name of the music, he was bemused to hear it was "American Seat". I still can't hear the difference.

Yours faithfully,
TERESA HICKLEY,
Lowestoft, Suffolk. June 13

From Mr Keith Kemp

Sir, Some years ago, a Scottish friend of my mother mentioned casually to her that the Countess of Ayr was coming for tea the following day.

It turned out to be the county surveyor.

Yours faithfully,
KEITH KEMP,
Frome, Somerset. June 13

From Miss Jane Asher

Sir, I claim personal mondegreen status, having recently received a letter addressed to "Mr J. Nasher" and opening with the greeting "Dear Mr Nasher".

Yours faithfully,
JANE ASHER,
London SW3. June 13

From Mrs Gwen Chessell

Sir, An eminent physician of my acquaintance told me some years ago of a delightful mondegreen perpetrated by his secretary. She misheard a word in a paper he was dictating to her for publication in a leading medical journal. She typed "jockstrap position" instead of "juxtaposition" (fortunately spotted by the editor).

Yours faithfully,
GWEN CHESSELL,
Uplyme, Devon. June 15

From Mr James N. D. Hay

Sir, Another (Lady) Mondegreen recollection:

I was once majestically written to by a colleague as James Hay, "Solicitor and not a republic". It caused some amusement in the office.   *Yours faithfully*,
JAMES N. D. HAY
(Solicitor and notary public),
Aberdeen. June 18

From Mr Gerry Hanson

Sir, As a civil servant in the 1950s I heard of an official who received a memo from his boss's secretary inviting him to attend a "haddock-stirring committee".

The puzzled official's superior had dictated "ad hoc steering committee".   *Yours truly,*
GERRY HANSON,
Iver Heath, Buckinghamshire. June 18

From Sir Antony Jay

Sir, The richest source of mondegreens is the transcription service for BBC live broadcast talks.

I once said: "To quote Clough, 'Say not the struggle nought availeth'," and found it transcribed as: "To quote fluff, 'Up the struggle naughty bailiff'." *Yours etc,*
ANTONY JAY,
Langport, Somerset. June 20

From Ms Helen Grayson

Sir, Here is a fine example, spotted by a friend. A teletext subtitler rendered an introduction to poet, essayist and critic Tom Paulin as "poet, SAS and critic".

Yours faithfully,
HELEN GRAYSON,
Horsforth, Leeds, West Yorkshire. June 21

From Mr Raj Kothari

Sir, I rang Directory Enquiries for The Wig and Pen Club. The operator apologetically informed me that there was no listing for a Pen Club in Wigan. *Yours faithfully,*
RAJ KOTHARI,
Bridport, Dorset. June 21

From Mr David Hide

Sir, Many years ago as a junior secretary my wife misread her shorthand for "quasi". Her episcopal boss was fortunately sharp-eyed enough to avoid the accusation that he had described the Church Lads' Brigade as a "crazy military organisation".

Yours sincerely,
DAVID HIDE,
Jesmond, Newcastle upon Tyne. June 21

From Mrs Jeannette Joiner

Sir, An advert in the *West Briton* (July 5) reads: "Competent chef required by quality restaurant . . . No time wasters or pre-Madonnas."

Was there life before Madonna?
JEANNETTE JOINER,
Falmouth, Cornwall. July 13

KIT AND CABOODLE

From Mrs Paddie Breeze

Sir, I keep two small screwdrivers in my kitchen to repair domestic appliances which my husband, who has 34 screwdrivers in his toolbox, borrows.

I recognise that men tend to hoard tools, but can a man ever have too many screwdrivers? *Yours faithfully,*
PADDIE BREEZE,
Hawksworth, Leeds, West Yorkshire. June 20

From Mr Peter Gathergood

Sir, Mrs Paddie Breeze asks if a man can have too many screwdrivers. Certainly not.

I have a comprehensive collection, displayed to good effect in a tasteful, recently extended, wooden rack in my garage.

The fact that I seldom use any of them is neither here nor there, and will not deter me from seeking more of these essential and useful implements. *Yours faithfully,*
PETER GATHERGOOD,
Kings Lynn, Norfolk. June 22

From Mrs Frances Stott

Sir, There is no need for Mrs Paddie Breeze to keep screwdrivers in her kitchen. The sharp end of a potato peeler serves admirably for all minor domestic screwdriving purposes. *Yours faithfully,*
FRANCES STOTT,
Devizes, Wiltshire. June 25

From Mrs Pauline Baycroft

Sir, We acquired a surprise addition to our assortment of screwdrivers when collecting from the police station our recovered stolen car radio. In the bag with it was a new screwdriver, presumably the one used by the thief to prise out the radio.

Yours faithfully,
M. P. BAYCROFT,
Potters Bar, Hertfordshire. June 27

From Mr Roger Guthrie

Sir, With regular application of the right type of screwdriver – three parts freshly

squeezed orange juice to one part vodka poured over crushed ice – those urgent household repairs can be prioritised, postponed, or indeed forgotten about altogether.   *Cheers,*
ROGER GUTHRIE,
Hexham, Northumberland. June 27

From Mr Frank P. Dilkes

Sir, Reading the several letters you have published about having a multiplicity of screwdrivers, reminds me of the old Irish saying: "It will come in handy, even if you never use it."   *Yours faithfully,*
F. P. DILKES,
Walsall, West Midlands. June 29

From Mr Peter Tray

Sir, As an avid follower of this correspondence, I am beginning to wonder whether an obsession with screwdrivers might stem from some subconscious Freudian fear of having a screw loose?   *Yours faithfully,*
PETER TRAY,
London N12. June 29

From Mrs Anna Conlong

Sir, As someone teaching Italian students about English language and culture, I have found your correspondence on screwdrivers an invaluable aid. It demonstrates both English eccentricity and the English sense of humour. It is also much easier to explain to foreigners than mondegreens.
Yours faithfully,
ANNA CONLONG,
Durham. July 2

MEASURE FOR MEASURE

From Mr Quentin Langley

Sir, For the first time today I heard the BBC (on the *Today* programme) using the size of Belgium as a unit of measurement instead of the traditional British measure, the size of Wales. Has there been a directive on European harmonisation? If so, will the French ignore it and carry on using the size of Corsica?

For those who are interested, there are 1.47 Waleses to the Belgium.   *Yours faithfully,*
QUENTIN LANGLEY,
Woking, Surrey. June 28

NATURE, RED IN TOOTH AND CLAW

From Mr David Crease

Sir, Many people compare the killing of foxes by dogs with killing by shooting, and conclude that shooting is more cruel. The comparison that is always omitted is the natural death of a fox, by disease, starvation or both. That is perhaps the most cruel.

Man may sometimes be cruel, but nature is never kind.   *I am, Sir, yours etc,*
DAVID CREASE,
Scampston, North Yorkshire. July 3

WARNING SIGNS

From Dr David Bryant

Sir, I have just returned from a shopping trip where I saw a large, bright yellow sign in the car park. The notice announced that the police were "Carrying out covert operations in the area".

No wonder crime detection isn't what it used to be.   *Yours,*
DAVID BRYANT,
St Margaret's, Twickenham. July 5

From Mr Stephen Hedley

Sir, Following the sign announcing that the police were "Carrying out covert operations in this area", I think I may have discovered their headquarters. It's located in Shropshire and is highlighted on a big yellow sign with an arrow, saying "Secret Bunker".   *Yours faithfully,*
STEPHEN HEDLEY,
Church Broughton, Derbyshire. July 12

HIGHLY STRUNG WINNERS

From Mr Greg Hopkins

Sir, Congratulations to the three Ivanisevics who, together with the epitome of sportsmanship, Pat Rafter, treated us to a Wimbledon Men's Final like never before.

In that final we saw Goran, the affable, talented and intense player; Groan, the player who, on repeated championship points, kept fans worldwide on the edges of their seats whilst he served double faults; and Organ (a euphemism for a more common Anglo-Saxon term), who swore and argued with the umpire.

Who, more than these three, deserved to achieve their lifetime ambition?

Yours sincerely,
GREG HOPKINS,
Beaconsfield, Buckinghamshire. July 11

From Mrs Christine Crispin

Sir, The stress of Tim Henman's matches caused my 33-year-old daughter to watch TV from behind the settee, something she has not done since the first appearance of the Daleks.   *Yours faithfully,*
CHRISTINE CRISPIN,
Saline, Fife. July 11

RULE OF THE ROAD?

From Mr John Clark-Maxwell

Sir, Nowadays it is clear that qualified drivers think their instructors have told them: "Your horn should be used only to signal your reproach."   *Yours faithfully,*
JOHN CLARK-MAXWELL,
Swallowfield, Berkshire. July 16

PERFECT TIMING

From Mr Tony Whelpton

Sir, That the femtosecond (report and leading article) is an incredibly tiny period of time is beyond dispute, but it has in fact been known in this household for some time as a "Gigi". The reason for this is quite simple: it is the time that elapses between our changing the cat's litter tray and the cat's (the eponymous Gigi) deciding that she desperately needs to use it.

Yours faithfully,
TONY WHELPTON,
Cheltenham, Gloucestershire. July 18

From Dr John Thurston

Sir, The femtosecond may be defined as the interval between the traffic light changing to green and the person in the vehicle behind sounding their horn.   *Yours faithfully,*
JOHN THURSTON,
Sevenoaks, Kent. July 24

From Dr Kieran Sweeney

Sir, In our house, the femtosecond denoted the time which elapsed between putting on a fresh nappy, and its being filled by a grateful, gurgling infant.   *Yours sincerely,*
KIERAN SWEENEY,
Exeter, Devon. July 24

From Mr David Colvin

Sir, The shortest perceptible slice of time is the ohnosecond: that infinitely painful moment between shutting the front door and realising that your keys are still inside the house.   *Your obedient servant,*
DAVID COLVIN,
London SW1. July 24

From Mr J. M. Yarnall

Sir, In my days as a civil servant, a femtosecond was the time it took at inter-departmental meetings for the Home Office representative to deny responsibility for any issue raised in discussion.

Yours faithfully,
J. M. YARNALL,
Kingston upon Thames, Surrey. July 25

From Mr Devsiri P. Hewavidana

Sir, A femtosecond is the period of time between water in the shower getting absolutely freezing cold and becoming burning hot. Ten years after installing the new shower I have yet to master the technique.

Yours sincerely,
DEVSIRI P. HEWAVIDANA,
Ashford, Kent. July 25

From Mr John Bell

Sir, The femtosecond is the time it takes for the smile to leave the face of an airline's chief flight attendant as he walks from Club Class to Economy Class.

> Yours faithfully,
> JOHN BELL,
> Wellington, Somerset. July 28

From Mr Evan M. Davies

Sir, In my street the shortest space of time is that between a car leaving a parking space and another occupying it.

> Your faithfully,
> EVAN M. DAVIES,
> Farnham, Surrey. July 28

From Mr John J. Carney

Sir, For a teacher, a femtosecond is the time it takes to prepare a lesson when asked to cover for an absent colleague.

> Yours faithfully,
> JOHN J. CARNEY
> (Teacher, Thanet College, 1964-96),
> Tankerton, Kent. July 28

From Mrs Maureen Nyazai

Sir, A femtosecond in this household is the time between asking for help with the washing up and teenagers finding an immediately urgent reason why they have to decline.   *Yours faithfully,*

> MAUREEN NYAZAI,
> Godalming, Surrey. August 2

From Mr Keith H. R. Cowell

Sir, The femtosecond is the interval between British manufacturers saying that a weak pound makes it difficult for them to buy raw materials overseas, and their saying that the strong pound makes it difficult to sell their goods overseas.   *Yours faithfully,*

> KEITH H. R. COWELL,
> Hayling Island, Hampshire. August 6

From Mr Stanley Armstrong

Sir, For cruciverbalists, to which fraternity I belong, a femtosecond is the interval between a clue being utterly obscure and blindingly obvious.   *Yours faithfully,*

> STANLEY ARMSTRONG,
> Malvern Link, Worcestershire. August 6

FAST DAY?

From Mrs R. Bennett

Sir, Spotted on a local takeaway menu: "Open 7 days a week including Bank Holidays, closed Tuesday."   *Yours faithfully,*

> R. BENNETT,
> Swadlincote, Derbyshire. July 21

NOT AS ADVERTISED

From Mrs Allison Walker-Morecroft

Sir, The label on my face cream affirms that it is "energizing". My shower gel claims to be "motivating". Neither works.

> Yours faithfully,
> ALLISON WALKER-MORECROFT,
> Norwich, Norfolk. July 23

From Mr David A. Leahy

Sir, I share something of Mrs Walker-Morecroft's frustrations with beauty products that fail to fulfil their promises. The vanishing cream I bought my wife hasn't worked, either.   *Yours faithfully,*

> DAVID A. LEAHY,
> Altrincham, Cheshire. July 26

TAKE NO NOTICE

From Mr Ray Perkins

Sir, I spied the following sign in a car park on the Isle of Wight:

Toilets Pay & Display

I declined.   *Yours faithfully,*

> RAY PERKINS,
> Kingsdown, Corsham, Wiltshire. July 28

SAFETY FIRST

From Mr R. V. Taylor

Sir, You report that the body of the Bronze Age hunter who was probably killed by an arrow in the back went on show "where tourists were able to view it through bulletproof glass".

Why do images of stable doors and bolting horses spring to mind?   *Yours sincerely,*

> R.V. TAYLOR,
> Radley, Oxfordshire. August 2

SPECIAL DELIVERY

From Mrs N. G. D. Sabin

Sir, We have today received a postcard addressed: "No 60, the road that Putney footbridge ends up on, on the opposite side of the river to Putney Bridge Station".

It was postmarked Paris, July 30.

Yours faithfully,
LINDSAY SABIN,
London SW15. August 4

From Sir Henry Marking

Sir, A few years ago, when I was on holiday in California, I sent a card addressed to "Tom, Fruit and Vegetable Stall at Corner of Oxford St and Orchard St, London W1".

Tom, a good-humoured Cockney, told me on my return: "I got yer card. Couldn't read it. You've got a doctor's 'andwritin."

Yours faithfully,
HENRY MARKING,
London W1. August 13

From Mrs Barbara Parkin

Sir, We were surprised and a little embarrassed to receive a postcard from Italy addressed:

Mr & Mrs P. Parkin, A 4 bedroomed detached house with 3 toilets, Up the hill from the showhouse, Evesham, Worcs.

Yours faithfully,
BARBARA PARKIN,
Evesham, Worcestershire. August 13

From Mrs Mary Caroe

Sir, A few years ago I bought a pair of shoes by mail order. I gave my address to the salesman, who remarked how wonderfully rural it sounded.

The parcel arrived the next day. The label read: "Mrs Caravan, Tumbledown, Surrey."

Yours faithfully,
MARY CAROE,
Vann, Hambledon, Surrey. August 16

From Mr David Walton

Sir, Some years ago when I lived in Livingstone, Zambia, I received a letter from Lusaka, the capital, correctly addressed but weeks late.

Among the numerous back stamps the envelope had collected in its travels the last was Livingstone, Canada, with an inscription "Try Livingstone, Zambia".

The letter had also visited Scotland and New Zealand.

Yours truly,
DAVID H. WALTON,
Crowland, Peterborough. August 24

From Mr K. R. Donald

Sir, In 1960 I received a letter addressed: "K. R. Donald, Windsor Castle." The envelope was marked: "Unknown in the Royal Apartments."

The letter was delivered to me on board the Union Castle mailship Windsor Castle in Cape Town where I was serving as Second Purser.

Full marks to the Royal Mail.

Yours faithfully,
KEITH DONALD,
Christchurch, Dorset. August 24

From Viscount Norwich

Sir, It may not have required any particular ingenuity on the part of the Post Office to deliver to me a letter addressed to "The Discount Norwich", but it certainly made my day.

Yours faithfully,
JOHN JULIUS NORWICH,
London W9. August 25

From Mr Shimon Cohen

Sir, When in 1949 Rabbi Immanuel Jakobovits (later Lord Jakobovits, Chief Rabbi of Great Britain and the Commonwealth, 1967–90) was appointed Chief Rabbi of Ireland, a newspaper there announced that "Jack O'Bovits is the new Chief Rabbi".

From that day on and for the next 40 years Lord Jakobovits's copy of Time magazine arrived addressed to "The Very Rev Jack O'Bovits, Chief Rabbi".

Yours etc,
SHIMON COHEN
(Private Secretary to Lord Jakobovits, 1983–90),
London WC2. August 25

GOOD HEALTH

From Mr John Wheeler

Sir, From time to time my wife emerges from behind some magazine or other to issue pronouncements on what is good or not good for my health.

Apparently, the consumption of five different fruits a day is a jolly good thing. I couldn't agree more. I assume that white grapes and red grapes can be counted separately, and that sparkling grapes qualify as a third. A wide selection of heavily distilled plums, apricots, oranges or peaches would make a splendid fourth, but for the fifth I have a small problem. Does the hop count as a fruit?   *Yours faithfully,*
JOHN WHEELER,
Walton-on-Thames, Surrey. August 13

TRICKY PROJECT

From Mrs Sara Mason

Sir, I was interested to read that B. Winder PhD, University of Sheffield, has been awarded a grant by the Leverhulme Trust to research the question: "Can old dogs be taught new tricks?"

Is this a canine research project, or can I put my husband up for study?   *Yours faithfully,*
SARA MASON,
Stroud, Gloucestershire. August 17

MOT JUSTE

From Mr Roger Foord

Sir, It was good to see that in the true manner of today's support for dead friends, the manager of the gravel pit where the giant carp died (report and photograph, August 20) said that he, personally, was "gutted".
Yours etc,
ROGER FOORD,
Chorleywood, Hertfordshire. August 22

VINTAGE PLANE CRASHES

From Group Captain John Featherstone, RAF (retd)

Sir, Given the very highest standards of airworthiness and the added benefit of the tender loving care lavished on them by their owners, it is not vintage aircraft that are a danger to the public at air shows. The real danger lies in the vintage pilots who insist on flying them.   *Yours faithfully,*
JOHN FEATHERSTONE,
Deal, Kent. August 27

UNDERSTANDING SPIN

From Professor Sir Alan Peacock, FBA

Sir, Establishing a "school of spin" in Downing Street (report, August 22) invites speculation about the difference between a diplomat and a spin-doctor. We know that the diplomat is sent to lie abroad for his country, whereas the spin-doctor is kept at home to lie to his country.   *Yours sincerely,*
ALAN PEACOCK,
Edinburgh. August 27

LEMON JUICE AND DVT

From Mr Stephen Phillips

Sir, Consumption of lemon juice has long been known to benefit scurvied wretches forced to subsist on lousy food whilst travelling in cramped, insanitary conditions.

No surprise, then, that lemon juice has been recommended to air travellers fearing deep vein thrombosis (report, August 20).
Yours faithfully,
STEPHEN L. PHILLIPS,
Longton, Preston. August 28

EQUAL FACILITIES

From Dr Andrew P. Brooks

Sir, The NHS should have no worries about its equal opportunities policy. A nearby hospital has the sign: "Nappy changing facilities are available in the gents toilet opposite the restaurant."
Yours faithfully,
ANDREW P. BROOKS,
Twyford, Winchester, Hampshire. August 28

UNDESIRABLES

From Ms Donna Lynde

Sir, In respect of Eric Bourlier's objections

to the enclosed millionaires' village being built in Provence (report, August 28), it has been my experience that such developments are a great help to local villages and customs. They keep the riff-raff in. *Yours*,

DONNA LYNDE,
Newark, Nottinghamshire. August 30

FOUR-MINUTE MILE AND GCSE MATHS

From Mr David Hibler

Sir, Before we take young Arran Fernandez's achievement in passing his maths GCSE as conclusive proof that the exam is in fact trivial, we should remember Groucho Marx's observation: "A child of five could understand this. Fetch me a child of five." *Yours faithfully*,

DAVID HIBLER,
Tenterden, Kent. August 31

CURIOUSER AND CURIOUSER

From Mr Nick Ingham

Sir, Today there were 18 1p coins on the grave of Ludwig Wittgenstein at the Parish of the Ascension Burial Ground in Cambridge. Originally – some days ago – there were four, spread about; and then five in a little pile to one side. This morning there were 15 neatly underlining his name. Now there are three more, still neatly lined up.

Over the years numerous small objects have been placed on the grave including a lemon, a pork pie, a Mr Kipling cupcake and a Buddhist prayer wheel. It is all very intriguing. *Yours faithfully*,

NICK INGHAM,
Cambridge. September 3

WASPS IN RETREAT

From Mr Alastair Hume

Sir, Whilst visiting an amusement park in France recently, our lunch at the open air cafe was disturbed by an hysterical small girl who had been stung on the foot by a wasp. The madame who ran the cafe lit a cigarette, which seemed rather offhand, but then she began to move it about immediately above the sting.

In an astonishingly short time the little girl was calm, and was able to put on socks and trainers and walk out of the cafe. Madame told me that it was "far better than any cream" and could be used generally for stings.

Given the presence of wasps in my garden, should I take up smoking for medicinal purposes ? *Yours faithfully*,

ALASTAIR HUME,
London N1. September 4

MARCONI'S WOES

From Mr Fraser Ashman

Sir I know that when in a hole I should stop digging.

As a Marconi shareholder who failed to sell at £12.50 I now also know that when I reach the summit, I should stop climbing.

Yours faithfully,
FRASER ASHMAN,
Altrincham, Cheshire. September 8

CURSE OF TERRORISM

From Mr Vikram Singh

Sir, Of all the words George W. Bush could have used to consolidate his response to these appalling events the most injudicious has to be "crusade" (report, September 17).

Yours faithfully,
VIKRAM SINGH,
Bristol. September 18

WHEELER-DEALING

From Mr Paul Gilbert

Sir, The reason so many people need to use large 4 x 4 "off-road" vehicles to deliver children to school is that very few manage to park with all four wheels on the road.

Yours sincerely,
PAUL GILBERT,
Solihull, West Midlands. September 19

A SEASONAL TIP

From Dr Arthur Hollman

Sir, To pick blackberries easily, get a 5in or larger plastic flowerpot and make two holes in the rim opposite each other. Attach a 3ft length of string to the holes and place the loop round your neck.

The flowerpot will hang at waist level, and leave both hands free for picking the fruit.

Yours faithfully,
ARTHUR HOLLMAN,
Pett, East Sussex. September 24

From Mr John McGuire

Sir, Dr Arthur Hollman's letter brings to mind our autumn family picnics. We lived in North Cheshire at the time, with an abundance of canals, and the best place in the world to pick the fruit was the bank opposite the towpath.

Using canoes, which we packed on the roofrack of the jalopy and hand-propelled through the water, pounds of berries could be picked in a short time. Only father was allowed the walking stick to reach the higher runners.

Did we fall in? Only the dog.

Yours faithfully,
JOHN McGUIRE,
Minehead, Somerset. September 29

From Commander M. F. Griffey, RN (retd)

Sir, In the midst of all the current doom and gloom, how refreshing to read Dr Hollman's letter. His scheme will certainly work if the drainage hole is not too big or the blackberries too small. I can't wait to see a row of pickers in our Somerset lanes with flowerpots suspended from their necks.   *Yours faithfully,*
M. F. GRIFFEY,
Peasedown St John, Bath. September 29

From Mr James Gibson

Sir, I staggered from one idiocy to another in dealing with the news in today's issue, and then reached this page with Dr Holl-man's "seasonal tip" on what to do with a plastic flowerpot.

Thank goodness for the English – it has set things in proportion for me. Do keep them coming.   *As ever,*
JAMES GIBSON,
Quorn, Leicestershire. September 29

From Mrs Sylvia Barry

Sir, Dr Hollman's blackberry-picking tip makes me wonder about juice dripping from the hole in the flowerpot. Maybe a large PVC apron would be useful?

Yours faithfully,
SYLVIA BARRY,
Harpenden, Hertfordshire. September 29

From Mrs Jo Miles

Sir, A small flowerpot is a waste of time when picking family-sized quantities of blackberries for the entire winter, plus all those needed for jelly. A decent-sized children's beach bucket is ideal, and you can loop it over your arm and still pick with two hands.

I don't have time to bother adapting a flowerpot!   *Yours productively,*
JO MILES,
Surlingham, Norfolk. October 2

From Mr J. G. Todd

Sir, The drawbacks in Dr Hollman's use of a flowerpot for blackberry-picking may be overcome by using instead a two or three-litre plastic milk container. Cut down between the hole and the handle for a few centimetres, then across to the side away from the handle, thus forming a large opening.

A piece of string through the handle completes a large, juice-tight container which is stable both on the ground and suspended round the neck.   *Yours faithfully,*
J. GEOFFREY TODD,
Harrogate, North Yorkshire. October 2

From Mr J. H. Anderson

Sir, Trials over the weekend show that Dr Arthur Hollman must be quite short. A 3ft length of string left the flower pot hanging well above my belly-button rather than at the waist, and I'm only 5ft 8$^{1}/_{2}$in.

I suggest the string should be 2x+3in long where x is the distance from the user's waist to the back of his neck (following the contours).
Yours faithfully,
JOHN H. ANDERSON,
Alciston, Nr Polegate, Sussex. October 2

From Mr David Wilson

Sir, Whatever methods your correspondents adopt to protect themselves from stains while picking blackberries should now be shelved till next summer: according to country lore, after September, blackberries are said to belong to the Devil.
Yours faithfully,
DAVID WILSON,
Bridell, Cardigan. October 2

DON'T TALK WET

From Mr John Scott Latham

Sir, I was intrigued to hear on the lunchtime forecast yesterday, Michael Fish say that "here would be the wettest rain". How is this measured?
Yours faithfully,
JOHN LATHAM,
Takeley, nr Bishop's Stortford, Hertfordshire.
September 27

From Mr Stephen Podger

Sir, Having stood out in many different types of rain, from a ten-minute tropical downpour in Sri Lanka to a "bracing" sea breeze on the beach at Skegness in February, I can assure Mr John Scott Latham that the wettest rain I have encountered by far is a good week-long Yorkshire drizzle when camping in the Dales.
Yours faithfully,
STEPHEN PODGER,
Newark-on-Trent, Nottinghamshire.
October 1

From the Reverend Iain K. Stiven

Sir, Poetry offers an insight into comparative wetness. Michael Fish says: "Here would be the wettest rain."

According to Rupert Brooke in his poem *Heaven*, fish say:
But somewhere, beyond space and time
Is wetter water, slimier slime
... in the Eternal Brook
Celestially wetter than any human worldly wettest rain?
Yours sincerely,
IAIN K. STIVEN,
Edinburgh. October 3

MOBILE ETIQUETTE

From Mr Ben Bolton

Sir, When the mobile telephone line goes dead, who should call whom back? Do class, rank or seniority have any relevance?
Yours faithfully,
BEN BOLTON,
Epsom, Surrey. October 5

From Dr Cris Whetton

Sir, Ben Bolton asks who should call back when a mobile telephone link is accidentally broken.

Here in Finland it is customary for those attending meetings to place their mobile telephones on the table at the end of business. Whoever has the oldest or least sophisticated model then pays for the first round of drinks. Perhaps the same principle could be adopted for restoring broken links.
Yours faithfully,
CRIS WHETTON,
Tampere, Finland. October 9

From Mr Lester May

Sir, Ben Bolton should follow the old rule I was taught as a midshipman: the caller must always reestablish the connection. Thus is avoided the possibility of both parties redialling only to hear the engaged tone.
Yours faithfully,
LESTER MAY,
Camden Town, London NW1. October 9

From Mr Rory Newman

Sir, When my girlfriend used to phone me, before we got a shared phone, the line used to go mysteriously dead as I answered. Seeing the name of my love on the screen, I

would immediately phone her back. It took me ages to work out why my bill was so much higher than hers. *I am, Sir, etc,*
RORY NEWMAN,
London E5. October 9

From Mr Christopher Barnett
Sir, Whoever disturbed the peace by calling in the first place. *Yours faithfully,*
CHRIS BARNETT,
Temple Ewell, Dover, Kent. October 9

From Dr Geoffrey R. Horton
Sir, While delayed for several hours recently in an airport departure lounge, I was able to formulate the First Law of Mobile Phone Etiquette.

This states that the volume with which an individual speaks into the phone is in inverse proportion to that individual's personal importance. *Yours slightly deafened,*
GEOFFREY HORTON,
Inverkip, Inverclyde. October 11

From Mr Richard Polkinghorne
Sir, The Second Law of Mobile Phone Etiquette appears to be that the length of the call is in inverse proportion to the meaningful content. *Sincerely,*
RICHARD POLKINGHORNE,
Dursley, Gloucestershire. October 13

From Mr Mike Chitty
Sir, Here in Somerset it is customary for those attending harvest to place their mobile telephones on the trailer at sunset. However, contrary to Dr Cris Whetton's Finnish experience, here whoever has the newest or most sophisticated model pays for all the drinks.

Mine's a pint of Barn Owl, please Cris.
Yours faithfully,
MIKE CHITTY,
Wells, Somerset. October 13

From Mr Michael Bland
Sir, Having on many occasions witnessed the frustration of mobile phone users cut off in the prime of an apparently vital conversation, I feel that it is time for someone to publish *The Mobile Phone User's Guide to the Tunnels of the British Railways.*
Yours faithfully,
MICHAEL BLAND,
Caversham, Reading. October 20

DEFINING TERRORISM

From Mr Roland White
Sir, How do you have a war on terrorism when history has shown in country after country that Monday's terrorists are Wednesday's freedom fighters and Friday's government ministers? *Yours faithfully,*
ROLAND WHITE,
Bognor Regis, West Sussex. October 8

RELIGION AND CONFLICT

From Mr Simon Kingsley–Pallant
Sir, In the current state of global anxiety, could you publish a map showing the whereabouts of the moral high ground?
Yours faithfully,
SIMON KINGSLEY-PALLANT,
Petersfield, Hampshire. October 9

From Mr Eric Humphreys
Sir, Mr Simon Kingsley-Pallant asks for a map showing the whereabouts of the moral high ground in the current crisis.

It has surely never been more straightforward to produce such a map. It would show New York City, highlighting the World Trade Centre – and the Statue of Liberty.
Yours faithfully,
ERIC HUMPHREYS,
Bury St Edmunds, Suffolk. October 11

From Mr Jim Harrison
Sir, I have just stumbled across the following maxim in *Black's Law Dictionary* (West Publishing Co, 1891):

Iniquissima pax est anteponenda justissimo bello ("The most unjust peace is to be preferred to the justest war").

Yours faithfully,
JIM HARRISON,
Muswell Hill, London N2. October 10

FUTURE OF RAIL INDUSTRY

From Mr Richard Posner

Sir, On the demise of Railtrack I was depressed to hear on the radio that rail services are expected to continue as normal.

Yours faithfully,
RICHARD POSNER,
West Bridgford, Nottingham. October 10

LIVING TOGETHER?

From Miss Sheila Thompson

Sir, Seeking a little light relief from the news bulletins I switched to a popular classical music programme. I was soon rewarded on hearing the presenter – anxious no doubt to place the music in its correct historical setting – tell us: "This piece was played for Queen Victoria and her partner, Prince Albert." *Yours sincerely,*
SHEILA THOMPSON,
Aylesbury, Buckinghamshire. October 18

EARNING OR LEARNING?

From Mr Bill Kirkman

Sir, As a schoolboy in the 1940s I heard the late Sir Robert Wood, Principal of the (then) University College of Southampton, proclaim at a school speech day:

The advantage of a classical education is that it teaches you to do without the money it makes you unable to acquire.

Yours faithfully,
BILL KIRKMAN,
Willingham, Cambridge. October 23

BY THE BOOKER

From Mr Richard J. Hildesley

Sir, Just when I thought I had mastered the semi-colon; they go and kill off the comma. *Yours faithfully,*
RICHARD J. HILDESLEY,
Windsor Forest, Berkshire. October 23

From Mr A. E. Grant

Sir comma I am not particularly bothered by the absence of commas since comma with Times Millennium font comma I can distinguish commas from full stops comma only with the use of a magnifying lens full stop *Yours faithfully comma*
A. E. GRANT,
Taunton, Somerset. October 26

WHOSE DAY IS HOLIER?

From the Reverend Ian C. Bell

Sir, I am puzzled. If it is wrong to bomb Afghanistan on the Muslim holy day, why is it right to bomb it on the Christian holy day? *Yours faithfully,*
IAN C. BELL,
Mildenhall, Suffolk. October 25

KEEP TRACK OF NATURE

From Mr Colin McLean

Sir, The latest rail timetable supplement from West Anglia Great Northern begins: "Dear passenger, The leaf-fall season is upon us."

This is preceded no doubt by the leaf-grow and full-leaf seasons and followed, surely, by the leafless season.

Vivaldi's Four Leaf-Lives, anyone?

Yours sincerely,
COLIN McLEAN,
Newmarket, Suffolk. October 27

GLOBAL CLIMATE

From Mr Barry Jones

Sir, Farmers thinking of grubbing up apple trees in favour of planting walnuts would do well to remember the old saying that if you plant a walnut tree when your son is born, it will bear its first walnuts when he is old enough to get married and yield just enough timber to make him a coffin at the end of his natural life.

Hardly a solution to an ailing agrarian economy! *Yours faithfully,*
BARRY JONES,
Bishop's Cleeve, Gloucestershire.
November 1

HONESTY IN POLITICS

From Mr Michael Hart

Sir, On the *Today* programme this morning in answer to a question by John Humphrys, Iain Duncan Smith replied: "I don't know."

These are not words I have ever heard a politician of any party utter before and Mr Duncan Smith immediately leapt upwards in my estimation.   *Yours faithfully*,
MICHAEL HART,
Mannings Heath, West Sussex. November 1

SLIPPING STANDARDS

From Professor Peter Lantos

Sir, Yesterday *The Sunday Times* reported the loss of confidential Whitehall documents in a Westminster pub. In the past confidential government papers were usually lost in one of the finer restaurants around St James's. Is this a further decline in the standard of our governance?   *Yours faithfully*,
P. L. LANTOS,
The Athenaeum, London. November 6

SHORT AND SWEET

From Mr D. C. Morris-Marsham

Sir, A jar of mincemeat I bought carried the following message: "The contents are sufficient for a pie for six persons or 12 small tarts."   *Yours faithfully*,
DAVID MORRIS-MARSHAM,
London SW12. November 21

JUMBOS NEVER FORGET

From Mr James Ferguson

Sir, I first bought your paper shortly after the 1939–45 war to strengthen my credentials for office advancement. One of the first crossword answers I encountered was "Lohengrin", the clue being "See chicken smile at the opera", or words to that effect.

Since then the doughty knight has reappeared every few years, but with ever more esoteric clues.   *Yours, etc*,
J. G. FERGUSON,

Moreton-in-Marsh, Gloucestershire.
November 22

TENTATIVE ADVANCE

From Mr Richard Goss

Sir, I note that scientists have developed "a pill to conquer shyness".

How will sufferers ask for it?
Yours sincerely,
RICHARD GOSS,
Lavenham, Suffolk. November 29

AUSTEN WIFE-SWAPPING

From Mr Hal Ewing

Sir, Oh dear (clue 14 down, Times 2 Crossword, November 28)! Poor Catherine Morland, dumped at Northanger Abbey as that rotter Henry Tilney scurries off to marry Fanny Price at Mansfield Park.

Yours faithfully,
HAL EWING,
Luton, Bedfordshire. November 28

From Mrs Susan Brittleton

Sir, Now that Jane Austen's characters are allowed to move around from book to book, may I make a plea for Marianne Dashwood, hitherto palmed off, by common consent, with a man twice her age, to be allocated a much younger soldier, the spirited Captain Frederick Tilney, thus leaving Colonel Brandon for her mother?

Yours faithfully,
SUSAN BRITTLETON,
Chipping Sodbury, Gloucestershire.
December 7

From Mr John Robinson

Sir, I take exception to the suggestion by Mrs Susan Brittleton that Marianne Dashwood be "allocated a much younger soldier" with Colonel Brandon receiving her mother's hand in exchange.

As is so often the case in these matters, the feelings of the male half of the couple are completely ignored; here he is forced to give up a spirited, pretty, intelligent young wife for a rather older, rather sillier woman.

Surely some better accommodation could be found for such a well-respected fellow?

Yours faithfully,
JOHN ROBINSON,
Baltimore, USA. December 10

From Mrs W. E. Balfour

Sir, Oh, what a delightful game! I seem to recall Jane Austen hinting that Jane Fairfax did not long survive her marriage to Frank Churchill. After a suitable interval can he find consolation with Mary Crawford?

He would make her a fitting husband, and I think Mary would be kind to the desolate Miss Bates.   *Yours faithfully,*
MARGARET BALFOUR,
Cambridge. December 13

From Mrs Penny Panman

Sir, I have always had misgivings about the lovely Lizzy Bennet's marriage to boring old Mr Darcy. I now realise that her true partner is the adventurous Captain Wentworth, with whom she can sail round the world and enjoy the comradeship of His Majesty's Navy.

This will have the added benefit of consigning elegant, wet Anne Elliot to Mr Darcy, no doubt to the great satisfaction of both their horrible families.   *Yours faithfully,*
PENNY PANMAN,
East Horsley, Surrey. December 15

From Ms Helen Corkery

Sir, In a 44-line poem Rudyard Kipling describes Jane Austen arriving in Heaven, where she is greeted by angels, welcomed by fellow writers and told that she may have her dearest wish. She asks for love.

The archangels search the heavens and in a corner of limbo find a Hampshire gentleman "reading of a book" called *Persuasion*, in which he finds his own love story faithfully reflected. Captain Wentworth, for it is he, did and still does love Jane and the angels bring them together in Paradise.

Yours faithfully,
HELEN CORKERY,
Reigate, Surrey. December 20

A HIGHER DEGREE

From Dr Gavin Westwood

Sir, "Stop hot flushes" (Times 2) reminds me of a patient who, following my inquiry, told me: "Toilets have flushes; I have tropical moments."   *Yours faithfully,*
GAVIN WESTWOOD,
Accrington, Lancashire. December 3

From Mrs Jo Buonaguidi

Sir, "Tropical moments" rather than hot flushes?

Personally I have "power surges".

Yours faithfully,
JO BUONAGUIDI,
Esher, Surrey. December 4

DEEP VEIN THROMBOSIS

From Mr Tony Pristavec

Sir, Alarmed by reports that deep vein thrombosis afflicts not only long-haul fliers but anyone immobilised for long periods in a sitting position, I have returned my tickets for *Parsifal*.   *Yours sincerely,*
TONY PRISTAVEC,
London SE16. December 4

TAKE A LETTER

From Dr John H. Greensmith

Sir, Databases for Christmas card addresses may not be so user-friendly in hands other than those of the compiler.

The daughter of the family, who had been seeking the address of a maternal aunt under various letters – S for the surname; D for Doreen; A for Auntie Doreen – sought her mother's help.

"Look under O," she replied.

"Why?"

"Our Doreen."   *Yours sincerely,*
JOHN GREENSMITH,
Downend, Bristol. December 18

From Mr John Lister

Sir, On my first day at work at the Plain English Campaign I was baffled to find the majority of files empty. The exception was one stuffed to the brim with all previous correspondence - filed under L for letters.

Yours faithfully,
JOHN LISTER
(Press Officer) Plain English Campaign,
High Peak. December 22

From Mrs Felicity Crawley

Sir, In pre-database days, the department of my office which prepared quiz questions made a search for the file on Napoleon. Not under N, nor France, nor Waterloo. On checking with the girl who filed, she replied: "Oh, I filed him under Lovers."

Yours faithfully,
FELICITY CRAWLEY,
London W4. December 24

From Mr Norman Ewles

Sir, Before the advent of word processors my wife was asked to retrieve an important document from the filing system of a fellow secretary who was off sick.

After two hours of fruitless search she had to call the unfortunate girl at home to ask its whereabouts. The reply came back: "I can't spell miscellaneous so I filed it under J for General."

Yours faithfully,
NORMAN EWLES,
Chelmsford, Essex. December 27

From Dr James Rogers

Sir, I streamlined my personal filing system a few years ago, thanks to the introduction of a new section labelled "Miscellaneous".

There has been a gratifying reduction in the time spent filing documents, but curiously I notice it now takes longer to find them again.

Yours faithfully,
JAMES ROGERS,
Bristol. December 29

From Mr Ken Wilkinson

Sir, During my National Service with the Royal Army Ordnance Corps I was a company pay clerk. My colleague and I frequently received unintelligible correspondence from the Royal Army Pay Corps HQ. At a complete loss as to where to file these letters we created a "File for Unfiled Documents", which became our reference in subsequent letters to HQ.

Their replies to us were always headed: "Ref your FFUD dated . . ." It was never queried.

Yours faithfully,
KEN WILKINSON,
Formby, Merseyside. December 29

From Mr Christopher Power

Sir, In 1956, on an expedition to Van in Eastern Turkey, we found that mail for Englishmen at the Poste Restante was always filed under E for Esquire.

An earlier English visitor had obviously not discovered this - his letter was still there, complete with a King George V stamp.

Yours faithfully,
CHRISTOPHER POWER,
Swanmore, Southampton. December 29

From Mrs Sian Flynn

Sir, Purchase of a second-hand filing cabinet delivered my favourite (and most used) file – it was labelled "Old Pending".

Yours (always trying to catch up),
SIAN FLYNN,
Woking, Surrey. December 31

From Mr Timothy Elliott

Sir, The standard definition of a filing cabinet was (and, I believe, still is) "a place where things get lost in alphabetical disorder". It is good to read that computers are not such new technology after all.

Yours faithfully,
T. J. ELLIOTT,
Haynes West End, Bedfordshire. January 3

From Mr Edwin Entecott

Sir, A friend had four trays labelled "In", "Out", "Pending" and "Too Difficult". The last was to store items which solved themselves if left long enough. They either became out of date and could be ignored, or were dealt with by some smart aleck trying to prove how clever he was.

I've tried it. It works.

Yours sincerely,
EDWIN ENTECOTT,
Nuneaton, Warwickshire. January 3

From the Rural Dean of Emlyn

Sir, Page 7 of the Llandaff Diocesan Year Book for 1995 is headed "Useful Addresses". The following page bears the heading "Other Addresses".
Yours faithfully,
HUGH JAMES,
Pencader, Carmarthenshire. January 3

From Major John FitzGerald (retd)

Sir, When I joined the 1st Battalion, The Royal Norfolk Regiment in 1950 my company commander showed me how he had cut "unnecessary" paperwork in his company office. He allowed only two files: "Rugger" and "Any Other Bumf".
Yours etc,
JOHN FITZGERALD,
York. January 5

From the Reverend Jack Scroggie

Sir, In 1844 Abraham Lincoln opened his own law office in Springfield, Illinois. His "filing system" was chaotic.

Papers were everywhere. Many were stuffed into a stovepipe hat. So difficult was the situation that Lincoln had a large envelope inscribed with the message:"When you can't find it anywhere else, look into this."
Yours sincerely,
JACK SCROGGIE,
Balmossie, Dundee. January 5

From Mr Geoffrey Bourne-Taylor

Sir, In a former life, I found myself in the presence of the great Field Marshal Earl Alexander of Tunis. My best attempt at small-talk was:"You must be very busy."

"My dear fellow," he replied, "at 1700 hours each day I transfer the contents of my In Tray to my Out Tray: you'd be surprised how little comes back!"
Yours faithfully,
GEOFFREY BOURNE-TAYLOR
(Bursar), St Edmund Hall, Oxford.
January 5

From Mr James Alexander

Sir, May one inquire as to how you propose to file the voluminous and oft-times banal correspondence on this subject? Oh for the good old days of a protracted dialogue in these columns on such weighty matters as making porridge.

Please feel free to shred this contribution after publication.
Yours faithfully,
JAMES ALEXANDER,
King's Lynn, Norfolk. January 5

COURT DOZING

From Mr Geoffrey W. Davey

Sir, The events at Gloucester Crown Court (report, December 18) remind me of an incident in Darlington County Court some years ago. I appeared as counsel in a turgid boundary dispute before the late Judge Cohen, who was listening to a less than enthralling closing speech from my opponent.

As he sometimes did, the judge closed his eyes. From the back of the court came the comment from a supporter of my opponent's client:"The old b****** has gone to sleep!" Judge Cohen opened one eye and replied: "The old b****** hasn't", and the trial continued to its appointed end.
Yours faithfully,
GEOFFREY W. DAVEY,
Northallerton, North Yorkshire.
December 19

From Mr Robin Miller, Recorder

Sir, During a trial recently I had noticed that a juror appeared to be dozing. Looking at the "culprit", I asked the jury whether anyone had difficulty in concentrating.

He immediately replied that, whenever he wished to concentrate, he closed his eyes. With such an alert juror, I felt it proper to continue, but warned the advocates that brevity was also an aid to concentration.
Yours faithfully,
ROBIN MILLER,
London EC4. December 24

IN THE CHAPEL

From Mrs Anne D. Cringle

Sir, "The white-collar union MSF, which

represents more than 1,500 clergy" (report, December 17). How very appropriate!

Yours faithfully,
ANNE D. CRINGLE,
Burnham Market, Norfolk. December 19

A LITTLE KNOWLEDGE

From Mrs Pauline Pearson
Sir, I, together with other easyJet passengers checking in at Luton airport recently, was asked: "Has anyone put anything in your luggage without you knowing?"

Yours faithfully,
PAULINE PEARSON,
Marlow, Buckinghamshire. December 26

WATER FEATURE

From Mr Roland White
Sir, I notice the trend to carry small bottles of water around. If this was Florence in August one could understand it, but London in December?

Is this a fashion statement I need to catch up with?   *Yours faithfully,*
ROLAND WHITE,
Felpham, West Sussex. December 28

From Mr Tony Harris
Sir, Mr Roland White asks if buying and carrying around bottled water is a fashion statement. Maybe. I can remember a comedy sketch in radio's *Round the Horne* in the Sixties, in which it was said: "We'd even buy water if they advertised it enough!"

It seemed ridiculous at the time.

Yours faithfully,
TONY HARRIS,
Royston, Hertfordshire. December 31

From Mr Benjamin John Sheriff
Sir, Were your correspondent a regular visitor to London, he would become aware that water portage is necessary to deal with Amazonian conditions on the Tube.

Yours faithfully,
BENJAMIN JOHN SHERIFF,
Sutton Coldfield, West Midlands.
December 31

HEIGHT OF FASHION

From Mr Matthew Wetmore
Sir, A back page headline today says: "Moss Bros extends ties."

Just how far will this go? Short people could trip up.   *Yours sincerely,*
MATTHEW WETMORE,
Halesworth, Suffolk. December 29

HAZARD LIGHTS

From Mr Geoff Watson
Sir, A new type of warning sign has been installed near here which flashes a "Slow Down" message when you approach it at more than 30 mph. My six-year-old daughter insists that we speed up as we approach it, "to make the pretty lights flash".

Yours faithfully,
GEOFF WATSON,
Downend, Bristol. December 29

CHURCH, STATE AND WORLD POLITICS

From Mrs Elizabeth Young
Sir, I liked Anatole Kaletsky's quoting of *The New York Times*'s Thomas Friedman's phrase "'Keep rootin' for Putin" (Comment, December 27) but may I suggest a possibly catchier way of putting it:

Whatever happens Putin's got
The oil and gas, and Bush has not.

Yours etc,
ELIZABETH YOUNG,
London W2. December 31

PROGRESS?

From Mr Nigel Hopkins
Sir, I was somewhat amused to receive a letter from Scottish Widows which concluded: "This information is handwritten in the interest of speeding up our customer service."   *Yours faithfully,*
NIGEL HOPKINS,
Sheffield, South Yorkshire. December 31

2002

SHOPS PREPARE FOR E-DAY

From Mr Christopher Meotti

Sir, When I asked my French associates what the euro is divided into, they said centimes.

Could it be that if we look after the pence the pound will look after itself?

Yours faithfully,
C. J. MEOTTI,
London W6. January 1

From Ms Christina Baron

Sir, Here in the centre of Paris it is already clear that the euro has brought a major advantage and a major disadvantage. The parking meters are out of order while they await conversion to euros, but so are the public lavatories.   *Yours faithfully,*
CHRISTINA BARON,
Paris, France. January 18

HEAVENLY SOUND

From Mr Richard Graham-Taylor

Sir, Canon Meirion-Jones asks, how is it that Welsh is the language of heaven? Perhaps because, for a non-Welsh speaker, it takes an eternity to learn that stuff.

Yours faithfully,
RICHARD GRAHAM-TAYLOR,
Douglas, Isle of Man. January 5

From Mr Hugh Tonks

Sir, If Welsh is the language of heaven, why does it have irregular verbs?   *Yours etc,*
HUGH TONKS,
Fulbourn, Cambridgeshire. January 5

From Mr Kenneth Vivian

Sir, It may take Englishmen an eternity to learn the language of heaven, but others will not be similarly handicapped in the after-life.

My adopted dog acquired a working knowledge of Welsh within the space of just a few months.   *Yours truly,*
KENNETH VIVIAN,
Garnant, Carmarthenshire. January 10

From Mr K. Beck-Andersen

Sir, Whenever I have prayed in Danish, my wishes have been met; but if I pray in English I have never had success. Do you think He could have difficulty with my accent?

Yours faithfully,
KAJ BECK-ANDERSEN,
Datchet, Buckinghamshire. January 10

From Mr Julian Thomas

Sir, My grandfather maintained that he always said his prayers in Welsh, because the good Lord would think he was showing off if he said them in English.

Yours faithfully,
JULIAN THOMAS,
Chobham, Surrey. January 11

From Mr David Wilson

Sir, If the language of Wales is that of heaven, does this apply to the weather too?

Yours faithfully,
DAVID WILSON,
Bridell, Cardigan. January 14

From Mr J. W. Simson

Sir, My great grandmother, who lived an eventful but blameless life into the early part of the 20th century, devoted her declining years to learning Hebrew, on the grounds that this was most likely to be the language spoken in Heaven and she would need to be able to get around.

Yours faithfully,
J. W. SIMSON,
Godalming, Surrey. January 17

From Mr Saifur Rahman

Sir, That great European, the Emperor Charles V, is said to have spoken to God in Spanish, to women in Italian and to men in French.

German he reserved for his horse.

Yours etc,
SAIFUR RAHMAN,
Wembley Park, Middlesex. January 17

From Sir Robert Sanders

Sir, I always pray to God in English and He always replies.

Sadly, very often He says: "No."

Yours faithfully.
ROBERT SANDERS,
Crieff, Perthshire. January 17

From Mr John Mills

Sir, Mr J. W. Simson's great grandmother's belief that Hebrew is the language of Heaven has literary support.

In Ronald Firbank's *Concerning the Eccentricities of Cardinal Pirelli*, the Cardinal's boy servant muses: "I hear it's the Hebrew in Heaven, sir. Spanish is hardly spoken." (5 Novels by Ronald Firbank, Duckworth, 1950, page 384). Yours faithfully,
JOHN MILLS,
London NW8. January 21

From Mr Hugh Leonard

Sir, The following is to be found in Kenneth Tynan's diaries. A journalist, on hearing of the death of General de Gaulle, passed the news on to Noel Coward and added: "I wonder what he and God are talking about in Heaven?"

To which the Master replied: "That depends on how good God's French is."

Yours faithfully,
HUGH LEONARD,
Dalkey, Co Dublin. January 21

FUSSY FELINES

From Mr Lionel Lane

Sir, A couple we know are owned by two cats. These animals will eat only good steaks and fine fish, but only from china plates, never from plastic, and they shy at cat food.

Recently their slaves bought a microwave. This has not gone unnoticed and the cats reject all offerings thus fast-cooked.

Why? What do they know?

Yours faithfully,
L. LANE,
Woking, Surrey. January 10

THE DIET TREADMILL

From Mrs Shirley Kennedy

Sir, To diet is not hard. All you do is refrain from buying anything tinned or packaged, laden with salt or sugar. Instead you cook with healthy ingredients.

I find that after hours of pummelling my (saltless) dough into loaves and rolling out and filling my (sugarless) tarte aux pommes, I am far too exhausted to eat either of them.

Yours faithfully,
SHIRLEY KENNEDY,
Clare, Suffolk. January 11

SELECTION PROCESS FOR ARCHBISHOP

From Mr Andrew Underwood

Sir, Why this fuss about the Bishop of Rochester being Roman Catholic in his younger days (report, January 12)? So was the Church of England. Yours faithfully,
ANDREW UNDERWOOD,
Ampthill, Bedfordshire. January 14

From Mr Philip Matthews

Sir, When Clement Attlee asked Churchill why, in 1942, he chose William Temple as Archbishop of Canterbury, he replied: "Because he was the only half-crown article in a sixpenny bazaar."

I wonder what our present Prime Minister will find in the ecclesiastical bazaar?

Yours faithfully,
PHILIP MATTHEWS,
Wilton, Salisbury. January 16

FAMILY MEDICINE

From Mr R. S. Atkins

Sir, As the father of two children aged nine and seven, I read with bemusement that family meals reduce stress in children.

Presumably the researchers were instructed to ignore the effect on the parents.

Yours faithfully,
R. S. ATKINS,
Pulborough, West Sussex. January 21

From Mr John Fender

Sir, Looking for signs of stress in our children, we concluded that they were immune, but carriers. *Yours faithfully,*
JOHN FENDER,
Solihull, West Midlands. January 24

A REALLY STIFF DRINK

From Mr Mike Shotton

Sir, Your report today about that noble beverage, the Bloody Mary, reminded me of a Russian recipe. It involves two minor amendments to the standard formula: 1) for vodka, substitute 95 per cent neat spirit; and 2) forget the tomato juice.

Yours faithfully,
MIKE SHOTTON,
Bodicote, Oxfordshire. January 22

From Mr Lev Zalessky

Sir, As I learnt it in Russia, for a Bloody Mary you first pour tomato juice (two thirds of the total amount), add salt and other ingredients to taste and stir well.

Then vodka (or spirit if you prefer) is carefully poured on top of the tomato juice along the glass wall using a knife or similar tool to smooth the flow, so that vodka and juice do not mix together. So if you drink it the Russian way, ie, in one go, you get your vodka shot washed down with tomato juice. Cheers! *Yours faithfully,*
L. ZALESSKY,
London NW3. January 30

From Mrs Claire Scott

Sir, A member of my family, writing home from Russia in 1915, reported that, in the absence of the neat spirit suggested by your correspondent, the natives would buy a bottle of furniture polish, put a lump of salt in it to soak up the heavy ingredients, and be left with the residue in the bottom of the bottle.

Has any reader tried it?

Yours faithfully,
CLAIRE SCOTT,
London SW1. January 30

From Commander T. V. G. Binney, RN (retd)

Sir, The only hope for those who follow Mr Lev Zalessky's instructions for a Russian Bloody Mary is a swift Prairie Oyster: an egg yolk floating in Worcester Sauce, to be swallowed in one without breaking the yolk.

The resulting feel-good factor lasts just long enough to get the victim from the bar by the fleet landing in Valetta, up the gangway past the stern eye of the Regulating Petty Officer and down to his messdeck, there to suffer as deserved for the remainder of the night.

It worked 45 years ago. *Yours faithfully,*
GILES BINNEY,
Rogate, Petersfield, Hampshire. February 4

A really stiff drink

From Commander David Philpott, RN (retd)

Sir, The concoction of Giles Binney was clearly the weak version. As I recall, the Prairie Oyster from Salvo's London Bar by Customs House Steps in Valletta contained not only a raw egg and Worcester Sauce but also a tot of sherry and some Cayenne pepper.

That really did temporarily remove the top of the head.   *Yours faithfully*,
DAVID PHILPOTT,
Tavistock, Devon. February 7

From Lieutenant-Colonel Robin Jackson (retd)

Sir, Why does it always seem to be the Royal Navy which has the greatest experience of evil concoctions?

I recall being introduced (inevitably, on board one of HM ships) to a particularly virulent strain of buck's fizz which went by the name of "Old Card Table", on account of its rapid effect of making your legs collapse and your tongue feel like green baize.
Yours faithfully,
ROBIN JACKSON,
Windsor. February 11

RELATIVE BARGAIN

From Mrs Barbara Peacock

Sir, I have just received a quotation from our plumber offering, as an added incentive, the following: "Plumber's mater £10 per hr + VAT."   *Yours faithfully*,
BARBARA PEACOCK,
Newcastle upon Tyne. January 31

ODD ARRANGEMENTS

From Mr Dermot Woolgar

Sir, I suppose it only takes one bigamist to explain your perplexing statistic that the number of people getting married rose from 263,515 in 1999, to 267,961 in 2000 (report, January 29).   *Yours faithfully*,
DERMOT WOOLGAR,
London EC4. January 31

WHAT'S IN A NAME?

From Mrs Julie Smith

Sir, Recently I sent my driving licence to the Driver and Vehicle Licensing Agency to record my change of address. When it was returned, I noticed that as well as changing my address they had also changed my name.

I am now told that to have my name corrected I must send in another form and use the name in which my licence is currently registered.

My husband quite likes the new name and is thinking of changing his to match.
Yours sincerely,
JULIE UNITED KINGDOM
(formerly known as Julie Smith),
Twickenham, Middlesex. February 2

From Mrs M. M. Robinson

Sir, Like Mrs Judith United Kingdom I also suffered an imposed change of name, possessing for several years a credit card in the name of Ju7dith Robinson.

I told those few people who noticed the unusual spelling that the 7 was silent.
Yours sincerely,
J. ROBINSON,
Ightham, Kent. February 6

LIFE IN THE BALANCE

From Mr Nigel Orchard

Sir, I have just been cold-called with the offer of a free 30-day trial of life assurance.

I am perplexed as to the criteria for a successful, or at least satisfactory, trial.
Yours faithfully,
NIGEL ORCHARD,
Salisbury, Wiltshire. February 5

From Mr Ken Deally

Sir, I can only imagine that the life assurance trial is offered to discover whether your beneficiary develops a tendency to leave rollerskates at the head of the stairs.
Yours faithfully,
K. P. DEALLY,
Harlow, Essex. February 6

SEA DOGS

From Mr F. Somerset

Sir, During the past 50 years I have owned a succession of working labradors, all named after sea areas (report, February 5). Their names were Rockall, Malin, Lundy, Finisterre, Shannon, Wight, and now Bailey.

I feel honoured that the Met Office has returned the compliment, and named one of its areas after me. *Yours sincerely*,
FITZROY SOMERSET,
Clapham, Worthing. February 8

DEATH OF A PRINCESS

From Lady Antonia Fraser

Sir, William Rees-Mogg looks to Henry IV of France to explain Princess Margaret's "romantic rather than practical" view of life as well as her attraction. If we are discussing genes, surely her Stuart ancestress Mary Queen of Scots may have had something to do with it?

Princess Margaret gave me her own view of history succinctly when my biography of the ill-fated Queen came out in 1969.

"Very nice," she told me. "And what are you writing about now?"

"Cromwell, ma'am."

"Not very nice," replied the Princess.
Yours faithfully,
ANTONIA FRASER,
London W8. February 12

OVERPROOF

From Mrs June Brough

Sir, While pouring a bottle of French wine (Chateau Picard, 1998) recently, I noticed that according to the back label the wine was "Made from a blend of 80 per cent merlot, 15 per cent cabernet sauvignon and 15 per cent cabernet franc". Is this an example of Euro-inflation?
Yours faithfully,
JUNE BROUGH,
Halesowen, West Midlands. February 13

From Dr John Burscough

Sir, The vignerons of Chateau Picard are to be toasted for producing a wine with 110 per cent grape content. This makes good the depredations from the bottle of the "angels' share" (evaporation from the top) and the voleur (dimple in the bottom).
Yours faithfully,
JOHN BURSCOUGH,
Wrawby, Brigg, Lincolnshire. February 18

TIMES CHANGE

From Mr Anthony Green

Sir, I see you have craftily introduced a new font to coincide with your makeover.

I think you should tell us a little more about it. At the moment I'm not sure it's quite my type. *Yours faithfully*,
ANTHONY GREEN,
Alwoodley, West Yorkshire. February 14

REPELLING BOYFRIENDS

From Dr David Hawson

Sir, Leo Cooper suggests some ways to get rid of unsuitable boyfriends. I find that a simple: "Have you seen my daughter's stamp collection?" is usually effective.
Yours faithfully,
DAVID HAWSON
(father of Iona, Ishbel, Celia and Verity),
Monymusk, Aberdeenshire. February 15

BREATH OF FRESH AIR

From Dr Philip Gait

Sir, Ramblers on the Pembrokeshire Coast Path who get a bit depressed (Alan Coren, February 13) at the brass plaques on benches should try walking the South West Coast Path instead.

There they may spot a plaque to a local resident stating: "Misbehaved all his life."
Yours faithfully,
PHILIP GAIT,
Holcombe, Bath, Somerset. February 18

From Mr Derek Payne

Sir, Walking down to Hope Cove for a glo-

rious view of the Seven Sisters, on the South Downs in East Sussex, we always enjoy a plaque on a seat in memory of a local resident: "Gone for a cup of tea and a slide down the banisters."   *Yours sincerely,*
DEREK PAYNE,
Tonbridge, Kent. February 20

From Mrs Suzanne Reeves

Sir, Delightful plaque to be seen on a bench overlooking Portsmouth and across to the Isle of Wight, in memory of a Mum from her loving daughter.

Enjoy your picnic,

Sit up straight,

And don't lick your knife.

Yours faithfully,
SUZANNE REEVES,
Fareham, Hampshire. February 22

From Mrs J. A. Berwick

Sir, Instead of having his name commemorated on a lamp or bench, in Cuffley Millennium Garden a recently departed, much loved member of the village has had his request granted that in his memory a rubbish bin be erected, with the inscription in blue and gold: "Still serving the community."

Yours faithfully,
JUDY BERWICK,
Cuffley, Potters Bar, Hertfordshire.
February 27

CROSSWORD BUG

From Mrs Penny Panman

Sir, So a "spotted insect" is a ladybug, is it (Crossword, February 16)?

It must be one of the bugs I see in my backyard before I mosey on down the sidewalk to the diner for a burger with regular fries. Hold the mayo.   *Yours faithfully,*
PENNY PANMAN,
East Horsley, Surrey. February 22

TO AND FRO

From Miss Jennifer R. McQueen

Sir, Philip Howard's report on palindromes (February 16) quoted Adam: "Madam, I'm

Adam," but failed to include the warning Eve found necessary to give him: "Sex at noon taxes."   *Yours faithfully,*
JENNIFER R. McQUEEN,
Lydeard St Lawrence, Somerset. February 22

A SHINING EXAMPLE

From Mr Hugh Fraser

Sir, Opening the drinks cupboard, a not unusual occurrence even in Lent, I had intended to replace the light bulb with a modern "long-life" bulb. On removing the bulb (which was still working), I was surprised to find written on it "Property of the War Department".

This house was last occupied by troops to June 1942, followed by the Canadian Forestry Corps to late 1945.

I now wish I knew how to obtain more of these sturdy objects.   *Yours faithfully,*
HUGH FRASER,
Beauly, Inverness-shire. March 1

IMPARTIAL CIVIL SERVICE

From Mr L. J. Middleton

Sir, Recent events once again call to mind the comments of the Major-General Jonathan Peel on the political manoeuvres of Disraeli:

Three things I have learnt . . . that there is nothing less vital than a vital point, nothing more insecure than security, and nothing so elastic as the conscience of a Cabinet Minister.   *Yours faithfully,*
L. J. MIDDLETON,
Oxford. March 5

THE GREAT AND THE GOOD

From Mr J. H. Ruston

Sir, Judging by reports in *The Times* today it may be prudent to alert your obituary writers to the impending death of the American adverb. On page 1 General Franks tells us that "the soldiers are performing great. The equipment is performing great" whilst on page 25 a peanut farmer from

Georgia reports that "our congressmen did as good as they could".

Should we welcome these grammatical grey squirrels or urge the customs officers at Heathrow to be vigilant?

Yours faithfully,
JOE RUSTON,
Wimbledon, London SW19. March 6

From Mr Roger Coombs

Sir, Adverbs are dying out in this country as well as in America, along with other grammar. We hear the increasingly frequent use of the word "less" in place of "fewer". But does it matter, except to English teachers?

Yours faithfully,
ROGER COOMBS,
Goudhurst, Kent. March 8

From Mr Anthony Messenger

Sir, Our weather forecasters have been advising us for some time now to wrap up warm.   *Yours faithfully,*
ANTHONY MESSENGER,
Windsor, Berkshire. March 8

From Mr E. C. McCarthy

Sir, As well as the increasing use of "less" in place of "fewer" we have the inelegant "going private" as an alternative to the NHS.

Your faithfully,
E. C. McCARTHY,
Stamford, Lincolnshire. March 9

From Mr John Campion

Sir, "Wrap up warm" is an ellipsis, not vulgarian for "wrap up warmly"; "so that you will be" is understood.

A favourite misprision of mine is "and, more importantly", which itself has an uncultivated ring; in "and, more important", what is understood is "what is". If this sets a bad example, it is to the grammarless.

Yours faithfully,
JOHN CAMPION,
London N21. March 12

From Lord Millett

Sir, It is good to be reminded of the ellipsis. "He done good" is not ungrammatical af-

ter all. It is an ellipsis, standing for "He (has) done (that which is) good".

Master the ellipsis, and you will never speak ungrammatical.   *Yours sincerely,*
MILLETT,
House of Lords. March 13

From Mr L. J. Stammers

Sir, Could ellipsis even render grammatical that drill sergeant's wonderful injunction: "Get fell in!"?   *Yours sincerely,*
L. STAMMERS,
Tadworth, Surrey. March 15

WRITTEN IN DUST

From Mr Geoffrey Bond

Sir, Your report on dust and the National Trust refers to Professor Peter Brimblecombe "condusting" experiments. Is this not a mite careless?   *Yours sincerely,*
GEOFFREY C. BOND,
Southwell, Nottinghamshire. March 8

WILD ABOUT FOOD

From Mr Oliver Chastney

Sir, Since chef Fergus Henderson's efforts to revive British cookery with the rustic delights of rook pie and baked squirrel are jeopardised by supply difficulties (report, earlier editions, March 13), I urge him to consider adding mole casserole to his menu.

Here, we seem to have an endless supply of essential ingredients which he is welcome to collect free of charge – if he can catch the little blighters.   *Yours faithfully,*
OLIVER CHASTNEY,
Cringleford, Norwich. March 18

SCHOOL SHAKESPEARE

From Mr Norman T. Shepherd

Sir, You state (Television Choice, T2, March 19) that King George V could not spell Shakespeare.

Neither could Shakspere.   *Yours etc,*
N. T. SHEPHERD,
Bristol. March 23

ENGLISH PRONUNCIATION

From the Reverend Dr Colin Sowter

Sir, Philip Howard lists six ways of pronouncing the letters "ough". There are two others – ought and borough.

I am constantly impressed by the ability of my continental friends to speak English and many other languages, but this must challenge even them.　　*Yours faithfully*,
COLIN SOWTER,
Guildford. March 26

From Mr Nicholas Pritchard

Sir, My late grandfather used to tell me that while there were only 36 words in English containing the letters "ough", there were nine different ways of pronouncing it, all of which could be found in the following rather obscure sentence: "Though a rough cough and hiccoughs ploughed through him, he houghed the horse with thorough thoughtfulness."

I wonder, however, where this leaves Lough Neagh, the largest lake in the United Kingdom?　　*Yours faithfully*,
NICHOLAS PRITCHARD,
Southampton English Language Centre,
Southampton. April 1

From Mr Dennis Gill

Sir, The inclusion of lough and hough gives a total of ten pronunciations, although Fowler, in my 1978 reprint of his *Modern English Usage*, does not accept hiccough, claiming it to be a misspelling of hiccup.
Yours faithfully,
DENNIS GILL,
Stockport, Cheshire. April 1

From Mr James W. Thirsk

Sir, These lines from an anonymous poem *Pronunciation for Foreigners* make one wonder whether the next Queen's Speech should include a Bill for spelling reform.

Beware of heard, a dreadful word,
That looks like beard and sounds like bird.
And dead: it's said like bed, not bead –
For goodness sake don't call it "deed"!

Watch out for meat and great and threat
They rhyme with suite and straight and debt.　　*Yours faithfully*,
JAMES W. THIRSK,
Tonbridge, Kent. April 1

From Mr John Goodhand

Sir, Three decades of my pupils have enjoyed and, I hope, benefited from Bennet Cerf's verses:

The wind was rough
And cold and blough;
She kept her hands inside her mough.
It chilled her through,
Her nose turned blough,
And still the squall the faster flough.
And yet although
There was no snough,
The weather was a cruel fough.
It made her cough,
(Please do not scough);
She coughed until her hat blew ough.

Yours faithfully,
JOHN T. GOODHAND
(English teacher),
Ipswich, Suffolk. April 6

From Mr Roger Bowmer

Sir, There are three places in the North West called, or at least spelt, Claughton. They are pronounced Clayton, Claffton and Clawton.　　*Yours faithfully*,
ROGER BOWMER,
Littleborough, Lancashire. April 6

From Mr J. L. Ransome

Sir, I have known three families with the surname Houghton, pronounced variously Howton, Horton and Hudgton.

Yours faithfully,
J. L. RANSOME,
Stanway, Colchester. April 11

From Mr Eric Rough

Sir, Would someone be kind enough to tell me how to pronounce my name?

Yours faithfully,
ERIC ROUGH,
Shrewsbury, Shropshire. April 11

From Mr William Knowles

Sir, Mr Eric Rough asks if someone would be kind enough to tell him how to pronounce his name. I am happy to oblige.

The answer is "Derrick", though he should of course leave the "d" silent as in, say, "Cholmondely". *Yours faithfully,*
WILLIAM KNOWLES,
Kingston Deverill, Wiltshire. April 13

From Mr Graham Garton

Sir, After knocking, a total stranger entered my office one day, stood confidently before me and loudly exclaimed, "Ow!" Somewhat nonplussed, I gazed at him uncomprehendingly for a moment when he again repeated his utterance,"Ow!", this time offering an extended hand. It turned out he was an army officer (in mufti) whose surname was Ough.

He certainly knew how to pronounce his own name. This may not help Eric Rough very much. Tough. *Yours sincerely,*
GRAHAM GARTON,
East Heckington, Lincolnshire. April 13

From Mr Peter Hitchmough

Sir, Enough! Some of your recent correspondents have given me an identity crisis. I was given a difficult start by my father Mr Arthur Hitchmough who, having the benefit of a Lancashire accent, always gave his name as "Itchmoor".

I find that pronunciation is no problem. However, I must spell my name many times a day in conversation. In this way, we Hitchmoughs, Whatmoughs, Oughs and Roughs find our names doubly cursed: you can't say it and you can't spell it.

Rescue comes by way of Homer Simpson. *Yours faithfully,*
PETER HITCHMOUGH (as in "Doh!"),
Disley, Cheshire. April 19

HOTTEST SHOW IN TOWN

From Mr Peter Hawkins

Sir, I have tickets for a concert which have the usual conditions printed on them, such as "No refund" and "No exchange", but in addition state: "Keep in a cool place."
Yours faithfully,
PETER HAWKINS,
Eye, Suffolk. March 28

From Mr Henry Robinson

Sir, Peter Hawkins, warned to keep his concert ticket "in a cool place", should surely put it in a hip pocket.
Yours faithfully,
HENRY ROBINSON,
Warblington, Hampshire. March 29

BBC ABANDONS GLOBE AS SYMBOL

From Mr Mike Storey

Sir, The Flat Earth Society must be delighted. *Yours, etc,*
MIKE STOREY,
Buckden, Cambridgeshire. March 29

BEST BEFORE

From Miss Geraldine Foy

Sir, I have recently been given notepaper bearing the legend "Best before June 2002" on the box.

I am therefore compelled to write to you amongst others before it goes off.
Yours faithfully,
GERALDINE FOY,
Horley, Surrey. April 8

WORK AND PLAY

From Mr Philip Johnston

Sir, Impressed by the morale-boosting success of the Sutton Coldfield heating company (report, April 5), I tried giving my workmates a daily hug too, but perhaps I should have told them about the article first – they are giving me a wide berth at the moment. *Yours,*
PHILIP JOHNSTON
(Director) Softwood Import Services Ltd,
Bury St Edmunds, Suffolk. April 10

TITLEHOLDERS

From the Reverend John B. Job

Sir, The letter from the International Consumer Services and Small and Medium Sized Enterprises Services Product Manager reminded me of naval days, when I was known as National Service Upper Yardsman Acting Petty Officer Coder (Special).

The length of this title was in precisely inverse proportion to its significance.

Yours faithfully,
JOHN B. JOB,
Chesterfield, Derbyshire. April 12

From Mr Leslie Howard

Sir, For many years I suffered under the somewhat misleading job title of "Secretary for the United Kingdom" within a commercial organisation with its main head office overseas.

This led to some interesting conversations with other organisations, especially government departments responding to me on behalf of a Secretary of State. *Yours faithfully,*
LESLIE HOWARD,
St Albans, Hertfordshire. April 12

From Mr Roger Ordish

Sir, When I was a BBC radio producer in the Sixties, I was occasionally summoned to meetings with the man who was in charge of the BBC World Service. He was always referred to internally as "Head of World".

I decided that, if I should meet a Martian who demanded "Take me to your leader", I knew where to send him. *Yours faithfully,*
ROGER ORDISH,
Lewes, East Sussex. April 16

From Mr Peter Mottley

Sir, Some 30 years ago, while working for the London office of an American advertising agency, I was introduced to the Creative Director of the World.

Brash and Bronx, she wasn't how I'd always imagined the Almighty to look.

Yours etc,
PETER MOTTLEY,
Pangbourne, Berkshire. April 17

From Mr Graham Matthews

Sir, On a visit to a university senior common room in the Seventies, I found that professors were known by their subject of specialisation.

"Music", with whom I was having lunch, made a somewhat startling reference to "God" sitting at another table. Such was the seniority and charisma of the Professor of Biblical Studies that there was no hint of facetious intention.   *Yours sincerely,*
GRAHAM MATTHEWS,
Dronfield, Derbyshire. April 17

From Rear-Admiral Richard Heaslip

Sir, Had Roger Ordish at the BBC found the "Head of World" was out, he could have brought his legendary Martian round to my office at the MoD.

In the Eighties there were two Directors of Defence Policy; my colleague was Director (Nato) whilst I rejoiced in the title of Director, Rest of the World.

Yours faithfully,
RICHARD HEASLIP,
West Parley, Dorset. April 18

From the Venerable George Austin

Sir, Creative Director of the World may seem hard to beat. However, some years ago I was chatting to a journalist and asked him what his other interests were.

"I'm Chairman of the Universe," he replied. It took me a few moments to realise I was not another Abraham who talked with God as a man talks to a friend, and that *The Universe* was the Catholic weekly broadsheet.

Yours,
GEORGE AUSTIN,
Wheldrake, York. April 19

From Dr Malcolm Windsor

Sir, Some years ago I phoned the, then, MAFF Fisheries Laboratory at Lowestoft and asked for a Mr Gray.

"Is he Pelagic or Demersal?" was the switchboard query. *Yours etc,*
MALCOLM WINDSOR,
Edinburgh. April 19

From Lieutenant-Colonel D. P. Earlam (retd)

Sir, At one time I was responsible for recruiting officers to one of the Corps in the British Army. Candidates were required to complete a form giving various personal details. In the box entitled "Father's Occupation" one candidate had entered "Recently retired from Mars".

I then noted he lived near Slough and, after he was commissioned, I am glad to say he proved to have both feet firmly on this planet. *I am, Sir, your obedient servant,*
DAVID EARLAM,
Canterbury, Kent. April 23

From Mr G. T. C. Musgrave

Sir, Our former rector, now retired, used to telephone an old Fleet Air Arm comrade, who was working for an insurance company in the City.

The friend would pick up the phone and give the name of his department: "Life."

Our rector would reply with his department: "Eternal Life." *Yours,*
GAVIN MUSGRAVE,
Westcott, Surrey. April 23

From Mr K. Thomas

Sir, Years ago in Foyle's bookshop I overheard a young lady apologising to a telephone caller for being unable to help. The caller seemed persistent, for the young lady's voice rose to a wail. "I should love to help you," she said, "but I am Philosopy: Religion has gone to lunch."

Yours faithfully,
K. THOMAS,
Northolt. April 23

From Mr Simon Brett

Sir, Further to your correspondence on strange titles, one of the greatest pleasures of many in my life as a writer occurred when BBC Television was making a series based on my book, *How To Be A Little Sod.*

Every time I rang the production team, the telephone would be answered with the deathless words, "Sod Office."

Yours faithfully,
SIMON BRETT,
Arundel, West Sussex. April 24

From Mr Malcolm Williams

Sir, Many years ago I was underwriting an insurance proposal for a class of business where the job status of the individual was a factor. The proposer was a professional footballer. His response to the question "Position Held" was "Left Back". Perfectly logical, but not quite what I or the author of the form was expecting. *Yours faithfully,*
MALCOLM WILLIAMS,
Raby Mere, Wirral. April 26

From Professor Graham Zellick

Sir, Mr Malcolm Williams's footballer who gave his "position held" as "left back" reminds me of the recent applicant for compensation under the Criminal Injuries Compensation Scheme who had been assaulted in a pub.

On the front page of the application form, in answer to the question "occupation at time of the incident", he wrote, admirably combining terseness with precision: "Drinking". *Yours faithfully,*
GRAHAM ZELLICK
(Vice-Chancellor), University of London,
London WC1E. April 27

From Mr Geoff Ledden

Sir, My general manager once reprimanded me for using the acronym SACE when reporting on a visit to the Italian export credit agency. As the full title is Sezione Speciale per l'Assicurazione del Credito all'Esportazione dell'Istituto Nazionale per le Assicurazioni, I think I should have been commended for saving time and ink.

Yours faithfully,
GEOFF LEDDEN,
Lingfield, Surrey. April 27

WIDER IMPLICATIONS OF LE PEN'S SHOWING

From Mr Barry Hyman

Sir, Obituaries today: Sir Michael Kerr, German refugee, Appeal judge and fighter pilot; Professor Victor Weisskopf, Austrian refugee and renowned physicist; Lewis Goodman, OBE, Polish refugee and noted textile technologist. Just shows you what can happen if you're not careful about the sort of people you let flood in to dilute the native population.   *Yours faithfully,*
BARRY HYMAN,
Bushey Heath, Hertfordshire. April 26

FIRST AMONG EQUALS?

From Mr Paul Pritchard

Sir, Having been reminded how our former Prime Ministers are on such bad terms with each other that they can hardly bear to sit at the same dinner table (reports and leading article, April 30), is it not rather worrying that we have been governed for so long by such childish people?
Yours faithfully,
PAUL PRITCHARD,
Dorchester, Dorset. May 1

From Mr Henry Brownrigg

Sir, It is unfair to say that the former Prime Ministers are childish because they are on bad terms with each other. Three of them are on bad terms with Baroness Thatcher. The rest get along famously.
Yours faithfully,
HENRY BROWNRIGG,
London SW6. May 4

MAY DAY MAYHEM

From Mr Richard Ploszek

Sir, I am pleased to report that the only significant police activity I witnessed on May 1 was a group of policemen escorting a family of ducks from Parliament Square to St James's Park. While I have no doubt that the ducks were anarchists, the incident appeared to pass off peacefully.
Yours faithfully,
RICHARD PLOSZEK,
London E14. May 3

FRIENDS AND RELATIONS

From Mrs Cheryl Bull

Sir, A few years ago I visited the Royal Academy with my teenage daughter and queued to gain entrance to the "Sensations" exhibition. There was a separate queue for Friends of the Royal Academy.

A member of staff who was trying to ensure we were standing in the correct queue asked us: "Are you Friends?" to which my daughter quickly replied: "No, she is my mother."   *Yours faithfully,*
CHERYL BULL,
Braintree, Essex. May 7

REPUBLICAN IDEALS

From Mr D. L. Bird

Sir, Matthew Parris (Comment, May 4) writes: "Constitutional monarchy comes closer to the republican ideal than any version of presidency on offer." This view was succinctly expressed by the former Foreign Secretary Michael Stewart when he lectured on my college courses.

"Britain," he would say, "is a crowned republic. And the USA is an elected monarchy."
Yours faithfully,
DENNIS L. BIRD,
Shoreham-by-Sea, West Sussex. May 9

EYE IN THE SKY

From Mr Peter Gillard

Sir, I was talking on the telephone this morning to a lawyer in the City. He broke off to tell me that a camera, on a pole in the street outside his window, had turned to contemplate him. He then asked the camera: "Can you lip-read?" The camera nodded.

My friend asks that his office not be identified further than his postcode, EC3, but I

suppose Big Brother will know the rest any-
way.   *Yours faithfully,*
PETER GILLARD,
Edlesborough Buckinghamshire. May 15

EARNINGS RELATED

From Mr John Bibby

Sir, You report (May 14) that "Eight directors at Tesco earn over £1m".

I do wish you would say "have been paid"
rather than "earn".   *Yours faithfully,*
J. M. BIBBY,
Wigton, Cumbria. May 15

ABOVE ONE'S STATION

From Mrs Sylvia Crookes

Sir, I have just visited 10 Downing Street's
website and note that it offers (lobby briefing, May 13) details of the "Lord's reform".

I wonder what He has in His mind on the
subject?   *Yours,*
SYLVIA CROOKES,
Bainbridge, Wensleydale. May 18

From Mr Mike Storey

Sir, The same 10 Downing Street website
tells me that copies of the Regional Governance White Paper are to be found in
"The Stationary Office".

Best place for them, I say.   *Yours, etc,*
MIKE STOREY,
St Neots, Cambridgeshire. May 21

GOOD NEWS FOR LAZY DAYS

From Ms Hilary Day

Sir, How pleasant your news has been recently. Forget the doom, gloom and football. I have learnt that red and white wine
are good for me; taking my dog for a walk
is more beneficial than household chores;
and wild gardens are back in fashion.

I am writing this as I sit sipping wine after
a long walk and I am ignoring the household chores and the gardening.

I feel better already.   *Yours sincerely,*
HILARY DAY,
King's Lynn, Norfolk. May 28

BYERS'S RESIGNATION

From Mr George Wake

Sir, Did I hear right? Someone called Darling has gone to the rescue of a crew whose
vessel has become stranded on rocks after
being pounded by a storm when drifting
off course.   *Yours faithfully,*
GEORGE WAKE,
Swalwell, Newcastle upon Tyne. May 31

ENGLAND'S STANDARD

From Mr Michael W. Painter

Sir, What an attractive object the once obscure flag of St George is. It has a fresh, un-
cluttered look, and a bold identity – something England itself once possessed.

Yours sincerely,
M. W. PAINTER,
Chandler's Ford, Hampshire. June 3

OUT OF THE MOUTH . . .

From the Reverend Dr Anthony Bash

Sir, The day after my fiftieth birthday, my
four-year-old son asked in a puzzled voice
how old I was.

"Fifty," I replied.

"But you're not very big," was his response.
Yours faithfully (at 5ft 7in),
ANTHONY BASH,
North Ferriby, East Yorkshire. June 7

POETIC LICENCE

From Sir George Engle

Sir, In your first leading article you quote
from T. S. Eliot's *Little Gidding* (1942) the
words "history is a pattern of timeless moments".

I was present when in 1943 Eliot gave a
talk on poetry to the Sixth Form at
Charterhouse and at the end was asked by a
"history specialist" (J. V. Judah) what he
meant by those words.

After a long pause Eliot replied: "I have
really no idea."   *Yours faithfully,*
GEORGE ENGLE,
London N6. June 8

SPORTING MOMENTS

From Mr Michael Mounsey

Sir, Argentina as England's "most dearly beloved enemy in sport" (report, June 8)? Whatever has happened to Australia?

Yours faithfully,
MICHAEL MOUNSEY,
Ollerton, Newark, Nottinghamshire. June 10

GOLDEN OLDIES

From Mr Michael Bland

Sir, Posters near my home have been offering an evening of "old school nostalgia" consisting of "Garage '93–'96".

Am I getting old?   *Yours faithfully,*
MICHAEL BLAND,
London, W5. June 10

From Mr Henry Adams

Sir, You know you are middle-aged when you write letters to *The Times*.

You know you are elderly when your letters are published.   *Yours in anticipation,*
HENRY ADAMS,
Eastham, Wirral, Merseyside. June 24

From Mr A. W. Hutt

Sir, Middle-aged is when you stop overnight when going from Lancashire to Normandy; elderly is when you go by coach; and senile is when you don't start.

Yours from Oxford overnight,
A. W. HUTT,
St Anne's-on-Sea, Lancashire. June 26

From Mrs Philip Trousdell

Sir, Twenty or so years ago my first port of call in *The Times* was the matches column. As years progressed I studied the hatches. I now scarcely glance at the former, rarely find friends' names in the latter and know I shall have reached maturity when I head straight for the dispatches.

Yours faithfully,
SALLY TROUSDELL,
Camberley, Surrey. June 29

RIGHT ON TRACK

From Mr Bruce Parker

Sir, I asked the man in the South West Trains ticket office if the 10.02 to Waterloo was a modern train or an old "slam-door". He replied that it was, indeed, a slam-door but they were now calling them "heritage trains".

Now there's spin, combined with humour.

Yours faithfully,
BRUCE PARKER,
Winchester, Hampshire. June 11

ALL YOU NEED IS LOVE

From Mrs Jenny McKitterick

Sir, Having agonised over being too young for Paul McCartney back in the Sixties, it is galling to discover, second time round and still eight years his junior, that I am now much too old.   *Yours faithfully,*
JENNY McKITTERICK,
Blagdon, Bristol. June 11

All you need is love

JUBILEE AND THE MONARCHY'S STANDING

From Mr Martin Fleming

Sir, Whilst it was wonderful to see the array of pop stars of previous decades performing some of their best-loved hits at the jubilee concert at Buckingham Palace, the Queen can take great encouragement that the monarchy seems far less outdated than most of the stuff happening on stage.

Yours,
MARTIN FLEMING,
Bwlch, Brecon, Powys. June 12

ONCE A KNIGHT . . .

From Mr C. P. Daynes

Sir, I was interested to learn from Robbie Miller's Sunday press review that Mick Jagger, who is described as a "58-year-old with seven kids by four women", may be given a knighthood. Would that be some proprietary brand of condom?

Yours faithfully,
C. P. DAYNES,
Orpington, Kent. June 13

EASTERN PROMISE

From Mr R. J. Mehta

Sir, Yesterday I, a typical Indian grandfather, asked my 10-year-old grandson, while he was wildly cheering England against Denmark, which team he would support if England and India were playing. "Of course, England" was the enthusiastic reply.

Noticing a tinge of disappointment on my face, he added: "Perhaps, it could be a draw."

Yours truly,
RAJNIKANT J. MEHTA,
Harrow on the Hill, Middlesex. June 17

UNWISE WORD

From Mrs T. A. Bond

Sir, This morning my husband received a letter from the Diocese of Bath and Wells asking if he could "diarise" a date.

Neologism or Bushism?

Yours faithfully,
TERRI BOND,
Highbridge, Somerset. June 19

From Mr Mike Nassau-Kennedy

Sir, A. P. Herbert's *What a Word!* (published 1935) contains the following entry under the (ironic) heading "Valuable Neologisms":

To diarize . . . not the casual aberration of a lowly clerk but the official invention of a great London bank...forced upon the defenceless staff and perpetrated with a rubber stamp!   *Yours faithfully,*
MIKE NASSAU-KENNEDY,
Sheffield, South Yorkshire. June 24

SIGN OF THE TIMES

From Mrs Antony Warren

Sir, On one corner of London's Russell Square – between London University's Institute of Education and the school examination board, Edexcel – a notice appeared briefly. It read: "Pedestrians please use other phootpath."

Dumbing down is an established phenomenon; is this a particularly ironically placed early example of dumbing up?

Yours sincerely,
VIRGINIA WARREN,
Cambridge. June 19

PAIN-FREE PARTING

From Mr Alan Millard

Sir, Although I have no answer to the question "Do faulty nerve cells cause migraine?" (Health, T2), I can report that after 20 years of regular migraine attacks my marriage ended in divorce and that, in the 20 years since the divorce, I have been completely free from headaches of any kind.

Would this information be of any help to Professor Goadsby and others in their search for a cure?   *Yours faithfully,*
ALAN MILLARD,
Lee-on-the-Solent, Hampshire. June 20

HOUSE PRICE HYSTERIA

From Dr Andy Bowman

Sir, While the Council of Mortgage Lenders is urging the Bank of England for a rate rise to dampen down the runaway property market, one of its largest members is fanning the flames of hysteria with advertisements urging first-time buyers: "Buy your first home before somebody else does." *Yours faithfully*,
ANDY BOWMAN,
Bestwood Park, Nottingham. June 26

MIDDLE EAST GAMES

From Mr Warren Williams

Sir, President Bush calls for Palestinian elections. The Palestinians announce that they are going to hold elections. And you report that the Palestinians have "called President Bush's bluff".

Boy, I'd sure like to play poker with you guys. *Yours sincerely*,
WARREN WELLDE WILLIAMS,
Mumbles, Swansea. June 28

WORLDCOM SCANDAL

From Mr Gordon Ferris

Sir, Another accounting-auditing scandal? Time for some ethic cleansing?
Yours faithfully,
GORDON FERRIS,
London SE16. June 28

"Just leave the books with the auditors."

Index of Letter Writers